Data Structures in C

Data Structures in C

Achuthsankar S. Nair
Honorary Director
Centre for Bioinformatics
University of Kerala
Thiruvananthapuram

T. Mahalekshmi
Principal
Sree Narayana Institute of Technology
Kollam, Kerala

PHI Learning Private Limited
DELHI-110092
2025

In fond memory of ***Shri Asoke K. Ghosh*** *(October 1942 – February 2024), Founder Chairman and Managing Director of PHI Learning, whose vision endlessly inspires.*

The Legacy Continues....

Published by Pushpita Ghosh, PHI Learning Private Limited, Rimjhim House, 111, Patparganj Industrial Estate, Delhi-110092 and Printed by Multi Colour Services, I-45, DLF Industrial Area, Sector-32, Faridabad, Haryana-121003.

₹695.00

DATA STRUCTURES IN C
Achuthsankar S. Nair and T. Mahalekshmi

ISBN-978-81-203-3642-1 (Print Book)
ISBN-978-93-5443-360-3 (e-Book)

The export rights of the book are vested solely with the publisher.

Contents

Preface

We have more than a passing interest in the pedagogy of programming languages. In 2004, we published a paper pertaining to Visualization of Data Structures in the ACM SIGCSE (Special Interest Group in Computer Science Education) Bulletin. Ever since that publication, we wanted to bring out a book which used such a visualization in explaining the various topics under a typical data structure course. Finding that these visualizations need to be explained starting from programming concepts such as arrays and pointers, we decided to include a brief introduction to programming languages also in this book. Except for the subtle attempt to visualize the memory in an arguably pedagogic improvement, this book does not boast of any novelty or specialty. Of course, the touch of personal style may always be there. Brief, purposeful, pedagogic and visual: that has been our *mantra*.

The book is organized into seven chapters. Chapter 1 gives an overview of the C language, which is the working language used in the text for implementing data structures. The most common concepts of C are discussed in a student-friendly manner. The approach of memory visualization, which is a special feature of this book, is introduced in this chapter. Pointer in C, very often a hard nut to crack for beginners, is explained clearly. Exercises based on memory diagrams add value to the discussions.

In line with the pedagogic approach used in Chapter 1, Chapter 2 deals with the linear static data structure and array, and focuses on the internal organization of arrays, two-dimensional arrays, and various operations associated with them. The unique approach of this book stands out in the section on handling arrays using pointers.

Dynamic memory allocation, which is memory allocated on the run time, is introduced in Chapter 3 in a simple visual manner and also with the help of analogies. The dynamic linked list and its variations such as doubly linked lists and circular linked lists are explained with the help of memory diagrams. Visual exercises for insertion, deletion, etc. preceding program implementation are special features of this chapter. Stacks and queues are discussed in detail in Chapter 4. Both static and dynamic implementations of these data structures are given. Chapter 5 on Tree Data Structures also is unique in the way visualization is exploited for introducing the concept. Conceptual exercises precede step-by-step implementation. Binary trees and binary search trees are also covered in this chapter. Chapter 6 deals with graphs. Breadth first search and depth wise searche, two common methods of searching a graph, are explained in this chapter. The study of structures is complete only when access and sorting methods are also studied. Chapter 7 deals with various types of searching and sorting techniques. These techniques are explained with the help of visual examples.

The book is intended for the undergraduate students of Engineering (Computer Science/Information Technology), and undergraduate and postgraduate students of Computer Applications, Computer Science, and Information Technology.

Any constructive criticism for further improvement of the book is most welcome.

Achuthsankar S. Nair
T. Mahalekshmi

Acknowledgements

I wish to thank, first and foremost, my programming teacher, Prof R.P. Rajagopalan Nair who kindled an interest in me in creative teaching of programming languages. I express my gratitude to all my fellow teachers and students who have supported, given critical feedback, and also encouraged during the development of core material of this book. In particular, I would like to thank D. Sajilal, Dr. Toufik Taibi, Dr. Prasad Krishna and Sumi Rao. My wife Hema Ramachandran, herself a teacher, deserves a special mention for bearing with me many inconveniences during the preparation of the manuscript.

Achuthsankar S. Nair

I wish to thank Dr. Satraj Sahini, who was my professor at the University of Minnesota, USA. His teaching of data structures as well as his book on the subject made a deep impact on me. During my association with Dr. Achuthsankar S. Nair, a lot of time was devoted discussing visualization. It was during these discussions that I fully appreciated the potential of visualization in pedagogy. I am deeply indebted to Dr. Achuthsankar S. Nair for infusing in me a fresh thinking on the subject. The feedback I received from my colleagues and student community was of great help. The advice received from Sri R.P. Lalaji and Sri R.P. Sugathan was invaluable. I would also like to thank Prof. K. Sasikumar and Sri D. Prasannan for their assistance. I will be failing in my duty if I do not mention the encouragement and support I got from my family members, especially Sri R. Thiruvenkitam, Dr. B.A. Rajakrishnan, and Sri T. Sivakumar.

T. Mahalekshmi

Chapter 1

Overview

1.1 INTRODUCTION

We begin with an introduction to C programming. Even if you are already familiar with C, it would still be ideal to go through this chapter, especially the second half of the chapter.

C is a computer programming language and, like every other language, the best way to learn it is by starting to use it. Indeed, this is the strategy we adopt throughout the book. You start learning C by writing some very simple programs. When you become familiar with the basic structure of C it will be easy to grasp the full details of the language.

Always remember that you have to be strong in C if you want to be good in Data Structures, C++, and Java. Isn't that enough motivation to learn C?

1.2 OUR FIRST C PROGRAM

Here is our first C program (Program 1.1).

Program 1.1

```
#include <stdio.h>
main( )

{
    printf("Namaste\n");
}
```

When you run the above program on your computer using your available C development environment, you will see the following result on the screen:

'Namaste'

An explanation of the **printf** command line is given below:

printf : C command to display something on the screen. Always followed by ( ).[1] Note that **printf** is a single word, not **print f,** and all the letters are lower case. Do not write as **Printf** since C is a highly *case sensitive* programming language.

" " : Inside the **printf** brackets, anything written inside these double quotes will be shown **as such** on the screen.

\n : The new line character (read as *back-slash-en*). Wherever this character appears, the computer proceeds to a new line on the screen. All **printf** statements, almost always, have a **\n** at the end.

; : Semicolon–required at the end of all C statements. Similar to period (**.**) in English. Also known as *delimiter*.

Example 1.1

1. Write a program to show your name on the screen.

```
#include <stdio.h>
main( )
{
    printf("Abdul  Kalam\n");
}
```

2. Write a program to show your name and address.

```
#include <stdio.h>
main( )
{
    printf("Sri.V.P.Gupta\n");
    printf("P.B.  No.  105,  Cochin,  682022\n");
}
```

Exercise 1.1

1. Write a program to display the address of the Chief Minister of your state along with the website address of the State Government.
2. Write a program to show on the screen the following: (a) all in one line, and (b) each word in a separate line.
   I Love my Country.

1.3 VARIABLE NAMES (IDENTIFIERS)

As in the case of algebra where we use variables, C also permits the use of variables.

[1] There are three types of brackets used in C programs as given below:
( ) *Parentheses* (or brackets)
{ } *Curly braces* (or simply braces)
[ ] *Square brackets*

Similar to the statement in algebra, "Let $a = 5$", we can have a C statement too. Here a is called a *variable name* or *identifier*. There are certain rules to be followed when naming variables. Variable names should:

1. use only alphabets, numbers and underscore '_'.
2. not begin with a number and must have at least one alphabet.
3. not be a reserved word (a word which has a special meaning in C).
4. not be longer than 32/256 characters.

The following are the reserved words in C (There is no need to remember all of these. Once you are familiar with C, the common reserved words can be easily recognized.):

auto	double	int	struct	break	else	long	switch
case	enum	for	typedef	char	if	return	union
const	float	short	unsigned	continue	do	signed	void
default	goto	sizeof	volatile	register	extern	static	while

Some examples of valid identifiers are:

average, main, print_main, number123, _temp

A few examples of invalid identifiers, along with the reasons, are:

print main	*space not allowed*
123number	*name should not begin with number*

Exercise 1.2

1. *Classify the following as valid or invalid C identifiers, giving reasons for each invalid case.*

Identifier	**Remarks**	**Identifier**	**Remarks**
Foo		a1,1	
a566		IBM/PC	
a10000		IBM_PC	
a1,0000		IBM-PC	
2ndtotal		1999total	
clanguage		Windows 95	
main		Main	
main( )		maiN	
26a		_o	
_a		_int	
firstsum		1stsum	
first sum		1st sum	

1.4 DATA TYPES AND TYPE DECLARATION

All the variables used in C program must be declared at the beginning of the program. This is for telling C in advance that certain variables are going to be used in the program. Not only should variable names be given, the type to which they belong should also be declared.

There are three popular basic data types in C:

1. **int** number without decimal part (whole number), e.g. 6273, 7986, –33
2. **float** number with decimal part (real number), e.g. 7.0, –2.3421, 1.123, 0.897
3. **char** character, any symbol on the keyboard, e.g. 'A', 'x', '+', '1', '*'

Once you decide the data type and the name of a variable, it can be declared as shown in (Table 1.1).

Table 1.1 Data type and name

Declaration	Explanation
int a;	**a** is an integer
int a,b;	**a,b** are integers
int a; int b;	**a** is an integer **b** is an integer
float speed;	**speed** is a float number
float velocity,cost;	**velocity** and **cost** are float numbers
float x,y,z; int student_id,mark;	**x, y, z** are float numbers **student_id** and **mark** are integers
char grade; char category, answer;	**grade** is a character **category** and **answer** are characters

Exercise 1.3

1. Decide the data type and variable names for each of the following. Then write the declaration. (Note that the choice between the integer and the float of the following cases is sometimes subject to interpretation.)
   (a) Student id, sex, marks, and grade are to be used in a program.
   (b) No. of units purchased, cost of items, amount at hand, and interest rate are to be used in a program.
   (c) Marks in Exam 1, Exam 2 and Exam 3 are to be used in a program.

	Variable Name	Data Type	C Declaration
a			
b			
c			

1.5 ASSIGNMENT STATEMENT

To assign a value to a variable, we normally say **variable = value**, as in the following examples.

Example 1.2

1. **integer** (Assume that the variables are declared as int.)

```
a = 5;
b = 250;
student_id = 25697;
```

float (Assume that the variables are declared as float.)

```
interest_rate = 3.5;
height = 1.6;
x = 1027.683;
```

character (Assume that the variables are declared as char.)

```
answer = 'y';
answer = 'N';
operator = '+';
grade = 'p';
```

Note: The character values should always be enclosed within single quotes. Only one character can be present inside the quotes.

1.6 PRINTING VARIABLE VALUES

So far, we have seen how **printf** can be used to print names, address, etc. on the screen by enclosing them inside " ". The values of variables can also be shown on the screen using **printf**. Study the following program (Program 1.2).

Program 1.2

```
#include <stdio.h>
main( )
{
    int a;
    a=5;
    printf (" The value of variable = %d\n", a);
}
```

Here is the explanation for the program: **int a; a = 5;** is already known. (a is an integer and let the value of a be 5). Inside **printf** brackets you find: **"The value of variable = %d\n", a** . We know that the **\n** is for effecting a new line. So, let us ignore that \n and have a look at the rest.

"The value of variable = %d", a

Here, we have something inside the double quotes, followed by a comma (**,**) and a variable name **a**. Inside the quote, we find something new: **%d**. You may always consider this as a *blank to be filled in*.

"The value of variable = ...", a

"%d" actually tells C to print an integer in its place. It is known as a **format string**. The format strings for different data types are different (see Table 1.2).

Table 1.2 Data type and format string

Data type	Format string
int	%d
float	%f
char	%c

The format strings %d, %f, %c all indicate blanks to be filled in. In addition, they indicate that the blanks have to be filled in by integer, float, and character values, respectively. We will see later that certain data types can be printed using more than one format with insightful use.

Example 1.3

1.
```
int a;
a = 5;
printf (" The value of a = %d\n",a);
float p;
p = 27.3;
printf ("The value of p = %f\n",p);
char x;
x = 'm';
printf ("The value of x = %c\n",x);
```

Exercise 1.4

1. Recall where you had decided data types and written the declaration for the following cases—in Exercise 1.3. Now write complete C programs to assign values for each variable and then print each of them using separate **printf** statements.
   (a) Student id, sex, marks, and grade are to be used in the program.
   (b) No. of units purchased, cost of items, amount at hand, and interest rate are to be used in the program.
   (c) Marks in Exam 1, Exam 2 and Exam 3 are to be used in the program.

1.6.1 More about printf

We can print out the values of more than one variable using **printf,** as in the following examples.

Example 1.4

```
1.  int  a,b,c;
    a  =  5;
    b  =  6;
    c  =  a;
    printf ("The value of a is %d, b is %d, c is %d\n", a, b, c );

2.  nt  a;
    float  p;
    char  x;
    a  =  5;
    b  =  10.56;
    x  =  'm';
    printf ("The value of a is %d, p is %f, x is %c\n", a, p, x);
```

You may note that the blanks inside the " " are filled in with the variable values in the order in which they are given. You must ensure that the appropriate format string is used for each variable type. Otherwise, unexpected results may follow.

Exercise 1.5

1. Write complete C programs to assign values for each variable and then print each of them using **single printf** statements for each of the following cases:
   (a) Student id, sex, marks, and grade are to be used in a program.
   (b) No. of units purchased, cost of items, amount at hand, and interest rate are to be used in a program.
   (c) Marks in Exam 1, Exam 2 and Exam 3 are to be used in a program.

1.7 ESCAPE CHARACTERS

We have already learnt about **\n** (*back-slash-n*) to print a new line on the screen. "\" is called an *escape character (or sequence)* and there are more:

\a	alert
\b	back space
\n	new line
\t	tab

Remember that escape characters always appear inside the double quotes " ", for example, printf("John\n"), not printf("John"\n). See an example for \t escape sequence. The effect is that in, there will be seven spaces between two variables.

Program 1.3

```
#include<stdio.h>
main( )
{   int a,b,c;
    a = 2;
    b = 3;
    c = 5;
printf ("a = %d,\t b = %d,\t c = %d",a,b,c);
}
```

Exercise 1.6

1. Write complete C programs to assign values for each variable and then print each of them using **single printf** statements, with \t for each of the following cases.
   (a) Student id, sex, marks, and grade are to be used in a program.
   (b) No. of units purchased, cost of items, amount at hand, and interest rate are to be used in a program.
   (c) Marks in Exam 1, Exam 2 and Exam 3 are to be used in a program.

1.8 SIMPLE ARITHMETIC IN C

For enabling us to practice writing programs, we need to know some simple arithmetic operators in C. A detailed study of operators will be done later. Right now, let us familiarize ourselves with some simple operators (see Table 1.3).

Table 1.3 Operators and its meaning

Operators	Meaning
+	Addition
–	Subtraction
/	Division (read *slash*)
*	Multiplication (read *star*)

If a and b are declared as integers, then we can use these operator as a + b, a – b, a/b, a*b. The following program lists how to compute the sum of the two numbers a and b.

Program 1.4

```
#include<stdio.h>
main( )
{   int a,b;
    a = 50;
    b = 60;
    printf (" Sum of a and b = %d\n", a+b);
}
```

Exercise 1.7

1. Write a program to declare two integer variables as **a** and **b**, assign values and then print out the result of **a – b**.
2. Write a program to declare two variables as **x** (integer) and **y** (float), assign values and then print out the result of **x** divided by **y**.
3. Write a program to declare two int variables as **n1** and **n2**, assign values and then print out the result of **n1** multiplied by **n2**.
4. Write a program to declare one int variable as **x**, assign value and then print out the result of the square of **x**.

1.8.1 Some More Examples

When a calculation is done, you may use a variable to store the result and then print out that variable. (This is actually required when the result is to be used for another calculation.) See the rewritten addition program in the following example, including a third variable **c**.

Example 1.5

1. Write a program to find out the value c = a + b , if a = 2 and b = 3. Then show the result on the screen.

```
#include<stdio.h>
main( )
{
    int  a,  b,  c;
    a  =  2;
    b  =  3;
    c  =  a+b;
    printf("%d\n",  c);
}
```

2. Use a variable y for the year of your birth and print out the age.

```
#include<stdio.h>
main( )
{
    int  y,  age;
    y  =  1979;
    age  =  1999  -  y;
    printf("I  am  %d  years  old\n",  age);
}
```

Exercise 1.8

Write a C program for the following cases, using a variable in each to store the result. You may name the third variable yourself.

1. Write a program to declare two integer variables as **a** and **b**, and then print out the result of **a – b**.

2. Write a program to declare two variables as **x** (integer) and **y** (float), and then print out the result of **x** divided by **y**.
3. Write a program to declare two int variable as **x** and **y**, and then print out the result of the sum of the square of **x** and the square of **y**.

1.9 THE scanf STATEMENT

So far, our programs were only showing something on the screen. They can also be made to *accept (read)* what you type through the keyboard, when the program runs.

For this, we have the **scanf** statement which is similar to the **printf** statement. Consider the following Program 1.5.

Program 1.5

```
#include <stdio.h>
main( )
{
    int  a;
    a  =  5;
    printf  ("  The  value  of  a  =  %d\n", a);
}
```

If the above program is to be run with a different value of a, we have to change the program and re-run it. Once the program is written, the value of **a** cannot be changed unless and until the program is altered. Now consider Program 1.6.

Program 1.6

```
#include <stdio.h>
main( )
{   int  a;
    scanf  ("  %d",&a);
    printf  ("  The  value  of  a  =  %d\n",  a);
}
```

The above program will accept (read) the value of **a** from the keyboard and then it will be used in the **printf** statement. While the program runs, it will wait for you to type an integer value. The program will not proceed until you type an integer. Suppose you type 10 (followed by return key), then the computer will take that as the value of **a**. That value of **a** will be printed out. **scanf ("%d",&a);** can be interpreted simply as "read the value of **a** from the keyboard".

Just like in **printf** statement, you need a format string (%d for integer) for each variable you read. Similar to **printf**, there can be more than one variable in **scanf.** For example **scanf("%d%d",&a,&b)** reads two variables a and b. There are two important things to note about **scanf**.

- There is always an '**&**' sign before the variable whose value is to be read*.

*We will later see that there is an exception for special kinds of variables.

- Inside quotes (" ") in **scanf, only** format strings will be present. No escape character like \n or any other message like "The value of a is %d" is permitted.

Example 1.6

1. Write a program to accept two integers and then print out the product of the numbers.

```
#include <stdio.h>
main( )
{
    int n1, n2;
    printf("Enter two integers\n");
    scanf("%d%d", &n1, &n2);
    printf("The product is %d\n", n1 * n2);
}
```

1.9.1 More about scanf

Given below is a summary of **scanf** and assignment statements for each data type (see Table 1.4).

Table 1.4 Scanf and assignment statement

Data type	Declaration	Example values	Scanf	Assignment
Integer	int num;	1, 0, 2312, 1000	scanf("%d", &num);	num = 1000;
Float	float velocity;	1.0, –0.2, 100.33	scanf("%f ", &velocity);	velocity = 1.0;
Character	char grade;	'A', '+', 'a', '–'	scanf("%c", &grade);	grade = 'A';

Exercise 1.9

1. Write a program to read two integer variables a and b, calculate their difference and display as shown below.

   Please enter two numbers > 50, 40
   The difference is 10.

2. Write a program to accept two integers and find the sum, difference, product and ratio. Then print the results.
3. Write a program to declare an integer variable b with value 9 and float variable x with value 9.0 and then print out the value of each variable divided by 2.
4 Write a program to accept the register number and grade of a student and then print it out.
5. Study the program below and predict the output.

```
#include <stdio.h>
main( )
{
printf("ABCDEFG\nABCDEF\nABCDE\nABCD\nABC\nAB\nA");
}
```

6. Write a program to read user data and calculate the age of the user. Then display as shown below.

```
Please enter your year of birth > 1977
You are 30 years old.
```

7. Write a program to accept working hours and rate. Then calculate the salary (working hours * rate) and print out the result as shown below.

```
Please enter your working hours > 80
Please enter your rate in Rs > 100
Your salary is Rs 8000.
```

8. Write a program to accept a number from the user. Then calculate the square of the number and print out as shown below.

```
Please enter a number > 8
Square of 8 is 64.
```

1.10 OPERATORS IN C

1.10.1 Introduction

There are three kinds of operators in C.

- Arithmetic: +, –, /, %, *, ++, – –
- Relational: >, <, >=, <=, ==, !=
- Logical: &&, | |, !

1.10.2 Arithmetic Operators

Arithmetic operators are applicable on integer/float data type. Some of these (+, –, ++, –) can be applied meaningfully on character data too. This is because characters are also integers internally (in memory).

+ : Addition
– : Subtraction (also unary minus)
/ : Division (different effects for int and float)
% : Modulus (works only on int)
* : Multiplication
++ : Increment (unary operator)
– – : Decrement (unary operator)

When the operators given above are applied on numbers, or variable names, or both, we get arithmetic expressions such as the following:

Addition: This is like ordinary + operator in algebra.

```
int a, b, c;
a = 5; b = 6;
c = a + b;
```

Subtraction: This is also like ordinary – operator in algebra.

```
(a) int a, b, c;
    a = 5; b = 6;
    c = a - b;
```

Here, c gets the value –1.

This operator can be used as a unary operator as well (i.e., needing only one operand).

```
(b) int a, b;
    a = 9;
    b = -a;
```

Here b gets the value –9.

Division: This has different effects on int and float data.

```
(a) int a, b, c;
    a = 7;
    b = 2;
    c = a/b;
```

c gets the value 3 (7/2 = 3.5, but the decimal part is ignored).

```
(b) float a, b, c;
    a = 7;
    b = 2;
    c = a/b;
```

c gets the value 3.5.

Modulus: This works on integer data only and gives the remainder of division.

```
int a, b, c;
a = 7;
b = 2;
c = a%b;
```

c gets the value 1 (7/2=3 and remainder 1).

Exercise 1.10

1. Fill up the following:

	Quotient	**Remainder**
10/2		
10%2		
25/2		
25%2		
3%7		
7%3		
3%3		
0%2		
10%100		

Note: Modulo division is usually used to check whether a number is a multiple of another number. If so, then modulo division gives zero result (completely divisible, so no remainder).

Multiplication: This is again like × operator in algebra.

```
int a, b, c;
a = 5; b = 6;
c = a*b;                          c gets the value 30.
float a, b, c;
a = 2.5; b = 4.0;
c = a*b;                          c gets the value 10.0.
```

Increment: ++ This is a unary operator (needs only one operand) which increments the value of the operand by 1. This can be used in two ways:

Post increment: e.g. a++; (i.e., use and then increment)

Pre increment: e.g. ++a; (i.e., increment and then use)

Consider the following examples.

Example 1.7

```
1. # include<stdio.h>
   main( )
   {
       int a, b, c;
       a = 5; b = 6;
       c = a * b++;
       printf("%d\n", c);
   }
```

The value of c will be displayed as 30. The variable *b* is used as 6 in the calculation, but the final value of b will be 7.

```
2. # include<stdio.h>
   main( )
   {
       int a, b, c;
       a = 5; b = 6;
       c = a * ++b;
       printf("%d\n", c);
   }
```

The value of *c* will be displayed as 35. The variable *b* is used as 7 in the calculation and the final value of *b* will be 7.

Decrement: This is similar to ++. It *decrements* the value of operand by 1. Decrement also can be used in two ways:

Post decrement: e.g. a–; (use and then decrement).

Pre decrement: e.g. – a; (decrement and then use).

Exercise 1.11

1. Predict the value of *p*, *q* and *r* after the execution.

```
(a) int p, q, r;
    p = 3;
    q = 2;
    r = p*q--;
(b) int p, q, r;
    p = 3;
    q = 2;
    r = p*--q;
```

2. Assume int a, b, c, d; float p, q, r, s; a = 100; b = 10; c = 3; d = 7; p = 20.5; q = 1.5; y = 6.5; s = 3.0;
   Predict the result of the following arithmetic expressions:

Expressions	Value
a + b	
p + q	
c – d	
q*r	
a/100	
r – s	
b*c	
s/q	
b/c	
p/r	
b%c	
100%r	
c%d	
a%++b	
a%b++	
b%d	
++a	
b+c --	

1.11 COMPLEX EXPRESSIONS (USE OF BRACKETS AND PRECEDENCE)

In the previous examples, we used only a few operators in each expression. You can use any number of operators and operands in an expression. For example:

```
a + b * c - d
a*b/c
p + q*2
a + b*c - d/d*e%f
```

However, there are some rules to be followed on such occasions. Suppose we want to calculate $\frac{a+b}{c}$. We may naturally write $a + b/c$. However, this may be confused (by you, not *C* !) with an expression such as $a + b/c$ which has a different meaning.

For $a = 6$, $b = 4$, $c = 2$

$$\frac{a+b}{c} = \frac{6+4}{2} = \frac{10}{2} = 5$$

whereas

$$a + \frac{b}{c} = 6 + \frac{4}{2} = 6 + 2 = 8$$

So, in C, if we write $a + b/c$ as in the above case, what could be the result ? 5 or 8? Before we answer that, we will learn how to avoid the confusion. Always put parenthesis to make clear to C what you mean.

(a) $\frac{(a+b)}{c}$ can be written as $(a + b)/c$.

(b) $a + \frac{b}{c}$ can be written as $a + (b/c)$.

Exercise 1.12

1. Write the C arithmetic expression for each of the following mathematical expressions. (Use parenthesis to ensure correctness.):

   (a) r^2

   (b) $\frac{a \cdot b}{a+b}$

   (c) $p + \frac{q}{r^2}$

   (d) $\frac{a-b}{a \cdot b}$

   (e) $(a + b)^2$

   (f) $\frac{\dfrac{a \cdot b + b \cdot c + c \cdot d}{a + b + c}}{a \cdot b \cdot c}$

2. Give the value of each of the following expressions:

   (a) ((1 + 2) * (3 – 4))

   (b) ((3 + 2)%5)

   (c) (–13/2)%(–3*2)

   (d) (3%5) + (5%3)

Let us now go back to the question what C will do with the expression $a + b/c$. If given without brackets, will C take it as $\frac{a+b}{c}$ or $a+\frac{b}{c}$? C will take it as the second one. This is because C has a standard order in which operators are applied. This standard order of arranging operators is known as C's precedence of operators (see Table 1.5).

Table 1.5 Precedence of operators

( )	Whatever is inside ( ) will be calculated first
++ --	Among these, whichever comes first from left
* / %	Among these, whichever comes first from left
+ –	Among these, whichever comes first from left

Example 1.8

1. Consider the following expression and see how the evaluation is taking place.

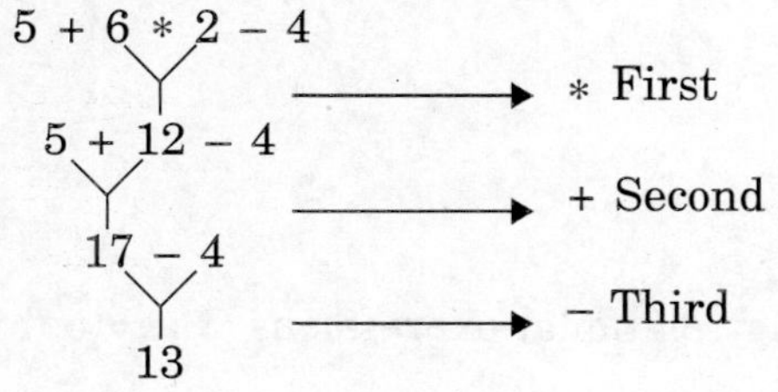

Exercise 1.13

1. Determine the value of each of the following C expressions using the precedence of operators.
   (a) 1 + 2 * 3 – 4, (b) 1 + 2 % 3 – 4, (c) 13/2 % 3 – 4, (d) 100/10/2 % 3, (e) (10 + 2)*3

1.12 RELATIONAL OPERATORS

Relational operators are used to compare(relate) values and they can be used in situations where we may need to ask questions such as *Is x greater than y?* The relational operators in C are given in Table 1.6.

Table 1.6 Relational operators

Symbol	Operator	Example
= =	Equality	x == y is x equal to y?
! =	Inequality	x != y is x not equal to y?
>	Greater than	x > y is x greater than y?
<	Less than	x < y is x less than y?
>=	Greater than or equal to	x >= y is x greater than or equal to y?
<=	Less than or equal to	x <= y is x less than or equal to y?

The result of a relational operation is TRUE or FALSE, represented in C by a non-zero value and zero value, respectively. Notice that characters are actually small integers and hence relational operators can be used on them too.

Example 1.9

```
1. int  a  =  5;  b  =  6;  c  =  7;
   a==5          true
   a==b          false
   a!=b          true
   a!=5          false
   char  c1,c2,c3;
   c1= 'p';  c2='q';  c3='r';
   c1>c2         false
   c2!=c3        true
   c3==  'r'     true
   c3!=  'p'     true
   c3!=  c1      true
   c1==c3        false
   c3>=c3        true
```

Exercise 1.14

1. Give the value of each of the following relational expressions if a = 5, b = 5, c = 7

Expression	**Value**	**Expression**	**Value**
a > 5		c < b	
a > = 5		c < = b	
a > b		c < a	
b > a		c! = b	
b > = a		c > = b	
b! = a		c == b	

2. Give the value of each of the following relational expressions:

```
If  char  c1,  c2,  c3;
c1  =  'm';
c2  =  'n';
c3  =  'o';
```

Expression	**Value**	**Expression**	**Value**
c1 > c2		c2 > c3	
c2 == 'o'		c2 < c1	
c2! = '0'		c1 > 'a'	
c2! = c1		c2 > 'A'	
c1! = c1		c3 <= 'a'	
c3> = c2		c1 == c3	
c2< = c2		c2 == 'A'	

3. For the following expressions, you need to refer to the ASCII table given in the Appendix. Write whether the expressions are True or False.

Expression	Value
‘+’ > ‘a’	
‘+’ == ‘A’	
‘–’ = ‘a’	
‘–’ = ‘A’	
“ ! ” = ‘a’	
‘>’ > ‘<’	
‘>’ > = ‘>’	

Note: There are two common mistakes.

(a) a == b being written as a = b. The first is a relational expression and the second is an assignment.

(b) 5 > 5 being evaluated as T. Note that 5 > 5 is false. 5 is not greater than itself. Similarly, 5 < 5 is also false.

1.13 LOGICAL OPERATORS

Logical operators can be used to combine relational expressions. There are three logical operators:

- && AND
- | | OR
- ! NOT

They can be used as in the examples below:

(A > B) && (A > C)

(A > B) | | (C > D)

!(A > B).

(exp1 && exp1)= **True** if both exp1 and exp2 are true.

(exp1 | | exp2) = **True** if either or both of exp1 and exp2 are true.

!(exp1) = **True** if exp1 is false; **False** if exp1 is true.

We usually summarize the explanation of AND, OR and NOT in **truth tables** which give the results in all possible cases. The truth tables for AND, OR, NOT are given in Tables 1.7, 1.8, and 1.9, respectively.

Table 1.7 AND (&&) Operator

exp1	exp2	exp1 AND exp2
F	F	F
F	T	F
T	F	F
T	T	T

Table 1.8 OR (| |) Operator

exp1	exp2	exp1 OR exp2
F	F	F
F	T	T
T	F	T
T	T	T

Table 1.9 NOT (!) Operator

exp1	NOT exp1
F	T
T	F

Example 1.10

1. Consider the logical expression (a > b) && (a > c), where a = 5, b = 4 and c = 7.

```
(a > b) && (a > c)
(5 > 4) && (5 > 7)
T && F
    = F
```

Exercise 1.15

1. Given i = 2, j = 3 and k = 6, what are the results of the following expressions?

```
(a) (i > j) && (i * j < = k)
(b) (!(i > j)) && (i * j < = k)
(c) (!(i > j))||( i * j < = k)
(d) ((i > j) && (i < = k))||(i * j < = k)
```

2. Actually, false has value 0 and true has value 1 (or any non-zero number). Hence, it is possible to print out the answer of the relational and logical expressions. Study the following program:

```
# include <stdio.h>
main()
{   int a, b, c;
    a = 5;
    b = 6;
    c = 10;
    printf("%d\n",a > b);
}
```

You now have a way of checking the value of any expression. Guess the value of the expressions given below and then test with a program similar to the above.

```
    int p, q, r, s;
    p = 5; q = 10; r = 15; s = 0;
(a) (p + q) > (r + s)
(b) (p/q) < (s/r)
(c) (p*q) == (r*s)
(d) (p + q + r)!=(r + q + p)
(e) (p + q)> = (s/r)
(f) ((p + q)>2) || ((p + r)>q)
    char x, y, z;
    x = 'A'; y = 'B'; z = 'C';
(g) x > y
(h) (x < y) && (y < z)
(i) (x < y) || (y > z)
(j) (x == y) || (y == 'B')
(k) ((x + 1) == y)
```

1.14 ASSIGNMENT STATEMENT REVISITED

Now that you have learnt the frequently used operators in C (there are many more!), we will take one more look at assignment statements. Recall that the general form of assignment statement is **variable = expression**.

Examples of valid assignment statements are:

```
x = y + 2;
a =(c + d)%k
b = 5;
sum = 0;
count = n + 1;
sum = sum + x;
a = 5;
b = 5 * 3;
c = a + b;
d = (a + b) * (x + y + z)/100;
```

Examples of invalid assignment statements are:

```
x + y = z
5 = x + y
(a + b)%c = x
sum + n = sum
3 = 5;
3 = a;
```

It may now be noticed that the interpretation of x = y, in C is not like in algebra (where it could mean the values of *x* and *y* are equal). In C, x = y means *store the value of the right-hand side* (y) *in the variable at the left-hand side* (x). As a result, x and y become equal. The meaning of the interpretation becomes clear when we look at the statement count=count+1. Mathematically, it is not meaningful. But in C, we have to consider it differently. Consider the following example:

```
count = 5;
count = count + 1;
```

In all assignment statements, always look at the right-hand side first. In this example, on the right-hand side, we have count + 1 which is 5 + 1 = 6. Now, store that value in the variable on the left-hand side. Hence, the count becomes 6. If a variable x appears on the left-hand side and right-hand side, you can read the right-hand side as the *current value of* x and the *left-hand side* as the new value of x. x = x + 1 may be read as (new value of x) = (current value of x) + 1.

Example 1.11

1. Write the values of a, b, c and d after the execution of each of the assignment statements.

Values of a, b, c, d

Assignment Statement	a	b	c	d	
	1	2	3	4	← Initial value
a = b;	(2)	2	3	4	
c = a;	2	2	(2)	4	
a = c + a;	(4)	2	2	4	
b = a++;	5	(4)	2	4	
d = d * 2;	4	5	2	(8)	
a = (a + b) * (c + d);	(90)	5	2	8	

Exercise 1.16

1. Write the values of a, b, c, d, e and f after the execution of each of the assignment statements.

	a	b	c	d	e	f
	5	6	3	10	2	3
a++;						
++b;						
a = ++c * e;						
a = c++ * f;						
f = f * e;						
d = a+b * c + e/f;						
a = a + 5;						
e = ++a /e++/f + d/d;						
a = 0;						

2. Study the program below and then predict the output of the program.

```
# include <stdio.h>
main( )
{
    int a, b, c;
    a = 12;
    b = 3;
    c = a + b;
    c = a - b;
    c = a * b;
    c = a / b;
    c = a % b;
    c = 12*a + b/2 - a*b*2/(a*c + b*2);
    c = c/4+13*(a + b)/3 - a*b + 2*a*a;
    a = a + 1;
    b = b * 5;
    printf("a = %d\n b = %d\n c = %d\n", a, b, c);
}
```

3. Study the program below and then predict the output of the program.

```
main( )
{
    int x = 0, y = 2, z = 1025;
    x = x + 1;
    x++;
    ++x;
    z = y++;
    z = ++y;
    printf("x = %d, y = %d, z = %d", x, y, z);
}
```

4. Study the program below and then predict the output of the program.

```
main( )
{
    int x = 0, y = 2, z = 1025;
    y = y - 1;
    y--;
    --y;
    y = 3;
    z = y--;
    z = --y;
    printf("x = %d, y = %d, z = %d", x, y, z);
}
```

1.14.1 Other Operators

Some of the other operators used in C language and their meaning with example are given in a tabular form below.

Operators	Meaning	Example	Action
+=	Addition then assignment	a + = b	a = a + b
–=	Subtraction then assignment	a – = b	a = b – a
*=	Multiplication then assignment	a * = b	a = a * b
/=	Division then assignment	a/ = b	a = a/b
%=	Modulus operation then assignment	a% = b	a = a%b
?:	Conditional operator	(i < 0)?0:100	If i < 0 the expression is 0 else the expression is 100
&=	a& = b	a = a&b	Logical bitwise AND of a and b
^=	a^ = b	a = a ∧ b	Logical bitwise exclusive OR of a and b
|=	a|= b	a = a|b	Logical bitwise OR of a and b
<<=	a << = b	a = a >> b	Left shift the elements of a by b number of displacement
>>=	a >> = b	a = a << b	Right shift the elements of a by b number of displacement

1.14.1.1 Bitwise operators

Bitwise operators are used to manipulate individual bits within a word of memory. They are divided into three types:

1. One's complement operator
2. Logical bitwise operator
3. Shift operator

One's complement operator. One's complement operator is usually denoted by ~. It is a unary operator. One's complement operator causes the bits of its operand to be inverted so that 1's become 0's and 0's become 1's.

Example 1.12

Sl. No.	Value	~Value
1	10110101	01001010
2	1111	0000
3	1010	1010

Logical bitwise operator. There are three operators in this type — bitwise and (&), bitwise exclusive or (^), and bitwise or (|). The working of these operators will be clear from the following examples.

Example	a	b	Expression	Output	Remark
1	0110	1010	a&b	0010	Returns 1 if both bits are 1
2	0110	1010	a^b	1100	Returns 1 if one bit is 0 and the other is 1
3	0110	1010	a|b	1110	Returns 1 if one or both bits are 1

Shift operator. There are two types of bitwise shift operators, viz. shift left (<<) and shift right(>>). These are binary operators. The first operand is an integer type that represents the bit pattern to be shifted. The second operand is an unsigned integer that indicates the number of displacement. The left shift operator results in the shifting of all of the bits in the first operand to the left by the number of positions indicated by the second operand. The right shift operator results in the shifting of all of the bits in the first operand to the right by the number of positions indicated by the second operand. The following examples will make it clear.

Example	a	Expression	Output
1	0110	a << 1	1100
2	0110	a << 2	1000
3	0110	a << 3	0000
4	0110	a >> 1	0011
5	0110	a >> 2	0001
6	0110	a >> 3	0000

In the above examples, consider the case when a = 0110; when it is shifted by one, all the bits are shifted to left and a zero is added to the empty position created at the right end. This is similar to multiplication of a number, say, 56, by 10 which gives 560. The digits 5 and 6 are shifted to left and a zero is added at end. So, the left shift is equivalent to multiplying by the base of the system.

When a is shifted to right by one, all the bits will be moved to right and a zero will be added to the left end. When a = 0011, "shift right" by one gives a = 0001. Consider the number 56 in the decimal system. When it is divided by 10, we get 5.6. In other words, an empty position is created at the left end. So, shift right is equivalent to divison by the base of the number system.

Exercise 1.17

1. Predict the output of the following operations.

Sl. No.	Initial value of a	Initial value of b	Operation	Final value of a	Final value of a
1	8		a+ = 5		
2	5.5	– 4.25	a– = b		
3	7	6	b* = (a – 2)		
4	6	3	a% = (b – 2)		
5	7.2		b/ = 4		

2. Predict the output of the following operations.

Sl. No.	a	Expression	Output
1	1110	a << 1	
2	0100	a << 2	
3	1010	a << 3	
4	1000	a >> 1	
5	1100	a >> 2	
6	0010	a >> 3	

1.14.2 Branching—Transfer of Control

In the C programs we have written so far, all the statements in the program were executed one after the other, in the order in which they appeared in the program. C permits this order to be changed, if desired. The statements used for this are known as **branching statements** or **conditionals**. There are two branching statements in C.

- if/if···else statement
- Switch statement

1.14.2.1 The if statement

The form of an **if** statement is as follows:

```
if (condition)
{
    statement 1;
    statement 2;
    :
    :
    statement n;
}
```

The **if** statement starts with the keyword 'if', followed by a condition inside ( ), then followed by any number of C statements inside { }. The condition is a relational or logical expression like (a > 5), (b == k), and (a > b) && (a > c). If the condition is true, then the statements inside the { } is executed and, if false, the statements are ignored.

Consider, as an example:

```
Fail_mark  =  30;
if  (mark_scored  <  Fail_mark)
{
    prinft("failed\n")
}
```

The program shown above checks if the mark scored by a student is less than the mark required for passing. If so, then it displays the message that the student has failed.

Here are some examples of how **if** statements begin:

```
if  ((a+b)==x)
if  ((a>b)&&(b>c))
if  (!(a>b))
if  ((a>b)||(c==d))
```

Whenever you face a situation where you need to say: *Do these only if a particular condition is true*, you will find an **if** statement appropriate.

Notes: 1. If there is only a single statement inside { }, the braces can be avoided. The above example can be written as if (m > 40) printf("Passed\n");. Students are strongly advised *not* to use this option as it is an easy way to make mistakes.

2. The **if** statement can be written in one line also, if found convenient, as follows:

```
#include <stdio.h>
main( )
{
    int  m;
    printf("Please  give  your  mark\n");
    scanf("%d",&m);
    if(m  >  40)     {printf("Passed\n");}
}
```

Example 1.13

1. Write a program to read the mark of a student and print out "First Class" if marks is more than 60.

```
#include <stdio.h>
main( )
{
```

```
    int m;
    printf("Please give your mark\n");
    scanf("%d",&m);
    if (m>60)
    {
        printf("First Class\n);
    }
}
```

2. Write a program to read two numbers and print out the smallest.

```
#include <stdio.h>
main( )
{
    int a, b;
    printf("Please give two integers\n");
    scanf("%d%d", &a, &b);
    if (a<b)
    {
        printf("%d is the smallest\n", a);
    }
    if (b<a)
    {
        printf("%d is the smallest\n", b);
    }
}
```

Note: Predict the results if (i) a = 15, b = 11, (ii) a = 25, b = 20, and (iii) a = 30, b = 30.

3. Write a program to ask for two numbers and let the user choose an arithmetic operator and then print out the answer.

```
#include <stdio.h>
main( )
{
    int a,b,c,choice;
    printf("1. Sum\n");
    printf("2. Difference\n");
    printf("3. Product\n");
    printf("4. Ratio\n");
    printf("Please choose an arithmetic that you want\n");
    scanf("%d",&choice);
    printf("Type in two value\n);
    scanf("%d%d",&a, &b);
    if (choice==1) {printf("The sum is %d\n", a+b);}
    if (choice==2) {printf("The sum is %d\n",a-b);}
    if (choice==3) {printf("The product is %d\n", a*b);}
    if (choice==4) {printf("The ratio is %d\n",a/b)}
}
```

Note: Predict the results if a = 5, b = 3, and the choices are: (i) 1; (ii) 22; (iii) 3; (iv) 4; and (v) 100.

Exercise 1.18

1. Identify and correct the errors in each of the following statements:

```
(a)  if (c<7);
     {
          printf("C is less than 7\n");
     }
(b)  if (c=>7)
     {
          printf("C is equal to or greater than 7\n);
     }
(c)  if (number=>largest)
     {
          largest==number;
     }
(d)  if (x=y)
     {
          printf("Reminder of %d divided by %d is %d\n",
          x,y,x%y);
     }
```

2. Write a C program that inputs two integers and then prints the larger number, followed by the words "is larger". If the numbers are equal, print the message "These numbers are equal".
3. Write a C program that inputs three different integers from the keyboard, and then prints the sum, the average, the product, the smallest, and the largest of these numbers. Display the information as shown below:

Input three different integers: 13 27 14
Sum is 54
Average is 18
Product is 4914
Smallest is 13
Largest is 27

4. Write a program to read three int numbers and print out the biggest.
5. Write a program that reads two integers and find if the first is a multiple of the second. (*Hint*: Use the modulus operator.)

1.14.2.2 The if···else statement

The form of an **if···else** statement is:

```
if (condition)
{
   statement 1;
}
```

⇒ *Do this if the condition inside ( ) is true*

```
else
{
    statement 2;
}
```

⇒ *Do this if the condition inside ( ) is false*

The above statement simply says that if the expression inside the parentheses is true, the first group of statement(s) inside { } is to be executed and, if false, the second group of statements following the 'else' is to be executed. Thus, one of the two set of statements will always be executed, whereas in the simple **if** statement, the statement inside { } is either executed or skipped.

Example 1.14

1. Write a program to read two numbers and print out the smallest. (Note the difference between this example and example 2 for simple **if**.)

```
#include <stdio.h>
main( )
{
        int a,b;
        printf("Please give two integers\n");
        scanf("%d%d",&a,&b);
        if (a<b)
        {
                printf("%d is the smallest\n",a);
        }
        else
        {
                printf("%d is the smallest\n",b);
        }
}
```

Note: Predict the result if (i) a = 15, b = 11; (ii) a = 25, b = 20; and (iii) a = 30, b = 30.

2. Write a program to ask the year of birth of a person and calculate the age in the year 2075, and if the result (age) is more than 90, then give the message that "It is likely that you may not be alive then".

```
#include <stdio.h>
main( )
{
        int year, age;
        printf("I will calculate your age in year 2075\n");
        scanf("%d",&year);
        age=2075-year;
        printf("Your age in year 2075 will be %d\n", age);
        if (age<90)
        {
```

```
        printf("I don't think you will be alive then\n");
    }
    else
    {
        printf("I think you will still be alive\n");
    }
}
```

3. Write a program to accept two integers and then print out either "the numbers are equal" or "the numbers are not eaqual".

```
#include <stdio.h>
main( )
{
    int a,b;
    printf("Input two integers\n");
    scanf("%d%d",&a, &b);
    if (a==b)
    {
        printf("Numbers are equal\n");
    }
    else
    {
        printf("Numbers are not equal\n");
    }
}
```

4. Write a program to accept the grade of a student and print out whether the student has a first class. (Only grade 'A' is first class.)

```
#include <stdio.h>
main( )
{
    char grade;
    printf("Please type in your grade\n");
    scanf("%c",&grade);
    if (grade=='A')
    {
        printf("You have a first class\n");
    }
    else
    {
        printf("You don't have a first class\n");
    }
}
```

5. Write a program to read the bank balance and category ('s' or 'o') of a person and then print out the interest (15% for category 's' and 10% for others).

```
#include <stdio.h>
main( )
{
    float balance;
    char cat;
    printf("Type in your bank balance>> ");
    scanf("%f",&balance);
    printf("Please type your bank category>> s or o\n");
    scanf("%c"&cat);
    if (cat=='s')
    {
        printf("Your interest is %f\n", (balance*0.15));
    }
    else
    {
        printf("Your interest is %f\n", balance*0.10);
    }
}
```

6. Write a program to accept three integers and then print out the biggest.

```
#include <stdio.h>
main( )
{
    int a,b,c;
    printf("Input three integers\n");
    scanf("%d%d%d",&a, &b, &c);
    if ((a>=b)&&(a>=c))
    {
        printf("%d is the biggest\n",a);
    }
    else
    {
        printf("%d is the biggest\n",c);
    }
}
```

Exercise 1.19

1. Write a program to accept the number of telephone calls made by a customer and then print out the rate as per the following rules:

Call	**Rate per call (Rs)**
Up to 100	1.0
100–300	0.9
301 and above	0.6

2. Write a program to accept the age and print out if the person is an adult (over 18) or a minor.
3. Write a program to accept three integer numbers and print out whether they are all equal.
4. Write a program to accept two character values and print out if they are the same.
5. Write a program to accept the choice of the user (0 or 1) and show a happy face ☺ for choice 0 and a sad face ☹ for choice 1.
6. Rewrite questions 1 – 5 given above using **if** statement only (no else part).
7. Write a program to read the age and mark of a student and then print out "selected" if the age is up to and including 25 and the mark is above 70.
8. Correct the following programs:

```
(a) if (gender == 1)
    {
         printf("Woman\n);
    }
    else ;
    {
         printf("Man\n");
    }
(b) if (age>=65);
    {
         printf("Age is greater than or equal to 65\n");
    }
    else
    {
         printf("Age is less than 65\n");
    }
```

9. Write an **if···else** statement to test if the current value of variable m is greater than twice the current value of variable v.

1.14.3 switch-case statement

Whenever we need to use a lot of **if** statements one after the other, the **switch-case** statement can be used more conveniently. The general form of the **switch** statement is as follows:

```
switch(x)
{
case n1: statement 1; break;    what to do if x==n1.
case n2: statement 2; break;    what to do if x==n2.
case n3: statement 3; break;    what to do if x==n3.
case n4: statement 4; break;    what to do if x==n4 etc.
default: statement; break       what to do if x!=n1, n2, n3,
                                and n4 etc.
}
```

The switch statement begins with the keyword 'switch', followed by a variable in parentheses which is the switching variable (should be an integer), in this case x. As many cases as needed are then enclosed within a pair of braces. The reserved word 'case' is used to begin each case, followed by the value of the variable for that case, then a colon, and the statements to be executed. Once an entry point is found, statements will be executed until a break is found or until the program drops through the bottom of the switch braces. The various case values can be in any order, and if a value is not found, the default portion of the switch will be executed.

Below are two programs (Programs 1.7 and 1.8) using **if···statement** and **switch-case** statement. First consider using **if** statement.

Program 1.7

```
#include <stdio.h>
main( )
{
    int choice;
    printf("Enter your choice 1,2,3, or 4\n");
    scanf("%d",&choice);
    if (choice==1) {  printf(":-)"); }
    if (choice==2) {  printf(":-o"); }
    if (choice==3) {  printf(":-("); }
    if (choice==4) {  printf(":-D"); }
}
```

The above program contains an **if** statement corresponding to each choice the user will have. Depending upon the choice of the user, the statement block contained in that **if** statement will take place.

Note: What will be the result if the user types choice as 25?
Note: What will be the result if the user types choice 4?

Now consider the same program rewritten into **switch-case**.

Program 1.8

```
#include <stdio.h>
main( )
{
    int choice;
    printf("Enter your choice 1,2,3, or 4\n");
    scanf("%d",&choice);
    switch(choice)
{
    case 1:
            printf(":-)");
            break;
    case 2:
            printf(":-o");
            break;
```

```
    case 3:
            printf(":-(");
            break;
    case 4:
            printf(":-D");
            break;
    default:
            printf("You type an invalid choice\n");
}
}
```

Note:

1. 'Break' can be written in the next line.
2. It is not necessary to have break after default.
3. What will be the result if a user types the choice as 25?

Example 1.15

1. Electricity consumers are divided into three categories 1, 2, and 3. Read each category and the number of units used and then print out the charge according to the following rates:

Category	Rate
1	Rs. 11/unit
2	Rs. 12/unit
3	Rs. 14/unit

```
#include <stdio.h>
main( )
{
    int cat, unit;
    printf("Please type in your category: 1, 2, or 3\n");
    scanf("%d",&cat);
    printf("Type in your number of units used\n");
    scanf("%d",&unit);
    switch(cat)
    {
    case 1:
            printf("Charge =Rs. %d\n", unit*11);
            break;
    case 2:
            printf("Charge=Rs. %d\n", unit*12);
            break;
    case 3:
            printf("Charge=Rs. %d\n", unit*14);
            break;
```

```
        default:
                printf("Sorry, no category like that \n");
                break;
        }
    }
```

2. Read the mark of a student. Give a bonus of 15 marks if it is a first year student, 10 marks if it is a second year student or 5 marks if it is a third year student. Print out the new mark.

```
#include <stdio.h>
main()
{
        int mark, year;
        printf("Type in your mark and your year\n");
        scanf("%d%d",&mark,&year);
        switch(year)
        {
        case 1:
                printf("Your new mark = %d\n", 15+mark);
                break;
        case 2:
                printf("Your new mark = %d\n", 10+mark);
                break;
        case 3:
                printf("Your new mark = %d\n", 5+mark);
                break;
        default:
                printf("Sorry, please type again\n");
        }
}
```

3. Write a program to scan a character and print out if it is a vowel.

(a) **Using if···else statement**

```
#include <stdio.h>
main( )
{
    char input;
    printf("Please enter a character that you like\n");
    scanf("%c",&input);
    if ((input=='a')||(input=='e')||)||(input=='i')||
          (input=='o')||(input=='u') )
        {
          printf("%c is a vowel\n", input);
        }
        else
        {
          printf("%c is not a vowel\n", input);
        }
}
```

(b) Using switch-case statement

```
#include <stdio.h>
main( )
{
    char input;
    printf("Please enter a character that you like\n");
    scanf("%c",&input);
    switch(input)
    {
        case 'a':
        case 'e':
        case 'i':
        case 'o':
        case 'u':
            printf("Vowel\n");
            break;
        default:
            printf("Not vowel\n"); break;
    }
}
```

Note: Trace the flow of execution for the following cases: (i) 'a'; (ii) 'o'; and (iii) 'k'.

Exercise 1.20

1. Write a program to read student category number and print out the fees to be paid according to the following table:

Category	Fee
1	Rs. 1000
2	Rs. 1200
3	Rs. 1300
4	Rs. 1400
5	Rs. 1400

2. Cricket players who hit sixes will be paid cash awards as follows:

No. of sixes	Cash award
0	–
1	Rs. 5000
2	Rs. 7500
3	Rs. 10000
4	Rs. 15000
> = 5	Rs. 20000

Write a program to accept the number of sixes and print out the cash award.

3. Study the program below, then predict the final value of the variables.

```
int x = 11, y = 11, z = 11;
char a = 40, b = 40, c = 40;
float r = 12.987, s = 12.987, t = 12.987
```

(a) First group of **if** statements

	x	y	z	a	b	c	r	s	t
Initial value	11	11	11	40	40	40	12.987	12.987	12.987
If (x==y){z=–13;}									
if(x>z){a='A';}									
if (!(x>z)){a='B';}									
if(b<=c){r=0.0;}									
if(r!=s){t=c/2;}									

(b) Second group of **if** statements

	x	y	z	a	b	c	r	s	t
Initial value	11	11	11	40	40	40	12.987	12.987	12.987
if (r!=s){z=1000;}									
if (x==y){z=222;}									
if (x!=0){z=333;}									
if (x){z=444;}									

(c) Third group of **if** statements

	x	y	z	a	b	c	r	s	t
Initial value	11	11	11	40	40	40	12.987	12.987	12.987
if ((x==y)&&(x==77)) {z=33;}									
if ((x>y)||(z>12)) {z=22;}									
if (x&&y&&z) {z=11;}									
if((x==1)&&(y==2)&&(z==3)) {r=12.00;}									
if((x==2)&&(y==3)&&(z==4)) {r=14.56;}									

(d) Fourth group of **if** statements

if (x==x){z=27.345; }
if (x!=x){z=27.345; }
if (x==0){z=27.345; }

	x	y	z	a	b	c	r	s	t
Initial value	11	11	11	40	40	40	12.987	12.987	12.987
if (x==x) {z=27.345;}									
if (x!=x) {z=27.345;}									
if (x==0) {z=27.345;}									

4. Assuming the values of x, y, and z as 1, 2, and 3, what will the following 'if statement' print out?

```
if  (y  >  z)
{
        if(y  >  z)
        {
              printf("%d\n",x);
        }
}
```

5. What, if any, is wrong with the following statement?

```
if  (x  =  y)
{
        printf("Equal\n");
}
```

6. Assuming x = 0, what will the following statement print out?

```
scanf("%d",&x);
switch(x)
{
        case  1:
              printf("one");
              break;
        case  2:
              printf("Two");
              break;
        default:
              printf("Neither  1  or  2");
              break;
}
```

7. Assuming the value of x to be zero, what will the following **switch** statement print out?

```
switch(x)
{
     case 1:
     case 2:
     case 3:
     case 4:
     case 5:
     case 6:
         printf("Less than or equal to 6");
         break;
     default:
         printf("Greater than 6");
}
```

8. Assuming the value of x= 3, and y=3, what will the following **switch** statement print out?

```
switch (x)
{
    case 1:
         if (x==y)
         {
              printf("Both one");
         }
         else
         {
              printf("Single one");
         }
    case 2:
         if (x==y)
         {
              printf("Both two");
         }
         break;
    default:
         if(x==y)
         {
              printf("Both equal but not one or two");
         }
         else
         {
              printf("Both Unequal");
         }
         break;
}
```

9. Write a program with **if···else** statement to accept an integer from the user. Then check whether it is an odd number or even number and print out the result in the following style: " - - - - is an odd number".
10. Rewrite the above program with a **switch** statement.
11. Write a program to read two int numbers, then print out the greatest among two numbers like the following using **if···else** statements in the following style:

" - - - - - is greater than - - - - - ".

12. Study the statement below and answer the following questions:

```
scanf("%d",&x);
switch(x)
{
    case1:
        printf("Good");
        break;
    case2:
        printf("Better");
    case3:
        printf("Best");
    default:
        printf("Out! Your choice is unacceptable"); break;
}
```

(a) What is the output if the user types 1?
(b) What is the output if the user types 2?
(c) What is the output if the user types 3?
(d) What is the output if the user types 4?

13. Study the statement below and answer the following questions:

```
if (category==1)
{
    if (age<18)
    {
        printf("You are not allowed to enter");
    }
    else
    {
        printf("You are allowed to enter");
    }
}
else
{
    if (category==2)
    {
        if (age<21)
        {
```

```
                printf("You are not allowed to enter");
            }
            else
            {
                printf("You are allowed to enter");
            }
        }
    }
```

(a) What is the output if category = 1 and age = 21?
(b) What is the output if category = 2 and age = 18?
(c) What is the output if category = 3 and age = 21?
(d) What is the output if category = 2 and age = 50?
(e) Rewrite the above with **switch** statements.

1.15 LOOPS: for, while AND do while

A loop is a facility to repeat a set of, statements as per the specified conditions. C gives you a choice of three types of loops, viz. **for, while,** and **do while**. The **for loop** is frequently used, usually where the loop is to be repeated for a fixed number of times. The **while loop** keeps repeating an action until an associated test becomes false. This is useful when the programmer does not know in advance how many times the loop will be repeated. The **do while loop** is similar to the while loop, but the test occurs after the loop body is executed. This ensures that the loop body is run at least once.

1.15.1 The for loop

A **for loop** statement has the following structure:

```
for (starting value; ending condition ; stepping)
{
    statement to be repeated; ⇒ Body of loop

}
```

Here is an example. The following loop will print the numbers from 1 to 10:

```
#include<stdio.h>
main( )
{
    int i; ⇒ i is known as loop index
    for (i= 1; i<11; i++)
    {                   ⇒ printf("%d\n", i) will be repeated 10 times
     printf("%d\n", i); while i=1,2,3......9,10 (one by one).
    }
}
```

The **for loop** consists of the keyword **for** followed by ( ), then by any number of C statements inside the curly brackets, { } . Inside the parentheses ( ), there are three parts separated by semi-colons. The first part defines the starting value through an initializing statement. This is executed prior to the first *pass* through the loop (*Several initializing statements can be placed in this field, separated by commas.*) The second part is the test which is done at the beginning of each pass through the loop. It can be any expression which will have a true or false value. The expression contained in the third part is executed after those statements inside { } are executed. (This field, like the first, can also be composed of several expressions separated by commas.)

The **for loop** is usually used in those cases where you are doing a fixed number of repetitions. The **for loop** is a very convenient loop because it has all the information about repetition in one place, rather than at both ends of the { } like in **while** and **do while** loops.

Example 1.16

1. Write a program to print out the numbers from 1 to 100.

```
# include <stdio.h>
main( )
{
    int i;
    for (i= 1; i<=100; i++)
    {
    printf("%d\n", i); ⇒ printf("%d\n", i) will be repeated 100 times
    }                        from i=1 to i=100, one by one
}
```

2. Write a program to print the numbers from 51 to 100.

```
# include <stdio.h>
main( )
{
    int i;
    for(i=51; i<101; i++)
    {
        printf("%d\n", i);
    }
}
```

3. Print the square of the numbers from 1 to 100.

```
# include <stdio.h>
main( )
{
    int i;
    for(i=1; i<=100; i++)
    {
        printf("%d\n", i*i);
    }
}
```

4. Print the odd numbers from 1 to 99.

```
# include <stdio.h>
main( )
{
    int i;
    printf("The odd numbers from 1 to 99 are:\n");
    for(i=1; i<100; i++)
    {
        if (i%2==1)
        {
            printf("%d\n", i);
        }
    }
}
```

Note: You can use the above approach to print out the numbers which are multiple of a specific number.

5. Write a program to print your name ten times on the screen.

```
#include<stdio.h>
main( )
{
    int i;
    for (i=1; i<11; i++)
    {
        printf(" Rama Varma\n");
    }
}
```

6. Write a program to find the sum of the first ten natural numbers.

```
#include <stdio.h>
main( )
{
    int sum,i;
    sum=0;
    for(i=1;i<11;i=i++)
    {
        sum=sum + i;
    }
    printf("Sum = %d",sum);
}
```

Note: The variable sum is initialized to 0 and the loop is repeated ten times. Each time the value of i is incremented—and in this program it is the number that is to be added to find the sum. Thus, by adding i to the sum each time in the loop, the final sum value will be obtained.

Exercise 1.21

Using **for loops,** write programs to print the sequence of numbers indicated below. You are advised to start with the first program and make modification for each of the rest.

1. Numbers from 1 to 50.
2. Numbers from 2 to 51.
3. Numbers from –5 to 15.
4. Numbers from 100 to 200.
5. Odd numbers from 1 to 50.
6. Even numbers from 1 to 50.
7. Multiple of 3, from 1 to 25.
8. Multiple of 5, from 10 to 70.
9. Multiple of 50, from 1 to 1000.
10. Multiple of 3 and also 5, from 1 to 25.
11. Multiple of 3 or 5, from 1 to 25.
12. Square of numbers from 1 to 10.
13. Square of odd number from 1 to 10.
14. Cube of numbers from 10 to 15.
15. Cube of odd numbers from 10 to 15.
16. Square and cube of numbers from 1 to 10.
17. Numbers from 1 to 10 along with square and cube.

Using **for loops**, write programs to print each of the following sequence of numbers:

18. 1,2,3,4,5,6,7,8,9
19. 1 2 3 4 5 6 7 8 9 10
20. 0 1 2 3 4 5 6 7 8 9
21. 1,3,5,7,9
22. 0,2,4,6,8
23. 0,2,4,6,8,10
24. 0,4,8,12,16,20
25. 10,9,8,7,6,5,4,3,2,1,0
26. 10,8,6,4,2,0
27. 9,7,5,3,1
28. Repeat Questions 1–17 to find and print the sum of the numbers indicated in the question.
29. Write a program to accept the value of two integers a and b and print all the multiples of 5 between a and b.
30. Write a program to accept the value of an integer N and then print all the odd numbers from 1 to N.
31. Write a program to accept the value of an integer N and then print all the numbers in the descending order (from N to 1).
32. Write a program to accept the value of an integer N and then print out the sum of all the numbers from 1 to N.

1.16 NESTED for LOOPS

A **for** statement can be executed within another **for** statement, which is called *nesting*. Let us take, as an example, the following program:

```
#include<stdio.h>
main( )
{
    int i, j;
    for (i= 0; i<4; i++)
    {
        for (j= 0; j<5; j++)
        {
            printf("i=%d, j=%d\n", i, j);
        }
    }
}
```

```
i = 0, j = 0
i = 0, j = 1
i = 0, j = 2
i = 0, j = 3
i = 0, j = 4
i = 1, j = 0
i = 1, j = 1
i = 1, j = 2
i = 1, j = 3
i = 1, j = 4
i = 2, j = 0
i = 2, j = 1
i = 2, j = 2
i = 2, j = 3
i = 2, j = 4
i = 3, j = 0
i = 3, j = 1
i = 3, j = 2
i = 3, j = 3
i = 3, j = 4
```

Note: In the above program, the outer loop will run 4 times, and the inner loop will run 5 times. Thus, the **printf** statement will run 4*5 = 20 times.

Example 1.17

1. Write a program to print out the multiplication table of numbers from 1 to 12.

```
# include <stdio.h>
main( )
{
    int i, j;
    for (i=1; i<=12; i++)
    {
        for (j=1; j<=12; j++)
        {
            printf(" %d times %d = %d\n", i, j, i*j);
        }
    }
}
```

2. Modify the above program so that a title is given for each table.

```
#include<stdio.h>
main( )
{
    int i, j;
    for (i=1; i<=12; i++)
    {
```

```
        printf("\nTable for %d\n", i);
        for (j=1; j<=12; j++)
        {
            printf("%d times %d = %d\n", i, j, i*j);
        }
    }
}
```

Exercise 1.22

1. Write a program to print out the multiplication table of numbers 10–20, starting from 5 and ending at 15. That is, the first output should be 5 × 10 = 50, and the last output should be 15 × 20 = 300. A title should be given for each table.

1.17 TIPS ON for LOOP AND NESTED for LOOP

1. It is not a good practice to use the index before and after the loop.

   Example:
   ```
   int i;
   printf("%d\n", i); ⇒ variable i is not meaningful before
   loop.
   for (i=0; i<10; i++)
   {
          printf("%d\n", i); ⇒ valid use of 1
   }
   printf("%d\n", i);
   ⇒ variable i is not meaningful after loop termination.
   ```

2. The same loop variable can be used for more than one loop, provided they are not nested.

   Valid example:
   ```
   int i, x;
   for (i=0; i<10; i++)
   {
       printf("%d", i);
   }
   for (i=0; i<3; i++)
   {
       printf("%d\n", i*x);
   }
   ```

   Invalid example:
   ```
   for (i=0; i<10; i++)
   {
   ```

```
    for  (i=0;  i<12;  i++)⇒  value for i is not clear
    {
        printf("%d * %d = %d\n", i, i, i*i);
    }
}
```

3. Some compilers may permit float data type for loop index.

```
Example
int i;
for (i=10.6; i<21.7; i=i+3.2)
{
    printf("%d\n", i);
}
```

4. A **for** loop can have more than one loop index and also can have any of the parts inside for ( ) missing, as long as the semicolon is still included between each part as in the following examples:

```
for (; i<10; i++)
for (i=0; ; i++)
for (i=0, j=0; i<10, j<10; i++, j++)
for (; ;)
```

5. There is no need for a { } if only one statement is there inside **for** loop. However, this is strongly discouraged.

```
Example
int i ;
for (i=0; i<10; i++)
printf("%d\n", i);  ⇒ i will be repeated 10 times
printf("%d\n", i*i);  ⇒ i*i will not be repeated 10 times
but only once.
```

6. Be careful not to put the semicolon (;) after the **for** loop. Such a loop will have no effect.

```
Example
for (i=0; i<10; i++); ⇒ will have no effect
```

1.18 THE while loop

The general form of the **while loop** is:

```
while (condition)
{       statement;
}
```

The **while loop** continues to repeat while the condition inside ( ) is true. When the condition becomes false, the repetition stops. Consider the following (Program 1.9).

Program 1.9

```
# include <stdio.h>
main ( )
{
    int i;
    i = 0;
    while (i<10)
    {
        printf("%d\n", i);
        i++;
    }
}
```

The program begins with an integer variable *i*. The variable is set to zero and we come to the **while loop** itself. The keyword **while** is followed by an expression ($i < 10$) in parentheses, followed by C statements inside the braces. As long as the expression in the parentheses is true, all statements within the braces will be repeatedly executed. In this case, since the variable *i* is incremented by one every time the statements are executed, it will eventually reach 10. At that time the statement will not be executed because $i < 10$ becomes false, and the loop will stop.

If the variable *i* were initially set to any number greater than 10, the statements within the loop would not be executed at all, so it is possible to have a **while** loop that is never executed. Also, if the variable was not incremented in the loop, the loop would never terminate, and the program would never complete. As in the **for loop,** if there is only one statement to be executed within the loop, it does not need {}. Again, this is strongly discouraged.

The **while loop** is very similar to the **for loop**. Their characteristics are similar as illustrated in the following figure.

```
for (i=0; i<10; i++)
{

    printf("%d\n", i);


}
```

```
i=0;
while (i<10)
{
printf("%d\n",i);
i++;

}
```

Example 1.18

1. Write a program to print the numbers between 0 and 9.

```
#include <stdio.h>
main( )
{
    int dig = 0;
    while(dig <= 9)
        printf("%d\n",dig++);
}
```

Note: In this program, while the value of the variable *dig* is less than or equal to 9, the value is displayed as well as *dig* is incremented in each step. When the condition fails, the program terminates.

2. Write a program by using the **while** loop to print all the odd numbers from 1 to 100.

```
#include<stdio.h>
main( )
{
    int  i;
    i=1;
    while  (i<100)
    {
      if  (i%2==1)
      {
         printf("%d\n",  i);
      }
      i++;
    }
}
```

Note: In this program, *i* is divided by 2 and the remainder of the division is used to verify whether *i* is an odd number or not. In the loop, *i* takes values from 1 to 100 and each time division operation is performed on it.

3. Write a program to accept an integer number n and then print out all the multiples of 7 from 1 to n using the **while loop**.

```
#include<stdio.h>
main( )
{
      int  i,  n;
      printf("Please  type  in  an  integer\n");
      scanf("%d",  &n);
      i=1;
      while  (i<=n)
      {
           if  (i%7==0)
           {
                printf("%d\n",  i);
           }
           i++;
      }
}
```

Note: As in the case of the Example 2, here too, the variable *i* is divided by 7 and its remainder is checked to find if it is zero. In that case *i* is a multiple of 7.

4. Write a program to accept the value of two integers a and b and print all the multiples of 5 between a and b by using the **while** loop.

```
#include <stdio.h>
main( )
{
        int i, a, b;
        printf("Type in two integers\n");
        scanf("%d%d", &a, &b);
        i=a;
        while (i<=b)
        {
              if (i%5= =0)
              {
                          printf("%d\n", i);
              }
              i++;
        }
}
```

5. Write a program to print whether a given integer is a prime.

```
#include <stdio.h>
main( )
{   int num=25, i;
    i=2;
    while(i<=num-1)
{
    if (num%i==0)
    {
        printf("Not a prime number");
        break;
    }
    i++;
}
if (i==num)
    printf("Prime number");
}
```

Note: A number 25 is selected at random. To check if the number num is a prime or not, it is divided by 2, 3 till 24. Each time the remainder is found and checked if it is zero. If it is zero, then the variable num is not a prime number and the process is terminated as indicated by the **break** statement. Otherwise, the process is continued.

Exercise 1.23

Using **while loops**, write programs to print the sequence of numbers indicated below. You are advised to start with the first program and make modification for each of the rest.

1. Numbers from 1 to 50.
2. Numbers from 2 to 51.
3. Numbers from –5 to 15.
4. Numbers from 100 to 200.
5. Odd numbers, from 1 to 50.
6. Even numbers, from 1 to 50.
7. Multiple of 3, from 1 to 25.
8. Multiple of 5, from 10 to 70.
9. Multiple of 50, from 1 to 1000.
10. Multiple of 3 and also 5, from 1 to 25.
11. Multiple of 3 or 5, which are from 1 to 25.

Using **while** loops, write programs to print the sequence of numbers indicated below.

12. Square of numbers from 1 to 10.
13. Square of odd numbers from 1 to 10.
14. Cube of numbers from 10 to 15.
15. Cube of odd numbers from 10 to 15.
16. Square and cube of numbers from 1 to 10.
17. Numbers from 1 to 10 along with square and cube.

Using **while** loops, write programs to print and to find the sum of the sequence of numbers indicated below.

18. 1, 2, 3, 4, 5, 6, 7, 8, 9
19. 1 2 3 4 5 6 7 8 9 10
20. 0 1 2 3 4 5 6 7 8 9
21. 1, 3, 5, 7, 9
22. 0, 2, 4, 6, 8
23. 0, 2, 4, 6, 8, 10
24. 0, 4, 8, 12, 16, 20
25. 10, 9, 8, 7, 6, 5, 4, 3, 2, 1, 0
26. 10, 8, 6, 4, 2, 0
27. 9, 7, 5, 3, 1
28. Predict the output of the following program segments.

Sl. No.	Program segment	Output

1	`int i=5;`
	`while(i>=1)`
	`{`
	`    printf("\n Namasthe !");`
	`    i=i-1;`
	`}`	

2	`int x=1;`
	`while(x=0;x<=255;x++)`
	`    printf("\nAscii value %d`
	`    Character %c",x,x);`	

3	`int counter;`
	`counter=0;`
	`while(counter!=25)`
	`{`
	`    printf("\n");`
	`    counter=counter+1;`
	`}`	

4	int j=1;
	while(j<=12)
	{
	    printf("\n%d",j);
	    j++;
	}	

1.19 do while loop

The **for loop** and the **while loop** that we have already discussed check the condition before the loop is executed each time. Therefore, the body of the loop may never be executed at all if the condition is false at the beginning. If we need to execute the body of the loop at least once, we can use the **do while** statement to achieve this. An example of the **do while** loop is given below. This prints numbers from 1 to 10.

```
i=1;
do
{
    printf("%d\n",i);
    i++;
} while(i< 10);
```

This program is identical to the **while** loop, except that the loop begins with the keyword **do**, followed by the statements to be repeated in braces, then the keyword **while**, and finally an expression in parentheses. The statements in the braces are executed repeatedly as long as the expression in the parentheses is true. When the expression in parentheses becomes false, execution stops. Since the test is done at the end of the loop, the statements in the braces will always be executed at least once. Also, if variable *i* was not changed within the loop, the loop would never terminate, and hence the program would never terminate.

```
i=1;
while(i<1)
    {
        printf("%d\n", i);
        i++;
    }
```

- It will not execute because i is not <1.

```
i=1;
do
{
    printf("%d\n", i);
    i++;
}while(i<1);
```

- It will execute only one time.

Example 1.19

1. Write a program using the **do while** loop to print all the odd numbers from 1 to 100.

```
#include<stdio.h>
main( )
{
      int i;
      i=1;
      do
      {
            if (i%2==1)
            {
                        printf("%d\n", i);
            }
            i++;
      }  while (i<=100);
}
```

2. Write a program to accept an integer number n and then print out all the multiples of 7 from 1 to n by using the **do while** loop.

```
#include<stdio.h>
main( )
{
      int i, n;
      printf("Please type in an integer\n");
      scanf("%d", &n);
      i=1;
      do
      {
            if (i%7==0)
            {
                  printf("%d\n", i);
            }
            i++;
      } while (i<=n);
}
```

Exercise 1.24

Using **do while loops,** write programs to print the sequence of numbers indicated below. You are advised to start with the first program and make modification for each of the rest.

1. Numbers from 1 to 50.
2. Numbers from 2 to 51.
3. Numbers from –5 to 15.
4. Numbers from 100 to 200.
5. Odd numbers from 1 to 50.
6. Even numbers from 1 to 50.

7. Multiple of 3 from 1 to 25.
8. Multiple of 5 from 10 to 70.
9. Multiple of 50 from 1 to 1000.
10. Multiple of 3 and also 5 from 1 to 25.
11. Multiple of 3 or 5 from 1 to 25.

Using **do while loops,** write programs to print the sequence of numbers indicated below.

12. Square of numbers from 1 to 10.
13. Square of odd numbers from 1 to 10.
14. Cube of numbers from 10 to 15.
15. Cube of odd numbers from 10 to 15.
16. Square and cube of numbers from 1 to 10.
17. Numbers from 1 to 10 along with square and cube.

Using **do while loops,** write programs to print and to find the sum of the sequence of numbers indicated below.

18. 1, 2, 3, 4, 5, 6, 7, 8, 9
19. 1 2 3 4 5 6 7 8 9 10
20. 0 1 2 3 4 5 6 7 8 9
21. 1, 3, 5, 7, 9
22. 0, 2, 4, 6, 8
23. 0, 2, 4, 6, 8, 10
24. 0, 4, 8, 12,16, 20
25. 10, 9, 8, 7, 6, 5, 4, 3, 2, 1, 0
26. 10, 8, 6, 4, 2, 0
27. 9, 7, 5, 3, 1

1.20 BREAK AND CONTINUE

Break and **continue** are two statements which can be used inside loops to control the behaviour of the loops as you desire. Note that the **break will jump out of the loop** and begin executing statements immediately following the loop, effectively terminating the loop. This is a valuable statement when you need to jump out of a loop, depending on the value of some results calculated inside the loop.

The **continue** statement does not cause termination of the loop but **skips the present iteration**. It always jumps to the beginning of the loop, skipping the statements after it for the current iteration. We will learn break and continue with examples. Consider the following example.

Example 1.20

1. Write a program to print the integer value from 1 to 10 using the **for** loop.

```
#include<stdio.h>
main( )
{
    int i;
    for(int i=1; i<=10; i++)
    {
        printf("%d\n", i);
    }
 }
```

2. Consider the following program when a **continue** statement has been added.

```
#include <stdio.h>
main( )
{
    int i;
    {
        for (int i = 1; i <= 10; i++)
        {
            if (i == 5)
            {
                continue;
            }
        printf("%d\t", i);
        }
    }
}
```

The output of the above program is:

1 2 3 4 ↑ 6 7 8 9 10

5 is skipped

Note: The new statement makes the program skip the print statement when i = 5. When i = 5, the **continue** statement will be executed such that the program will skip the following print statement. Thus, 5 was not printed out. The **break** statement, in comparison, breaks out of the loop.

3. Consider the following program when a **break** statement has been added.

```
#include <stdio.h>
main( )
{
int i;
    {   for (int i = 1; i <= 10; i++)
        {
            if (i == 5)
            {
              break;
            }
            printf("%d\t", i);
        }
    }
}
```

The output of the above program is:

1 2 3 4

Note: We can clearly see the difference from the outputs. The **continue** statements will skip all the following statements in the loop and continue with the new value. The **break** statement will terminate the loop immediately.

1.21 COMPARISON BETWEEN LOOPS

The **while** loop is convenient to use when you do not have any idea as to how many times the loop will be executed, and the **for** loop is usually used in those cases when you are doing a fixed number of iterations. The **for** loop is also convenient because it moves all of the control information of the loop into one place, rather than at both ends of the code. Depending on how they are used, it is possible with **for** and **while** loops to never execute the statement within the loop at all. This is because the test is done at the beginning of the loop, and the test may fail during the first iteration. The **do while** loop, however, will always execute the code at least once because statements are executed prior to the test.

Exercise 1.25

1. How many times does each of the following loops repeat ?

```
(a) for  (j=0;  j<8;  j++)
     { printf("%d\n",j); }
(b) for  (k=1;k<=8;  k++)
     { printf("%d\n",k); }
(c) for  (i=10;  i<=10;  i++)
     { printf("%d\n",i); }
(d) for  (i=10;  i<10;  i++)
     { printf("%d\n",i); }
(e) for  (i=10;  i>=1;  i=i-4)
     { printf("%d\n",i); }
(f) for  (i=10;  i==1;  i=i-4)
     { printf("%d\n",i); }
```

2. Are the following loops equivalent?

```
(a) for  (j=65;  j<72;  j++)
     { printf("%c",j); }
(b) int  k=65;
    while  (k<72)
     { printf("%c",k);  k++;  }
```

3. What will be printed out by the following loops?

```
(a) int  k=100;
    while  (k<100)
    { printf("%c",k);
      k++;
    }
```

```
(b)int  k=100;
   do
   {
      printf("%c",k);
      k++;
   } while  (k<100);
```

4. Write programs for the following using *(i)* **while** loops and (ii) **do while** loops.
   (a) scanf and printf characters until the character 'x' is typed in.
   (b) scanf and printf integers until a negative integer is typed in.
   (c) scanf and printf integers until the square of the integers read is > 1250.
   (d) scanf and printf integers until the number read is <100 or > 200.

5. Write **for** loops for the following situations, making use of **continue** or **break** as required.
   (a) Print numbers from 1 to 100 except 75.
   (b) Print characters from 'a' to 'z' except 'p'.
   (c) Print numbers from 50 to 100 except 56 and 79.
   (d) Print characters from 'A' to 'Z' except 'P', 'Q' and 'R'.
   (e) scanf and printf numbers until a negative number is typed in. However, the printing should stop if the number is a multiple of 7.
   (f) scanf and printf lower case alphabet characters, but stop printing if the character is 'm' or 'n'.

1.22 ARRAYS

An array is an ordered arrangement of data elements. It can be either single dimension or multidimension.

1.22.1 Single Dimension Arrays

Here are some key concepts about arrays:

- Arrays are a collection (group) of data of the same type, e.g. integer, real.
- Arrays are referred to by a single name such as A, sales, marks.
- Each element (member) of the group is referred to by an **index,** as in: A[0], A[1], sales[5], marks[j], etc.
- 0, 1, 5 and j inside the square brackets given above are examples of **indices.**
- Arrays can be handled easily and efficiently by using **for** loops (or **while/do while** loops also).
- Memory is allocated for arrays during compilation (hence arrays are known as *static data structures*).

Arrays can be declared as follows:

int	a	[100];
↓	↓	↓
data type	name	size (number of elements)

Example 1.21

char name [25]; ⇒ name is an array of 25 characters, (name[0],name[1],..... name[24])
float height [12]; ⇒ height is an array of 12 floats, ([height[0],height [1],...height[11])
int x [33]; ⇒ x is an array of 33 integers, (x[0],x[1],....x[32])

Arrays are stored in the memory in consecutive locations. It may be useful (perhaps later) to know how an array is stored in the memory (Figure 1.1), e.g. int x[3].

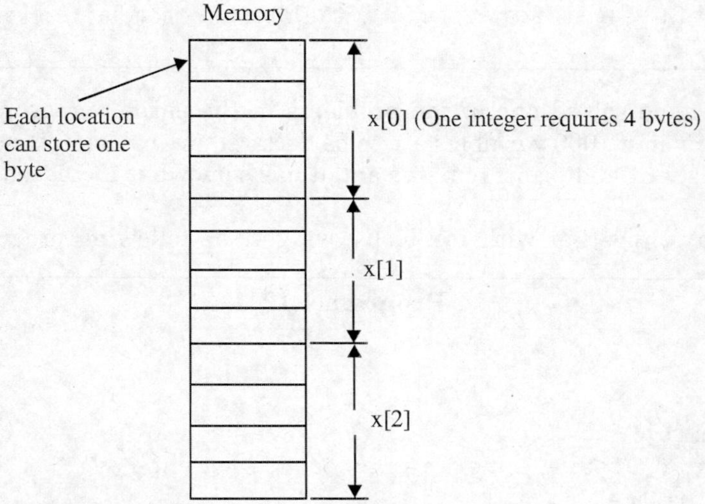

Figure 1.1 Visual representation of an array in memory.

Note: The first element of an array is actually 0th element since C uses indexing beginning from 0.

To appreciate the need and significance of arrays, we will consider a program written

- Without using arrays,
- Using arrays, but no **for** loops, and
- Using arrays with **for** loops.

A program is written to read the marks of five students, without using arrays (Program 1.10).

Program 1.10

```
#include<stdio.h>
main( )
{   int m1, m2, m3, m4, m5;
    printf("Please enter 5 student's marks\n");
    scanf("%d%d%d%d%d", &m1, &m2, &m3, &m4, &m5);
    printf("%d%d%d%d%d",m1, m2, m3, m4, m5);
}
```

Note: We will face two difficulties if we want to read marks of 1000 students this way:

- Declaring 1000 variable names and
- Writing **scanf** and then **printf** for 1000 variables.

Now, another program is given using arrays without **for** loops (Program 1.11).

Program 1.11

```
#include<stdio.h>
main( )
{  int  m[5];
   printf("Please  enter  5  marks\n");
   scanf("%d%d%d%d%d", &m[0], &m[1], &m[2], &m[3], &m[4]);
   printf("%d%d%d%d%d", m[0], m[1], m[2], m[3], m[4]);
}
```

Note: Here, we have solved one of the problems in the earlier program, i.e. declaring 1000 variables. Even if 1000 variables are to be declared, we can simply say m[1000]. But the difficulty in **scanf** and printf remains and it has somewhat increased due to so many [ ] being used.

Using arrays, together with **for** loops, we get the following program.

Program 1.12

```
#include<stdio.h>
main( )
{
   int m[5], i;
   printf("Please enter marks of 5 students\n");
   for (i=0; i<5; i++)
   {
   scanf("%d", &m[i]);
   }
   for (i=0; i<5; i++)
   {
   printf("%d\n", m[i]);
   }
}
```

Note: Here not only declaration but **printf** and **scanf** have become simple. For changing this program to work with marks of 1000 students, we just have to change the declaration and the ending values of the loops.

Example 1.22

1. Write a program to read five integer numbers and print them out using arrays.

```
#include<stdio.h>
main()
{
     int  n[5],  i;
```

```
    printf("Enter 5 integers\n");
    for (i=0; i<5; i++)
    {
        scanf("%d", &n[i]);
    }
    for (i=0; i<5; i++)
    {
        printf("%d\n", n[i]);
    }
}
```

2. **Write a program to read ten integers into an array and then print their squares.**

```
#include<stdio.h>
main( )
{
    int a[10], i;
    printf("Enter 10 integers\n");
    for (i=0; i<10; i++)
    {
        scanf("%d", &a[i]);
    }
    for (i=0; i<10; i++)
    {
        printf("Square of %d = %d\n", a[i], a[i]*a[i]);
    }
}
```

3. **Write a program to read seven integers into an array and then print out all the elements which are greater than 25.**

```
#include<stdio.h>
main( )
{
    int a[7], i;
    for (i=0; i<7; i++)
    {
        scanf("%d", &a[i]);
    }
    for(i=0; i<7; i++)
    {
        if(a[i]>25){ printf("%d\n", a[i]); }
    }
}
```

Exercise 1.26

1. Write a program to read 10 float numbers into an array **x** and then print them out.
2. Write a program to read 15 characters into an array **letter** and then print them out.
3. Write a program to read 10 int numbers into an array **N** and then:
   (a) Print out all the numbers.
   (b) Print out the numbers greater than 25.
   (c) Print out the numbers not less than 50.
   (d) Print out the numbers greater than 25 and less than 50.
   (e) Print out the numbers which are greater than 25 and less than 50 or greater than 75 and less than 100.
   (f) Print out the numbers which are odd.
   (g) Print out the numbers which are even.
   (h) Print out the numbers which are multiples of 7.
   (i) Print out the numbers which are multiples of 3 and 6.
   (j) Print out the numbers which are multiples of 3 or 5.
4. Write a program to read 10 characters into an array x and then:
   (a) Print out all the characters.
   (b) Print out all upper case characters.
   (c) Print out all lower case characters.
   (d) Print out all non-alphabetic characters.
   (e) Print out all alphabetic characters.
   (f) Print out all lower case vowels.

1.22.2 Initializing the Arrays without scanf

When declaring an array, the elements can also be initialized by listing the values separated by commas inside the braces, { }. Consider the following program.

Program 1.13

```
main( )
{
    int  a[5]={100,101,102,103,104};
    int  i;
    for  (i=0;  i<5;  i++)
    {
       printf("%d\n",  a[i]);
    }
}
```

Note: The number of values inside the braces should match the number of elements in the declaration. If more values are given, C will give an error message. If less values are given, the remaining values will be taken as zero.

Example 1.23

1. Write a program to declare and initialize an array **num** of 10 integers and then print the elements in reverse order.

```
#include<stdio.h>
main( )
{
    int num[10]={11,22,33,44,55,66,77,88,99,111}, i;
    for (i=0; i<10; i++)
    {
        printf("%d\n", num[9-i]);
    }
}
```

Note: You can also do this by rewriting the **for** loop as for (i=9; i>=0; i--).

2. Scan two arrays a and b (both 5 integers) and calculate array c (5 integers) = a + b. Then print out the elements of c.

```
#include<stdio.h>
main( )
{
      int a[5], b[5], c[5], i;
      printf("Type in 5 integers for array a\n");
      for (i=0; i<5; i++)
      {
          scanf("%d", &a[i]);
      }
      printf("Type in 5 integers for array b\n");
      for (i=0; i<5; i++)
      {
          scanf("%d", &b[i]);
      }
      for (i=0; i<5; i++)
      {
          c[i]=a[i] + b[i];
      }
      printf("a+b=\n");
      for (i=0; i<5; i++)
      {
          printf("%d\n", c[i]);
      }
}
```

Note: The first **for** loop is used to get the elements of array a, the second loop is used to collect the elements of array b, and the third **for** loop is used to find the sum of the corresponding elements and store it in array c. The same result can be obtained by using a single **for** loop. But in this case, the elements entered should be as follows:

The first element of array a
The first element of array b
The second element of array a
The second element of array b
. . . .

The program segment for this is:

```
for( i=0;i<5;i++)
{
    scanf("%d", &a[i]);
    scanf("%d", &b[i]);
    c[i]=a[i] + b[i];
}
```

3. Initialize an array of 10 integers and print out the elements in the following format:

```
a[0] = 25
a[1] = 37
a[2] = 49
a[3] = 11
a[4] = 22
a[5] = 44
a[6] = 39
a[7] = 95
a[8] = 99
a[9] = 42
#include<stdio.h>
main( )
{
    int a[10]={25,37,49,11,22,44,39,95,99,42}, i;
    for (i=0; i<10; i++)
    {
        printf("a[%d] = %d\n", i, a[i]);
    }
}
```

4. Initialize an array of 6 integers with the values of your choice. Then find the count of numbers which is greater than 25. Then print out the count.

```
#include<stdio.h>
main( )
{
    int a[6]={5,46,23,18,25,30}, count, i;
    count=0;
    for (i=0; i<6; i++)
    {
```

```
        if  (a[i]>25)
        {
            count++;
        }
    }
    printf("Count  =  %d\n",  count);
}
```

5. **Initialize an array of 6 integers with the values of your choice. Then find out the sum of the numbers in the array.**

```
#include<stdio.h>
main( )
{
     int  a[6]={5,46,23,18,25,30},  sum,  i;
  sum=0;
     for  (i=0;  i<6;  i++)
     {
         sum=sum+a[i];
     }
     printf("Sum  =  %d\n",  sum);
}
```

6. **Initialize an array of 6 integers with the values of your choice. Then find out the average of the numbers in the array.**

```
#include<stdio.h>
main( )
{
     int  a[6]={5,46,23,18,25,30},  sum,  i;
     sum=0;
     for  (i=0;  i<6;  i++)
     {
         sum=sum+a[i];
     }
     printf("Average  =  %f\n",  sum/6.0);
}
```

7. **Count the number of occurrences of a character in a given string.**

```
main( )
{
     char  str[]={"Data  Structures  Gently  Through  C  &  C++"},
     check_char  ='t';
     int  i,  count;
     count  =0;
     for(i=0;  i<strlen(str)  -1;  i++)
     {
         if  (str[i]  ==  check_char)
                   count  =  count  +  1;
     }
     printf("%c=%d\n",  check_var,  count);
}
```

8. Find the sum of the numbers in the odd positions of a given array of integers.

```
main( )
{
      int  arr[]={31,3,6,7,10},sum,i;
      sum=0;
      for(i=0;i<5;i=i+2)
      {
          sum+=arr[i];
      }
      printf("\nSum of the elements in the odd position is
%d",sum);
}
```

9. Count and print the odd numbers in a given array of integers.

```
main( )
{     int  arr[]={31,3,6,7,10,99,1001},i=0,count=0;
      printf("\n\tOdd Numbers\n");
      for(i=0;i<7;i++)
      {
          if  (arr[i]%2==1)
          {
              printf("\n%d",arr[i]);
              count++;
          }
      }
      printf("Total odd numbers in the array is %d\n", count);
}
```

Exercise 1.27

1. Declare an array of ample size to store characters in your name and initialize it with the characters in your name. Then print out the array.
2. Declare an array x[10] of type float and initialize it with the value of your choice.
3. Declare an array a[10] of type integer and initialize it with values: 15, 3, 7, 23, 44, 36, 22, 4, 29, 97. Now write **for** loops to print out:
   (a) All the values
   (b) Values greater than 19
   (c) Sum of the values greater than 19
   (d) Average of the values greater than 19
   (e) Count of the values greater than 19
   (f) Sum of the values greater than 20 and less than 40
   (g) Average of the values greater than 22 [*Hint*: For this, you need to calculate both count and sum.]
4. Declare an array x[19] of character and initialize it with the values: "C++ V1 . 0 Released !". Now write **for** loops to print out:
   (a) All characters

(b) Alphabet characters
(c) Non-alphabet characters
(d) Numeric characters
(e) Non-numeric characters
(f) Count of alphabets
(g) Count of non-alphabets
(h) Count of numeric characters
(i) Count of non-numeric characters
(j) Count of lower case characters
(k) Count of upper case characters
(l) Count of upper case vowels

1.22.3 Two-Dimensional Arrays

The arrays we have already considered are known as *one-dimensional arrays*. Two-dimensional (2-D) arrays are used to store a group of data arranged in rows and columns, all of the same type, and called by a single name. The array elements are referred to by two indices: **row index** and **column index**. Like one-dimensional arrays, two-dimensional arrays are also handled easily and efficiently by **for** loops. However, since both rows and columns are to be handled, we need **nested for** loops.

Example 1.24

1. Data of marks of three students in three examinations are given below:

Student \ Exam	0	1	2
0	25	36	41
1	55	96	69
2	33	92	14

Write a program to read the marks into a 2-D array and then print them out.

Data type = int
Name of array = m
No. of rows = 3
No. of columns = 3

```
#include<stdio.h>
main( )
{
int  m[3][3],i,j;
for (i=0;  i<3;  i++)
    {
      for  (j=0;  j<3;  j++)
         {                               ⇒ Scan all elements row by row
        scanf("%d",  &m[i][j]);
         }
    }
```

```
for  (i=0;  i<3;  i++)
{
    for  (j=0;  j<3;  j++)
    {
        printf("%d\n",  m[i][j]);
    }
             }
}
```

Note: As in the case of one-dimensional arrays, we can initialize the array without **scanf**. The data of each row has to be given in separate { }. For the above example:

```
int  m[3][3]={{25,36,41},{55,96,69},{33,92,14}};
```

2. The sales data of three salesmen in four cities are as follows:

Salesman \ City	0	1	2	3
0	6	7	5	9
1	3	2	8	11
2	22	6	0	7

Write a program to initialize an array with this data and then print it out.

```
#include<stdio.h>
main( )
{
    int  s[3][4]={{6,7,5,9},{3,2,8,11},{22,6,0,7}},  i,  j;
    for  (i=0;  i<3;  i++)
    {
        for  (j=0;  j<4;  j++)
        {
           printf("%d\n",  s[i][j]);
        }
    }
}
```

Note: The elements are displayed one by one in each line.

3. The sales data of three salesmen in four cities are given below:

Salesman \ City	0	1	2	3
0	6	7	5	9
1	3	2	8	11
2	22	6	0	7

Write a program to initialize an array with this data and then print out the numbers row by row.

```
#include<stdio.h>
main( )
{
    int s[3][4]={{6,7,5,9},{3,2,8,11},{22,6,0,7}}, i, j;
    for (i=0; i<4; i++)
    {
        for (j=0; j<3; j++)
        {
            printf("%d ", s[j][i]);
        }
        printf("\n");
    }
}
```

Note: The first **printf** displays each element in a row in the same line. The second **printf** is used to start a new line.

4. Initialize an array marks to store marks of three students in four exams and print out all marks >=40.

Student \ Exam	0	1	2	3
0	40	60	70	35
1	65	15	36	95
2	77	93	13	22

```
#include<stdio.h>
main( )
{
    int m[3][4]={{40,60,70,35},{65,15,36,95},{77,93,13,22}}, i, j;
    for (i=0; i<3; i++)
    {
        for (j=0; j<4; j++)
        {
            if (m[i][j]>=40)
            { printf("%d\n", m[i][j]);
            }
        }
    }
}
```

Note: Inside the **for** loop, the 'if condition' checks if the mark of the student satisfies the required condition and if so, the mark is displayed.

5. Read marks of three students in four exams into an array. Give a moderation of five marks for students with marks less than 40. Then print out all marks.

```
#include<stdio.h>
main( )
{
    int m[3][4], i, j;
    for (i=0; i<3; i++)
    {
        for (j=0; j<4; j++)
        {
            scanf("%d", &m[i][j]);
        }
    }
    for (i=0; i<3; i++)
    {
        for (j=0; j<4; j++)
        {
            if (m[i][j]<40)
            {
                m[i][j]=m[i][j]+5;
            }
        }
    }
    for (i=0; i<3; i++)
    {
        printf("\n");
        for (j=0; j<4; j++)
        {
            printf("%d\t", m[i][j]);
        }
    }
}
```

6. Read a 3 by 3 matrix a and then print out the values in the following way.

```
a[0][0] = 5
a[0][1] = 3
a[0][2] = 17
  .
  .
  .
```

```
#include<stdio.h>
main( )
{
  int a[3][3], i, j;
  for (i=0; i<3; i++)
  {
```

```
    for  (j=0;  j<3;  j++)
    {
          scanf("%d",  &a[i][j]);
    }
  }
  for  (i=0;  i<3;  i++)
  {
    for  (j=0;  j<4;  j++)
    {
       printf("a[%d][%d]\n",  i,  j,  a[i][j]);
    }
  }
}
```

7. Read a 3 by 3 matrix **a** and add five to each element in row 1 and then print out all the elements.

```
#include<stdio.h>
main( )
{
    int  a[3][3],  i,  j;
    for  (i=0;  i<3;  i++)
    {
        for  (j=0;  j<3;  j++)
        {
            scanf("%d",  &a[i][j]);
        }
    }
    for  (i=0;  i<3;  i++)
    {
        for  (j=0;  j<4;  j++)
        {
            if  (i=  =1)
            {
                a[i][j]  =  a[i][j]+5;
            }
        }
    }
    for  (i=0;  i<3;  i++)
    {
        for  (j=0;  j<3;  j++)
        {
            printf("%d",  a[i][j]);
        }
    }
}
```

Note: Suggest a better way to write the second loop.

8. **Read a 3 by 3 matrix c and print out its diagonal elements.**

```
#include<stdio.h>
main( )
{
    int  c[3][3],  i,  j;
    for  (i=0;  i<3;  i++)
    {
        for  (j=0;  j<3;  j++)
        {
            scanf("%d",  &c[i][j]);
        }
    }
    for  (i=0;  i<3;  i++)
    {
        for  (j=0;  j<3;  j++)
        {
            if  (i=  =j)
            {
                printf("%d\n",  c[i][j];
            }
        }
    }
}
```

Note: **Suggest an alternate way for the second nested loop.**

9. **Read a 3 by 3 matrix a, then calculate the sum of all the elements and print out the sum.**

```
#include<stdio.h>
main( )
{
  int  a[3][3],  i,  j,  sum;
  for  (i=0;  i<3;  i++)
  {
              for  (j=0;  j<3;  j++)
              {
                    scanf("%d",  &a[i][j]);
              }
  }
  sum  =  0;
  for  (i=0;  i<3;  i++)
  {
              for  (j=0;  j<3;  j++)
              {
                      sum  =  sum+a[i][j];
              }
  }
    printf("%d\n",  sum);
}
```

10. Read a 5 by 5 matrix a and print out all the elements of even numbered rows.

```
#include<stdio.h>
main( )
{
    int  a[5][5],  i,  j;
    for  (i=0;  i<5;  i++)
    {
        for  (j=0;  j<5;  j++)
        {
            scanf("%d",  &a[i][j]);
        }
    }
  for  (i=0;  i<5;  i++)
  {
        for  (j=0;  j<5;  j++)
        {
            if  (i%2=  =0)
            {
                  printf("%d\n",  a[i][j];
            }
        }
  }
}
```

11. Read a 3 by 3 array and print out the row number and the column number of all the elements with the value greater than 40.

```
#include<stdio.h>
main( )
{
    int  b[3][3],  i,  j;
    for  (i=0;  i<3;  i++)
    {
        for  (j=0;  j<3;  j++)
        {
            scanf("%d",  &a[i][j]);
        }
    }
    for  (i=0;  i<3;  i++)
    {
        for  (j=0;  j<3;  j++)
        {
            if  (a[i][j]>40)
            {
                printf("i  =  %d,  j=%d,  value=%d\n",i,j,  a[i][j]);
            }
        }
    }
}
```

12. Given a two-dimensional array of integers, find the columnwise sums.

```
main( )
{
    int  arr[][3]={{3,4,5},{6,9,1},{5,3,7}},i,j,sum;
    clrscr( );
    for(i=0;i<3;i++)
    {
        sum  =  0;
        for(j=0;j<3;j++)
        {
            sum+=arr[i][j];
        }
        printf("\nThe  sum  of  %d  -  column  is  %d",i+1,sum);
    }
}
```

Exercise 1.28

1. Write a program to initialize an array a of size 4 by 3 with the following values:

21	32	57
93	20	69
37	66	17
11	3	94

Write **for** loops to:

(a) Print out all the elements of the array, each row in a separate line.
(b) Print out all elements > 50
(c) Print out all elements > 50, with a zero in the position of other elements.
(d) Print out all elements > 50 and < 60.
(e) Calculate and print out the sum of all elements.
(f) Calculate and print out the count of all elements.
(g) Calculate and print out the average of all elements.
(h) Calculate and print out the sum of elements > 50.
(i) Calculate and print out the count of elements > 50.
(j) Calculate and print out the average of elements > 50.
(k) Print out the odd valued elements.
(l) Print out the elements which are multiples of 6.
(m) Calculate and print out the count of odd valued elements.
(n) Print only the elements in row 1 and column 2.
(o) Print only the elements which are not in row 2 and column 1.

2. Write a program to initialize an array a of size 4 by 3 with the following values:

'h'	'a'	't'
'm'	'a'	't'
's'	'a'	't'
'b'	'a'	't'

Write **for** loops to:

(a) Print out all the elements of the array, each row in a separate line.
(b) Print out all vowels.
(c) Print out all vowels, with a space in the position of others.
(d) Print out all elements which are equal to 'a', 'b', 'c', or 'd'.
(e) Calculate and print out the count of all vowels.
(f) Calculate and print out the count of non-vowels.

1.23 STRUCTURES

The basic idea behind C structures is to **put related data together** as one unit. This is a simple but very important concept. You can think of **struct** statement in C as a sort of stapler. Just as a stapler is used to pin together related sheets, **struct** statement puts together related data. The class concept in C++ is basically an expansion of this (though puritans may not agree). In classes, we put together related data and functions as a single unit.

A struct definition has the following general form:

struct *name* {
______ ______
______ ______ *Structure members.*
______ ______};

Let us study an example of reading id and mark of students without structure and with structure

```
main( )
{      int  id;
       int  mark;

       scanf("%d%d",  &id,  &mark);
       printf("%d,  %d\n",  id,  mark);
  }
main( )
  {
       struct  student  {
       int id;
       int mark;
       };

       struct  student  s1;
       scanf("%d%d",  &s1.id,  &s1.mark);
       printf("%d,  %d\n",  s1.id,  s1.mark);
  }
```

- The reserved word **struct** introduces the structure definition.
- "struct student" type consists of two integers: the first one is id and the second one is mark. Any variable of type "struct student" will have these parts.

- Variables declared inside the { } are the **structure members**. Structure members in the above program are id and mark.
- "struct student" is structure type. Once it is defined, we can use it the same way we use int, float, etc. We can have variables of type struct student just like we have variables of type int, char, etc.
- To access the members of the structure, the dot (.) operator is used, e.g. s1.id and s1.mark.
- Note the semicolon in **struct** definition after the }. It is unusual.

Example 1.25

1. For the following **struct** definitions, (a) What is the name of the structure? (b) How many members are there? (c) What are their names and types?
   (a) Storing student id and mark in 3 exams and grade ('P', 'F', 'C' or 'D').

```
struct  student
{
       int  id;
       int  mark1,mark2,mark3;
       char  grade;
};
```

Ans: Name of the struct : student

No. of members : 5

Name of member	Type
id	int
mark1	int
mark2	int
mark3	int
grade	char

Exercise 1.29

1. For the following **struct** definitions, (a) What is the name of the structure? (b) How many members are there? (c) What are their names and types?
   (a) Storing x and y coordinates of a point.

```
struct  point
{
       int  x;
       int  y;
};
```

   (b) Storing cost, number of wheels, type of fuel ('p'/'d'), weight and speed of a vehicle.

```
struct vehicle
{
    int wheel;
    int speed;
    float cost;
    float weight;
    char fuel;
};
```

(c) Storing age, height and sex ('m'/ 'f') of a person.

```
struct people
{
    int age;
    float height;
    float weight;
    char sex;
};
```

1.23.1 Declaring Structure Variables

Once a structure type has been defined, it can be used to define variables of this structure type. In the previous example, **structure student** has been defined. We can now define a variable "John" of this type as follows:

struct student John;

To access the components of this structure, the dot operator is used, as given below:

John.id, John.mark1, John.mark2, John.mark3, John.grade.

1.23.2 Initializing Structure Variables

Like in arrays, structure variables can also be initialized when they are declared. For this, we just need to give the value of each of this member inside { } as below:

```
struct point
{
    int x;
    int y;

};
    struct point A= {5 , 6};
```

This would make A.x = 5 and A.y = 6

See the following example:

```
struct stud
{
    int id;
    int marks;
    char grade;
};
```

```
struct stud john={250671, 75, 'A'};
```

This would make john.id=250671, john.marks=75, john.grade= 'A'

Consider the following declaration:

```
Struct vehicle
{
    char color[6];
    float price;
    char type[4];
};
struct vehicle car={"Blue", 300000.0, "XX"}
```

The components of this structure can be accessed as vehicle.color, vehicle.price, and vehicle.type.

Example 1.26

1. Using the above **vehicle** structure declaration, store information about three vehicles and retrieve them.

```
#include <stdio.h>
main( )
{
    int i;
    struct vehicle
    {
        char color[6];
        float price;
        char type[4];
    };
    struct vehicle car[]={"Blue", 300000.0, "SL",
                          "Red", 170000.0, "UNO",
                          "Black",700000.0, "2000"};
    for(i=0;i<3;i++)
    {
        printf("\n%s\n%0.2f\n%s\n",car[i].color,car[i].price,
        car[i].type);
    }
}
```

Note: The way the character array is handled here is different from the approach so far.

2. The employee number and the salary of an employee are to be read and printed out. Write a program by using structure.

```
#include<stdio.h>
main( )
{
    struct emp
    {
```

```
        int  num;
        float  salary;
    };
    struct  emp  john;
    scanf("%d%f",  &john.num,  &john.salary);
    printf("Employee  number  =  %d  and  salary  =  %f\n",
    john.num,  john.salary);
}
```

3. **Modify the above program to read and print data of two employees.**

```
#include<stdio.h>
main( )
{
    struct  emp
    {
        int  num;
        float  salary;
    };
    struct  emp  john,  mary;
    scanf("%d%f%d%f",  &john.num,  &john.salary,  &mary.num,
    &mary.salary);
    printf("%d,  %f  and  %d,  %f\n",  john.num,  john.salary,
    mary.num,  mary.salary);
}
```

4. **Modify the above program to read and print number, salary and tax of one employee.**

```
#include<stdio.h>
main( )
{
    struct  emp
    {
        int  num;
        float  salary;
        float  tax;
    };
    struct  emp  john;
    scanf("%d%f%f",  &john.num,  &john.salary,  &john.tax);
    printf("%d\t%f\t%d\n",  john.num,  john.salary,
    john.tax);
}
```

5. **Write a program to read data of ten students. Data are id, mark, and fees.**

```
#include<stdio.h>
main( )
{
```

```
        struct student
        {
            int id;
            int mark;
            int fee;
        };
        struct student s[10];
        int i;
        for (i=0; i<10; i++)
        {
            scanf("%d%d%d", &s[i].id, &s[i].mark, &s[i].fee);
        }
        for (i=0; i<10; i++)
        {
            printf("%d%d%d", s[i].id, s[i].mark, s[i].fee);
        }
    }
```

Note: This example demonstrates that just as arrays can be made out of int, char, and float elements grouped together, structures can also be grouped together.

Exercise 1.30

1. Give **structure** declaration for the following case:
   (a) A vehicle name, colour, model and price.
   (b) Your address, value of the residence, and your bank account number with balance.

   Read and print data for each of the above cases.
2. Initialize a structure suitable to store employee data such as name, salary, extra hours worked and rate per hour. Then calculate overtime income as the product of extra hour worked and rate.
3. Define a structure **employee** with name, category, salary and tax as members. Read the name, category and salary of an employee and calculate the tax as below:

Category	
A	10% of salary
B	15% of salary
C	20% of salary
Others	30% of salary

1.24 POINTERS

1.24.1 Introduction

Pointers are one of the most basic features of C. They are both the strength and the weakness of C. The full appreciation of the use of pointers will be possible only when you read the chapters that follow. However, to start using pointers, all you need to know is a clear picture of the computer's memory. Let us learn that first.

1.24.2 The Main Memory

All the variables we have been using (and indeed, the program itself) reside in the memory when the program is executed. The organization of the memory is rather straightforward. You may imagine it to be similar to a hotel with a sequence of rooms, each with a room number (address) and in which numbers (not persons!) can stay. That is, it is a sequence of large number of memory locations, each of which has an address. Each memory location is capable of storing a small number (0 – 255), which we call a **byte**. A character data is 1 byte in size and hence needs one location of the memory. Both integer and float need 4 bytes each, or 4 locations. (Please note that this could be different from computer to computer. You should write a C program with a single statement as follows to check the size of int in your computer:

```
printf("%d\n", sizeof(int));
```

The technique can be applied to any data type or structure.) Note that even if the actual value of an integer/float number is small, it will still occupy four locations. Figure 1.2 represents these facts.

How an integer or float occupies four locations together is not important in this context. You may note that even if the integer value is small, say 100, which can be stored in one location, it would still occupy four locations since it is declared as an integer.

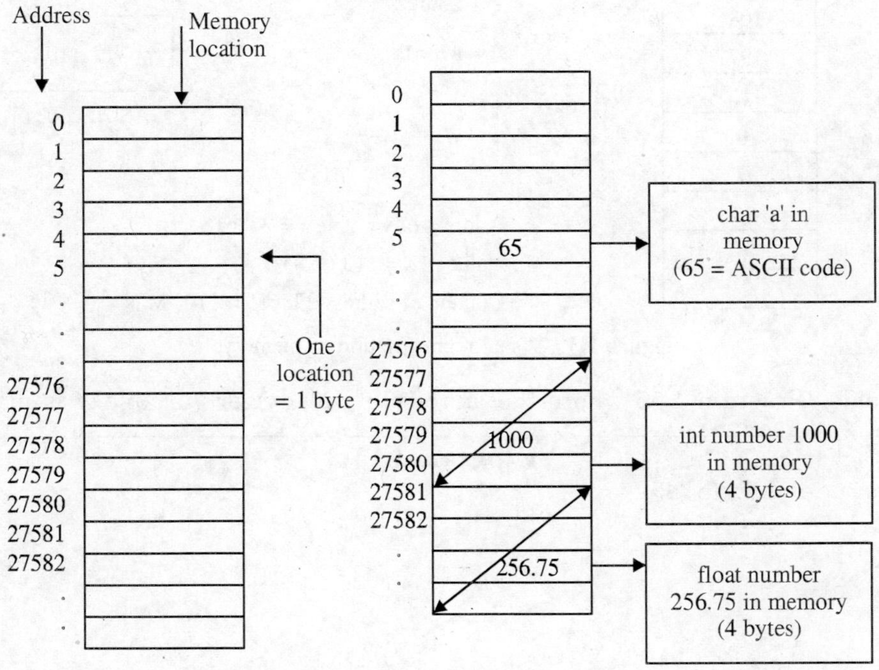

Figure 1.2 Visual representation of an array in memory.

1.24.3 The Address of Variables

All the variables that you declare in programs are allocated addresses in the memory. You can print that out using the **&** operator which you have already been using in **scanf** statements. Study the following program (Program 1.14).

Program 1.14[2]

```
#include <stdio.h>
main( )
{
    char  x;
    x  =  'M';
    printf("x  =  %d\n",  x);
    printf("Address  of  x  =  %d\n",  &x);
}
```

The exact output of the above program cannot be predicted, but it would be a number like, say, 27861S. If it were possible to peep into a computer memory, what is going on there could be represented graphically as given below (Figure 1.3).

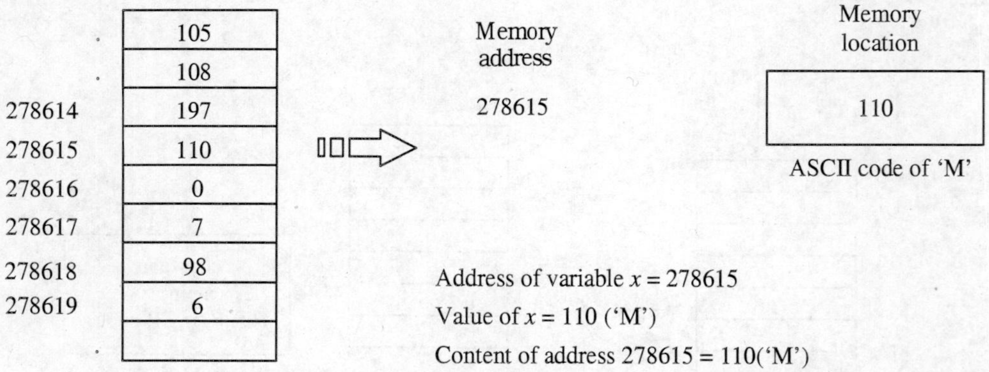

Figure 1.3 Visual representation of memory.

Consider Program 1.15 where the address of an integer variable *X* is printed.

Program 1.15

```
#include <stdio.h>
main( )
{
    int  X;
    X=1000;
    printf("X=%d\n",X);
    printf("Address  of  X  =  %d\n",  & X);
}
```

[2]If your computer prints negative value, use %u instead of %d.

Let us assume that the output of the above program is 278614. Now let us see what is happening in the computer memory. Its graphical representation would be as follows (Figure 1.4).

In this case, the value will be stored in four locations, not one, since the integer requires four bytes to store. How 1000 is 'sliced' into 4 pieces, you need not bother now.

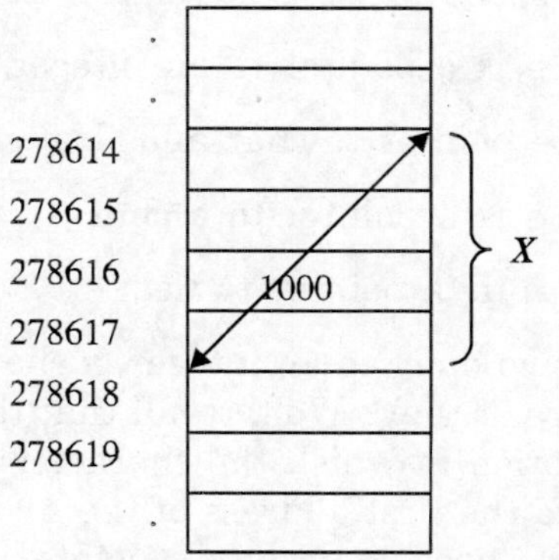

Figure 1.4 Visual representation of an integer in memory.

Here, what are the addresses of *X*? Actually it is 278614, 278615, 278616 and 278617. However, in C, we consider the address of *X* as 278614, the address of first of the 4 locations. This is an important thing to remember and crucial to the understanding of pointers.

Whenever variables are declared, some memory locations get allocated for them. It will be helpful to assume some addresses and draw the picture of the memory to answer the questions on pointers.

1.24.4 The Pointer Variable

One of the most surprising things for a beginner is that a memory location can contain a memory address. For example, assume in a memory location 273616, we have 97. This can be a data for a program, or it could be the address of location 97. By inspecting the memory, it would not be possible to distinguish what the content is. Let us look at this possibility now.

In the previous section, we printed out & X, which is the address of X. Suppose we need to store that address in a variable. Then we need a special variable called the **pointer**. A pointer variable is one which can store the addresses of another variable. Study the following program (Program 1.16), which uses a pointer variable *p*.

Program 1.16

```
#include <stdio.h>
main( )
{
    int x;
    int *p;
    x=1000;
    p=&x;
    printf("x=%d\n", x);
    printf("Address of x=%d\n",p);
}
```

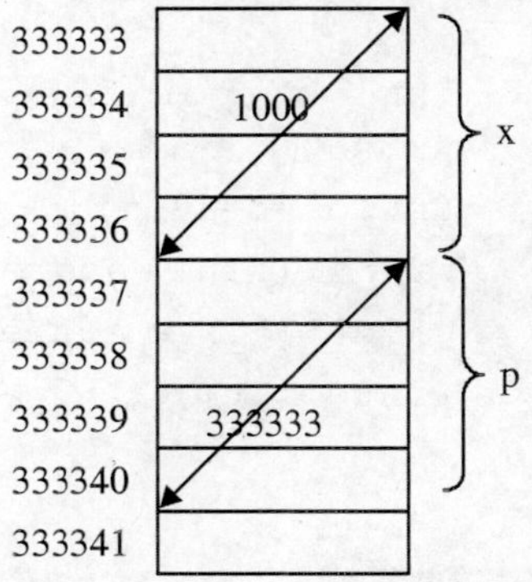

When you declare x, it gets allocated a memory, say, 4 locations starting from 333333. When pointer p is declared, it also gets allocated a memory, say, from 333337. When you assign x =1000, the value occupies the memory from 333333 to 333336. Let us see what happens when you assign p = &x. As in any assignment statement, look at the R.H.S. first. &x is the address of x, which is 333333. This value now occupies the memory location starting from 333337 to 333340. The pointer declaration is given as follows:

int *p; ⟶ p is a pointer to an integer.

We can similarly declare pointer to char and float.

char *q; ⟶ q is a pointer to a char.

float *fp; ⟶ fp is a pointer to float.

What is common among pointers to an integer, a character and float? They are all storing memory addresses, aren't they? Well, recall that the address of the character is the address of the single location in which the character is stored. But the address of the integer/float only refers to the first address of the 4 locations in which the integer/float is stored. That is why we need to declare a pointer as pointing to a certain data type. In general, we can declare pointers as:

data type *pointer-name;

When assigning values to pointers, we have to take note of the data type to which the pointer points. For example:

(a) int x;
    int *p;
    p=&x; ⟹ Correct, p is a pointer to an int and &x is the address of an int

(b) int x;
    char *p;
    p=&x; ⟹ Not correct, p is a pointer to a char and &x is the address of an int

Exercise 1.31

Predict the output of the following programs, or point out mistakes, if any. Draw the picture of the memory for each and assume memory addressess shown consecutively.

1.
```
#include <stdio.h>
main( )
{
    int  num;
    int  *intpoint;
    num=50;
    intpoint=&num;
    printf("The  address  of  num  is  %d\n", &num);
    printf("The  address  of  intpoint  %d\n",
    &intpoint);
}
```

223278	
223279	
223280	
223281	
223282	
223283	
223284	
223285	
223286	
223287	

2.
```
#include <stdio.h>
main( )
{
   char grade;
   char *cp;
   grade='D';
   cp=&grade;
   printf("Grade is %c\n", grade);
   printf("Address of grade is %d\n", &grade);
   printf("cp is %d\n", cp);
   printf("Address of cp is %d\n", &cp);
}
```

234555	
234556	
234557	
234558	
234559	
234560	
234561	
234562	
234563	
234564	

3.
```
#include <stdio.h>
main( )
{
   int a;
   char b;
   float c;
   int *ap;
   char *bp;
   float *cp;
   ap=&a;
   bp=&b;
   cp=&c;
   printf("The address of a, b and c are
   %d %d %d", ap, bp,cp);
}
```

234555	
234556	
234557	
234558	
234559	
234560	
234561	
234562	
234563	
234564	
234565	
234566	
234567	

1.24.5 Pointer Arithmetic

Pointer arithmetic is an interesting aspect of pointers. In some sense, pointers are very much like integers. They are, after all, string memory addresses which are numbers. C permits the use of some arithmetic operators on pointer variables. One can meaningfully apply addition and subtraction on pointers (+, –, ++ and - -). The results are pleasant surprises. Study the following program (Program 1.17).

Program 1.17

```
#include <stdio.h>
main( )
{
   char x;
   char *p;
   x='M';
   p=&x;
   printf("Pointer value =%d\n", p);
   printf("Pointer plus one =%d\n", p+1);
}
```

223455	77
223456	
223457	
223458	
223459	
223460	
223461	

An example output will be:

Pointer value = 234555
Pointer plus one = 234556

Of course, there is nothing surprising here. Now, change the data type to integer and try Program 1.18.

Program 1.18

```
#include <stdio.h>
main( )
{
    int x;
    int *p;
    x=1000;
    p=&x;
    printf("Pointer value = %d\n",p);
    printf("Pointer plus one =%d\n",p+1);
}
```

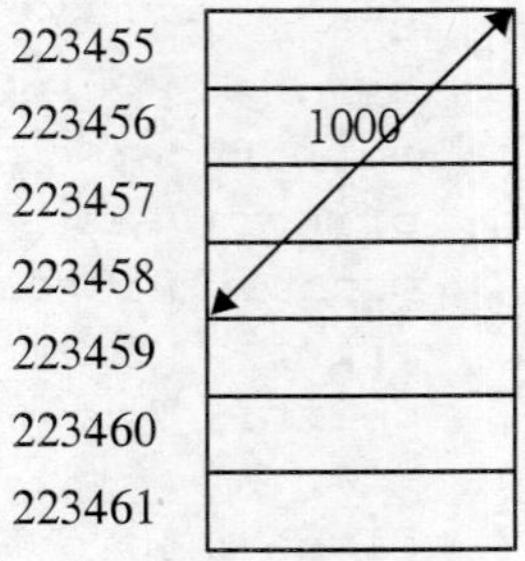

An example output will be:

Pointer value = 223455
Pointer plus one = 223439

223455+1=223439 ! That is pointer magic! How does C justify that? Well, 223455 is not just a number; C knows it is the address of an integer that takes 4 locations. So, 223455, 223456, 223457 and 223458 are all held together by the integer x. So, C interprets +1 as the next free location and gives the answer 223459.

Since float also takes 4 bytes to store, a pointer to float will also show the same effect. We can say that +1 is interpreted as follows by C:

char address + 1 ⟹ char address + 1

integer address + 1 ⟹ integer address + 4

float address + 1 ⟹ float address + 4

In general, address of any data type + 1 = address of the data type + (size of the data type in byte). This behaviour of C is described as *pointer arithmetic in C being scaled according to the data type.*

1.24.6 Pointer De-referencing

So far, we have only assigned values to pointers and tried incrementing them. There is another operation you can do with pointers, known as de-referencing. Before we proceed, be aware that '*' symbol appears in the C language in four different situations with four different meanings. Three of these we have already seen.

- Comments/*...*/
- Arithmetic operator for multiplication as in a*b
- Declaring pointer variables as in int *p
- De-referencing.

Now we will consider the fourth situation. Comment is easily recognized and so is multiplication. The rest of the two situations are related to pointers. When it appears in a declaration "int *p", we just read it as "p is a pointer to an integer". After the declaration, in the body of the program we can use the * with p as *p, which is read as *de-reference* p. De-referencing can be explained as follows. Every pointer stores some address, *p means *the value stored in that address*. To understand *p, we can replace p with some assumed address. *(333375) means the value stored in location 333375. In this sense, * works in a way exactly opposite to &.

&x = address of variable x.

*p = content of location whose address is stored in p.

See Program 1.19.

Program 1.19

```
#include <stdio.h>
main( )
{
    int  x;
    int  *p;
    x=100;
    p=&x;
    printf("x=%d\n",x);
    printf("p=%d\n",p);
    printf("*p=%d\n",*p);
}
```

```
x=100
p=223455
*p=100
```

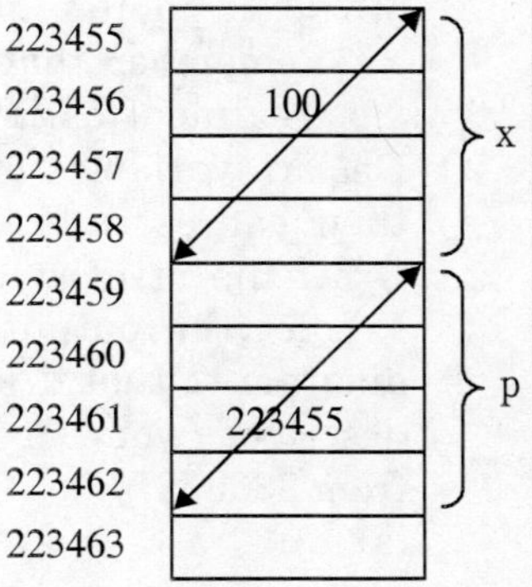

Before you decide the format string for printing *p, please check the data type that p is pointing to.

Before we end this section, the final question—What is *(&x) in the above program? Remember, & and * are opposing operators. You should be able to guess now.

1.24.7 The Usage of a Structure Pointer

Consider the following program:

```
#include <stdio.h>
main( )
{
    struct  book
    {
        char  name[35];
        char  author[25];
        int  price;
    };
    struct book b1={"Data Structures Gently Through C","ASSN", 180};
    struct  book  *ptr;
    ptr=&b1;
    printf("\n%s  %s  %d\n",b1.name,  b1.author,  b1.price);
    printf("\n%s  %s  %d\n",ptr->name,  ptr->author,  ptr->price);
}
```

Note: This example demonstrates that pointers to **struct** variables are possible. However, doing de-referencing, instead of using the notation (*ptr).name, we find a new notation used : ptr->name

Exercise 1.32

1. Write the following pointer declarations:
   (a) p, a pointer to an integer
   (b) q, a pointer to a character
   (c) p1, a pointer to a float
   (d) sp, a pointer to struct student which has already been declared. [*Hint:* Remember that once a structure is declared, it can be given the same treatment as int, float, char.]
2. Declare variables of type int, char, float and struct student and then assign their addresses to the respective pointers declared in Questions.
3. Draw the memory diagram for each of the above cases.
4. Predict the output of each of the following programs (draw the memory diagram so that it will be easy to answer). Where memory addresses are to be described, you can assume any 6-digit number. Assume numbers starting from 333333.

   (a)
```
int a;
int *integer_pointer;
a=222;
integer_pointer=&a;
printf("The value of a is %d\n", a);
printf("The address of a is %d\n",&a);
printf("The address of integer_pointer is %d\n",
&integer_pointer);
printf("Star integer_pointer is %d\n", *integer_pointer);
```
   (b)
```
char a;
char *char_pointer;
a='b';
char_pointer=&a;
printf("The value of a is %d\n", a);
printf("The address of a is %d\n", &a);
printf("The address of char_pointer is %d\n",
&char_pointer);
printf("Star char_pointer is %d\n", *char_pointer);
```
   (c)
```
float a;
float *float_pointer;
a=22.25;
float_pointer=&a;
printf("The value of a is %d\n", a);
printf("The address of a is %d\n", &a);
printf("The address of float_pointer is %d\n",
&float_pointer);
printf("Star float_pointer is %d\n", *float_pointer);
```

(d)
```
int a, b;
int *ip1, *ip2;
a=5;
b=6;
ip1=&a;
ip2=ip1;
printf("The value of a is %d\n", a);
printf("The value of b is %d\n", b);
printf("The address of a is %d\n",&a);
printf("The address of b is %d \n"&b);
printf("The address of ip1 is %d\n", &ip1);
printf("The address of ip2 is %d\n", &ip2);
printf("The value of ip1 is %d\n",ip1);
printf("The value of ip2 is %d\n", ip2);
printf("ip1 dereferenced is %d\n",*ip1);
printf("ip2 dereferenced is %d\n", *ip2);
```

(e)
```
int i, j, *ip;
i=1;
ip=&i;
j=*ip;
*ip=0;
printf("The value of i is %d\n", i);
printf("The value of j is %d\n", j);
```

(f)
```
int x, y;
int *ip1, *ip2;
y=1;
ip2=&y;
ip1=ip2;
x=*ip1+y;
printf("The value of x is %d\n", x);
printf("The value of y is %d\n",y);
```

1.25 FUNCTIONS

1.25.1 The Concept of Functions

So far the programs we have written were all rather simple and small. (In fact, mostly trivial.) In large software projects, programs will be large and complex. There are many methods used to manage such complexity. One of them is to divide a program into many parts and name each of the parts. Such a named part of a program is called a **function**. Even though the use of functions is more relevant for large programs, we will learn them using small programs themselves, for the sake of clarity and simplicity.

Function is a group of statements with a single name, having some unique purpose. Some programs require a group of same instructions at different places within the program. Such instructions can be placed within a single function, which can be accessed at the required places in the main program by calling its name.

Functions are classified as *library functions* and *user defined functions*. Library functions are available in the system ready-made, whereas user defined functions are created by programmers for individual use.

Every C program consists of one or more functions. One of these functions must be called main( ). The execution of the program will always begin by carrying out the instructions in main( ). You may now realize why all programs we wrote so far contain main( ). Additional functions will be subordinate to main( ).

Every function is capable of accepting some data and then performing some processing (e.g. calculation) and then giving back (return) the result. The data that goes into a function is known as its *argument* or *parameter* (with a slight difference in meaning which can be ignored in the beginning), and the data that comes out is known as *return value*. Functions are given names in the same way variables are named. When functions are defined, the return type is mentioned just before the name and the arguments are given inside brackets after the function name. When a function is made use of, we say a 'function call' has been made. With this much basic information, let us look at an example for calculating the sum of two numbers, with and without the use of functions.

1. Program to calculate the sum of two int numbers **without** using functions.

```
# include <stdio.h>
main ( )
{
    int a, b;
    scanf("%d %d", &a, &b);
    printf("sum=%d\n", a+b);
}
```

2. Program to calculate the sum of two integer numbers **using** functions.

```
# include <stdio.h>

void showsum (int x, int y)
{
printf("sum=%d\n",x+y);
}

main ( )
{
   int a, b;
   scanf("%d %d", &a, &b);
      showsum(a,b);
}
```

This gets executed with x = a and y = b

Both the above programs give the same result. In the second program, we see the statement showsum(a, b); in place of a printf("sum=%d\n",a+b);. This is a function call. When C finds a function call, it executes the function defined earlier. In the example above, the arguments are x and y, both integers. This means that the function needs two integers x and y to work with. We say, we *call* the function 'showsum' by passing a and b as *arguments/parameters*. *Return type* of the function is *void* (=nothing). Although the function calculates and prints out a + b, the result is not given back to the main( ) function. Let us look at the function definition once again. The different parts of a function definition are shown below:

```
void    showsum(int x, int y)        ← Return type (void), Function name (showsum), Arguments (int x, int y)
{
   printf ("sum is"........);        ← Function body
}
```

Return type
Function name
Arguments
Function body

```
So, the format of a function definition is:
        Return_type function_name (arguments)
        {
            statement(s);
        }
```

Exercise 1.33

1. Write a function similar to the example above to:
   (a) Show the difference between two int numbers.
   (b) Show the product of two float numbers.
   (c) Show the sum of three int numbers.
   (d) Show the square of an int number.
   (e) Show the result of modulus division of two int numbers.
   (f) Show the ASCII code of a character (*Hint*: Print it using %d.)

1.25.2 User Defined Functions

From the foregoing discussion, it is clear that a function can be accessed (called) by specifying its name, followed by a list of arguments enclosed in parenthesis and separated by commas. The arguments appearing in the function call are referred to as *actual arguments,* and the arguments defined in the function definition are called *formal arguments*. In normal function call, there will be one *actual argument* for each formal argument. The value of each actual argument is transferred into the function and assigned to the corresponding formal argument.

User defined functions are developed by the programmer at the time of writing programs. If a program contains multiple functions, their definitions may appear in any order, but they must be independent of one another, i.e. one function definition cannot be embedded within another. The same function can be accessed from several different places within a program. After performing the desired operation, the control will be returned to the point from which the function was called.

Notes:

1. The actual arguments must be the same as the number of formal arguments and each actual argument must be of the same data type as its corresponding formal argument.

2. They are usually written at the beginning of a program ahead of any user defined function (including main). Function prototype ends with a semicolon . The names of the arguments within the function prototype need not be declared elsewhere in the program.
3. The argument names are usually included and are often the same as the names of the actual arguments appearing in one of the function calls.

Example 1.27

1. To find factorial of an integer quantity using functions.

```
#include <stdio.h>
int factorial (int n)
{
     int i;
     int fact=1;
     if (n>1)
          for(i=2;i<=n;++i)
               fact*=i;
     return(fact);
}
main( )
{
     int n = 5;

     printf("\n n ! =%d", factorial(n));
}
```

2. To find the reverse of a given number. For example, if the number is 2345, the output should be 5432.

```
#include <stdio.h>
#include <conio.h>
int reverse(int n)
{
     int digit, s=0;
     while(n!=0)
     {
          digit=n%10;
          s=s*10+digit;
          n=n/10;
     }
     return (s);
}
main( )
{
     int p = 2341, q;
     q=reverse(p);
     printf("Reverse of %d is %d\n", p, q);
}
```

1.25.3 Library Functions

Library functions are the inbuilt functions provided with the compilers. These functions carry out various commonly used operations or calculations. Library files are obtained as part of C compiler. The following table (Table 1.10) gives examples of library functions.

Table 1.10 Some Library Functions in C

Function	Type of function	Purpose	Type of argument
abs(i)	integer	Return the absolute value of i	integer
exit(u)	void	Close all files and buffers, and terminate the program	
fabs(i)	double	Return the absolute value of i	float
free(p)	void	Free a block of allocated memory whose beginning is indicated by p	
getc(f)	int	Enter a single character from file f	file
getchar()	int	Enter a single character from the standard input device	
gets(s)	char*	Enter a string from the standard device	string
islower(c)	int	Determine if the argument is lower case. Return a nonzero value if true; 0 otherwise	character
isspace(c)	int	Determine if the argument is a whitespace character. Return a nonzero value if true; 0 otherwise	character
isupper(c)	int	Determine if the argument is upper case. Return a nonzero value if true; 0 otherwise	character
malloc(u)	void*	Allocate u bytes of memory. Return a pointer to the beginning of the allocated space	
putc(c,f)	int	Send a single character to file f	character, file
putchar(c)	int	Send a single character to the standard output device	character
puts(s)	int	Send a string s to the standard output device	string
scanf(.....)	int	Enter data items from the standard input device	
sqrt(d)	double	Return the square root of d	float
strcmp (s1,s2)	int	Compare two strings lexicographically. Return a negative value if s1<s2; 0 if s1 and s2 are identical; and a positive value if s1>s2.	Two strings
strcpy (s1,s2)	char*	Copy string s2 to string s1	Two strings
strlen(s)	int	Return the number of characters in a string	string
toascii(c)	int	Convert the value of argument to ASCII	character
tolower(c)	int	Convert the letter to lower case	character
toupper(c)	int	Convert the letter to upper case	character

Exercise 1.34

1. For the following functions, specify the return type, formal agruments, actual arguments and predict the output of the program.

<table>
<tr><th>Sl. No.</th><th>Program segments</th><th>Output</th></tr>
<tr><td>1</td><td><pre>int function(int y)
{
     int x;
     x=y*y;
     return(x);
}
main()
{
     int a, cnt;
     for(cnt=1;cnt<=5;++cnt)
     {
          a=function(cnt);
          printf("%d ", a);
     }
}</pre></td><td></td></tr>
<tr><td>2</td><td><pre>int function(int no)
{
     if(no>0) return(no+function(no-1));
}
     main()
{
     int no=5;
     printf("%d ", function(no));
}</pre></td><td></td></tr>
<tr><td>3.</td><td><pre>int function(int no)
{
     if(no>0) return(no+function(no*no);
}
main()
{
     int no=5;
     printf("%d ", function(no));
}</pre></td><td></td></tr>
</table>

1.26 THE EVOLUTION OF C LANGUAGE

C was originally developed by Dennis Ritchie of the Bell Laboratories in 1972. The language was named "C" because it was the successor to a language named "B". C was developed as a high-level language that could be used to rewrite the Unix operating system. Today, most of the Unix operating system and most of the programs that run under Unix are written in C.

The standard for C programs was originally written by Brian Kernighan. Later, an international standard was developed by the American National Standards Institute (ANSI), which is the existing standard today.

We briefly list some of C's important characteristics:

- C has an extensive library for mathematical computations, character analysis, input and output functions, hardware management and graphics.
- C is not tied to any particular hardware or system. This makes it easy for a user to write programs that will run without any changes on practically all machines. This is referred to as C's portability.
- C allows the manipulation of bits, bytes and addresses—the basic elements with which the computer functions.
- C is often called a middle-level computer language as it combines the elements of high-level languages with some features of the assembly language.
- C offers the speed of the assembly language, has high-level constructs and can handle low-level activities.
- C is prone to errors, especially in relation to direct memory access and pointers.
- C programs are also sometimes too 'complicated' for beginners if written without proper style.
- C is a structured language.

C++ and JAVA are both successors of C which retain many basic features of C. C++ is an enhanced version of the C language. C++ includes everything that is part of C and adds support for object-oriented programming (OOP). In addition, C++ also contains many improvements and features independent of object-oriented programming. C++ is actually an extendable language since we can define new types in such a way that they act just like the predefined types which are part of the standard language. Some of the new features include encapsulation, inline function calls, overloading operators, inheritance and polymorphism.

JAVA is sometimes referred to as C+– since it takes away some of the features from C which are error-prone, especially pointers and direct memory manipulation. In addition, JAVA is a net-centric language which is used to write both applications (stand-alone program) and Applets which run on web pages.

The C language, along with its evolved and transformed cousins, has been holding the centre stage of the programming world for close to three decades now, and this scenario seems all set to continue in the near future.

1.27 DATA STRUCTURES: SOME BASIC IDEAS

Mathematically, we can define **type** as a set and the elements of the set are called the **values** of the type. In any programming language when we define data types, it means the set of all data belonging to that type (see Table 1.11).

Table 1.11 Data type and their meaning

Data Type	Meaning
int	Set of all integers
char	Set of all characters
real	Set of all real numbers

In every programming language, some basic types of data are defined (Table 1.11). These basic data types cannot be divided further. They are used to build new types called **data structures**.

A brief mention about 'abstract data type (ADT)' is necessary before we proceed further. The word *Abstract* means *existing in idea only*. A formal description of the data type, independent of its implementation, is known as ADT. An ADT can be implemented in the chosen programming language in the way the programmer wants. For example, a *stack* data structure can be abstractly considered as a sequence of data items and associated functions which can be applied on the sequence of data: push( ) to add data to the sequence, pop( ) to remove data from the sequence. This, as we will see soon, can be implemented in two different ways.

Table 1.12 shows the basic classification of data types and structures in C.

Table 1.12 Classification of data type and data structure

Basic data types	Internal level	bits Bytes (8 bits) **Words (16, 32, 64, etc., typically 32)**
	Program level	char (signed/ unsigned) float (signed/ unsigned) double (signed/ unsigned) int (signed/ unsigned) short int (signed/ unsigned) long int (signed/ unsigned) **pointers (Short, Far)**
Data structures	Non-user defined (supported directly by C)	arrays enum struct union **files**
	User defined	stacks queues trees binary trees octal trees linked lists graphs **heaps ....**

There are two further classifications of data structures, which are discussed in detail in succeeding chapters, are mentioned briefly here:

- Static and dynamic data structure
- Linear and non-linear data structure.

1.27.1 Static and Dynamic Data Structure

Data structures which have fixed size and have their memory allocated during the time of compilation of the program are called *static data structures*. Typically, the elements (nodes) of a static data structure will have consecutive addresses in the memory. An array is an example of the static data structure.

A data structure that can grow and shrink, with memory allocated during the execution of the program is known as a *dynamic data structure*. Typically, the elements are stored wherever there is a free space. A linked list is an example of the dynamic data structure.

1.27.2 Linear and Non-linear Data Structure

If the elements of a data structure form a sequence, then it is said to be a *linear data structure*. That is, there is an order between the elements of the data structure. Given an element of the data structure, there exists a previous element and a successive element for the given element, provided this element is not the first or last element of the sequence. Examples of linear data structures are arrays, linked lists, stacks and queues.

On the other hand, if the elements of the data structures do not form a sequence, it is said to be a *non-linear data structure*. That is, there does not exist an order between these elements. Different type of sequences can be formed with the elements of the non-linear data structure. Examples of non-linear data structures are trees and graphs.

As a C programmer, you are already familiar with data types such as int, char, float, etc. These are basic building blocks of a programming language. For the real-world programming problems, it would not be possible to proceed with the basic data types alone. We will, for the sake of easiness of reference, repeat the example given earlier. Consider the following C program (Program 1.20) which reads 5 integer numbers using **scanf** and then prints them out.

Program 1.20

```
#include <stdio.h>
main ( )
{
    int a, b, c, d, e;
    scanf("%d %d %d %d %d", &a, &b, &c, &d, &e);
    printf("%d %d %d %d %d\n", a, b, c, d, e);
}
```

Try extending the above program to read 1000 integer numbers! Obviously, using separate names for 1000 variables and reading all of them using a **scanf** similar to the above is unthinkable to any programmer. This situation is easily handled with arrays (see Program 1.21)

As you already know, an array is a group of data all of the same type, referred to by a single name (say, *a*) and each separate element of the group referred to by an index (say, a[0], a[15], a[998], etc.).

An array is an example of building *structures* using existing data types. **struct** in the C language is another example that you are already familiar with. Both are examples of *data structures*—structures built from the existing data types. Whereas arrays and struct are supported directly by the C language, programmers are free to create their own data structures to suit their requirements. Such data structures are known as *user defined data structures,* which are the major focus in this book. They are: Linked lists, Stacks, Queues, Trees, Graphs and Files.

Program 1.21

```
#include <stdio.h>
main ( )
{
    int a[1000];
    int i;
    for (i=0; i<1000; i++)
        {
            scanf ("%d", &a[i]);
        }
        for (i=0; i<1000; i++)
        {
            printf ("%d", a[i]);
        }
}
```

An analogy may be helpful here. Human beings use the basic building materials such as wood, metal, plastic, etc. But they always make *structures* of different shapes suited for different situations. Wood can be used to build a box as well as a shelf. Which is better? Well, that depends on what you want to do with them. Imagine keeping books in a shelf and also in a box (Figure 1.5).

Figure 1.5 Two real-world data structure analogies.

Obviously, for library use, it is more convenient to keep the books in a shelf. In data structures also, similar situations arise. We can keep a sequence of numbers stored in an array or a linked list. The way they can be used and the convenience of using each are different.

Your program's complexity and efficiency critically depend on the selection of the appropriate data structures. (If we were to keep all books in boxes, it would cause long delays for users in searching and locating books they want to refer.) The selection of this data structure is closely related to the way in which data is used. (In a warehouse of a printing company, multiple copies of the same books can well be stored in a box without any problem.)

The main objective of this book is to familiarize the student with the most popular data structures so that they can choose the most appropriate one for the problem at hand. Keep this perspective in mind during further reading.

Exercise 1.35

1. Consider the following program:

```
#include <stdio.h>
void main( )
{      int x;
       printf(" size of x in bytes = %d ", sizeof(x));
}
```

Modifying this program for each of the following data types, find out the size of these types or structures:

(a) int, short int, long int (both signed and unsigned)
(b) char (both signed and unsigned)
(c) float, double
(d) int *, char *, float*
(e) struct A

```
{
       int x;
       int y;
};
```

(f) struct B

```
{
         int x;
         char y;
};
```

(g) struct c

```
{
       struct A;
       struct B;
       int i;
       float c;
}
```

(h) int a[10];
(i) int a[10][10];

(*Note:* In the case of structures, the size of the structure need not always be the sum of the member structures, since C might use memories which are multiples of the word length, typically 4 bytes.)

2. Fill up the following table using the results from question 1.

Data type/Structure	Size in bytes	Remarks
1. char		
2. short int		
3. int		
4. long int		
5. float		
6. double		
7. struct A		
8. struct B		
9. struct C		
10. pointer to int		
11. pointer to float		
12. pointer to char		
13. pointer to struct A		
14. pointer to struct B		
15. pointer to struct C		

EXERCISES

1 Write minimal number of statements to accomplish each of the following. Assume that

c is of type char
x, y, and z are of type int
d, e and f are of type float
ptr is of type char *
s1[100] and s2[100] are arrays of type char.

(a) Convert the character stored in variable *c* to an upper case letter. Assign the result to variable *c*.
(b) Determine if the value of variable *c* is a digit. Use the conditional operator to print "is a" or "is not a" when the result is displayed.
(c) Convert the string "1234567" to long and print the value.
(d) Determine if the value of variable *c* is a control character. Use the conditional operator to print "is a" or "is not a" when the result is displayed.
(e) Read a line of text into array s1 from the keyboard. Do not use scanf.
(f) Print the line of text stored in array s1. Do not use printf.
(g) Assign to ptr the location of the last occurrence of c in s1.
(h) Print the value of variable *c*. Do not use printf.
(i) Convert the string "8.63582" to double and print the value.
(j) Determine if the value of c is a letter. Use the conditional operator to print "is a" or "is not a" when the result is displayed.

(k) Read a character from the keyboard and store the character in variable *c*.
(l) Assign to ptr the location of the first occurrences of s2 in s1.
(m) Determine if the value of c is a printing character. Use the conditional operator to print "is a" or "is not a" when the result is displayed.
(n) Read three float values into variables *d*, *e*, and *f* from the string "1.27 10.3 9.432".
(o) Copy the string stored in array s2 into array s1.
(p) Assign to ptr the location of the first occurrences in s1 of any character from s2.
(q) Compare the string in s1 to the string in s2. Print the result.
(r) Assign to ptr the location of the first occurrence of c in s1.
(s) Use sprintf to print the values of integer variable x, y, and z into array s1. Each value should be printed with a field width of 7.
(t) Append 10 characters from the string in s2 to the string in s1.
(u) Determine the length of the string in s1. Print the result.
(v) Convert the string "–21" to int and print the value.
(w) Assign ptr to the location of the first token in s2. Tokens in s2 are separated by commas (,).

2. Show two different methods of initializing character array vowel with the string of vowels, "AEIOU".

3. What, if anything, will be printed out when each of the following C statements is performed? If the statement contains an error, describe the error and indicate how to correct it. Assume the following variable declarations:
char s1[50] = "jack", s2[50] = "jill", s3[50], *sptr;
(a) printf ("%c%s, toupper(s1[0], &s1[1]);
(b) printf ("%s, strcpy(s3,s2));
(c) printf ("%s, strcat(strcat(strcpy(s3,s1), " and "),s2));
(d) printf ("%u, strlen(s1)+strlen(s2));
(e) printf ("%u, strlen(s3));

4. Find the error in each of the following program segments and explain how to correct it:
(a) char s[10];
strncpy(s, "hello", 5);
printf("%s\n", s);
(b) printf ("%s", 'a');
(c) char s[12];
strcpy(s, "welcome home");
(d) if (strcmp(string1, string2))
printf ("The strings are equal\n");

5. Write a program that inputs a line of text with function 'gets' into character array s[100]. Output the line in upper case and lower case letters.
6. Write a program that inputs four strings that represent integers, converts the strings to integers, sums the values, and prints the total of the four values.
7. Write a program that uses function 'strcmp' to compare two strings input by the user. The program should state whether the first string is less than, equal to, or greater than the second string.

8. Write a program that inputs several lines of text and a search character, and uses function 'strchr' to determine the total occurrence of the character in the lines of text.
9. Write a program that reads a series of strings and prints only those strings beginning with the letter "b".
10. Write a program that reads a series of strings and prints only those strings end up with the letters "ing".
11. Write a program that inputs an ASCII code and prints the corresponding character. Modify this program so that it generates all possible three-digit codes in the range 000 – 255 and attempts to print the corresponding characters. What happens when this program is run?
12. Using the ASCII character chart given in the Appendix as a guide, write your own version of the character handling functions.
13. Write two versions of function 'strlen'. The first version should use array subscripting, and the second version should use pointer and pointer arithmetic.

Chapter 2

Arrays

2.1 INTRODUCTION

In Chapter 1, we discussed the simple processing of one-dimensional and two-dimensional arrays. In this chapter, we focus on two things: (i) internal organization of arrays and (ii) handling of arrays using pointers.

2.2 INTERNAL IMPLEMENTATION

2.2.1 Simple One-Dimensional Arrays

Study Program 2.1 and the corresponding memory diagram (Figure 2.1). (Please notice that when you run the program, the address value you get could be different. Also, you may use **%u** to print addresses if you get negative values in the output.)

Program 2.1

```
#include<stdio.h>
main ( )
{
int a[5] = {100, 200, 300 ,400, 500};
int i;
for (i=0; i<5;i++)
  {
      printf("Address = %d, value = %d",
      &a[i], a[i])
  }
}
Output:
Address = 276314 value = 100
Address = 276318 value = 200
Address = 276322 value = 300
Address = 276326 value = 400
Address = 276330 value = 500
```

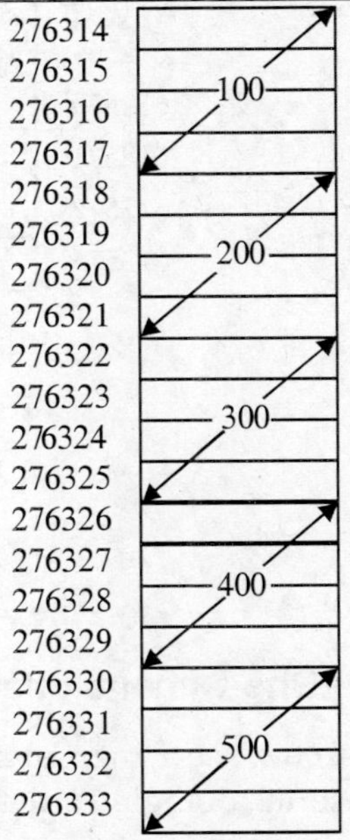

Figure 2.1 Visual representation of one-dimensional array in memory.

Exercise 2.1

1. Draw the memory diagram for the arrays declared in the following program and predict the output of the program. Assume that memory locations starting from 333333 are in use. (Please make use of the ASCII table given in the Appendix for finding ASCII code of characters.)

(a)
```
#include <stdio.h>
main  ( )
{    char a[8]  = {'g', 'o', 'o', 'd', 'l', 'u', 'c', 'k'};
     int  i;
     for  (i=0;  i<8;i++)
     {    printf("Address  =  %d,  value  =  %d",  &a[i],  a[i])
     }
}
```

(b)
```
# include <stdio.h>
main( )
{    float  x[3]={20.5,  300.2,  28.7};
          int  i;
          for  (i=0;i<8;i++)
          { printf("Address=%f,  Value=%d",  &f[i],  x[i]);
     }
}
```

2. Given the memory diagram, write the corresponding 'C' array declarations and initializations.

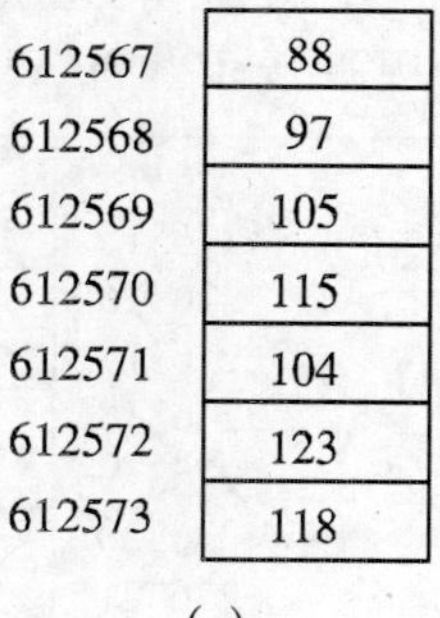

(a)

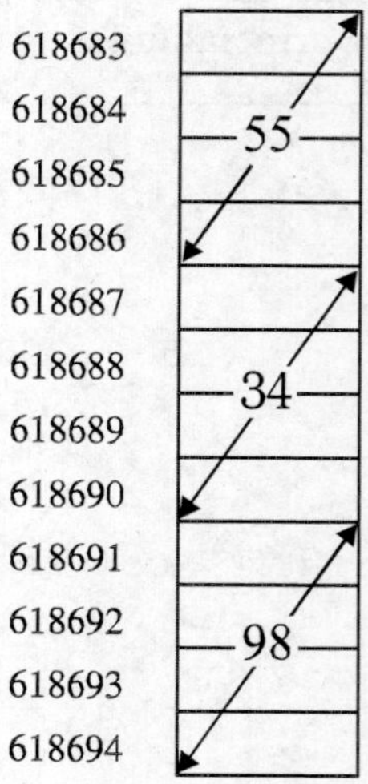

(b)

2.2.2 One-Dimensional Array of Structures

Let us now see Program 2.2, which deals with the array of structures. First consider the case of a single structure variable (Figure 2.2).

Program 2.2

```
#include<stdio.h>
main( )
{
struct point {
    int x;
    int y;
};
```

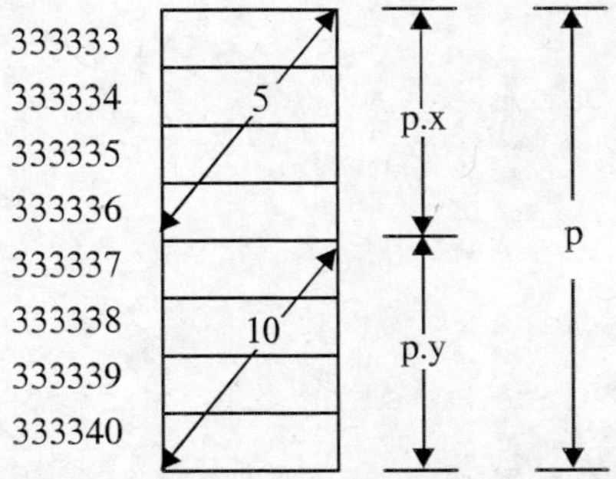

Figure 2.2 Visual representation of a structure variable in memory.

```
struct point p = {5,10};
printf("Address of whole structure = %d\n", &p);
printf("Address of p.x= %d\n", &p.x);
printf("Address of p.y= %d\n", &p.y);
printf("Value of p.x = %d, p.y= %d\n", p.x, p.y);
}
```

Output:

Address of whole structure = 333333
Address of p.x= 333333
Address of p.y= 333337
Value of p.x = 5, p.y= 10

We will now extend Program 2.2 to an array of structures (Program 2.3). Try to understand the output by referring to the memory diagram given in Fig. 2.3.

Program 2.3

```
#include<stdio.h>
main( )
{   int i;
    struct point
    {
        int x;
        int y;
    };
    struct point p[5] = {{5,10}, {6,11}, {7,12}, {8,13}, {9, 14}};
    for (i=0; i<5;i++)
    {
        printf("Address of p[%d] = %d\n", i, &p[i]);
    }
    for (i=0; i<5;i++)
    {
        printf("Address of p[%d].x=%d\n", i, &p[i].x,);
    }
    for (i=0; i<5;i++)
    {
        printf("Address of p[%d].y=%d\n", i, &p[i].y);
    }
}
```

Output:

```
Address of p[0]  =  333333
Address of p[1]  =  333341
Address of p[2]  =  333349
Address of p[3]  =  333357
Address of p[4]  =  333365

Address of p[0].x  =  333333
Address of p[1].x  =  333341
Address of p[2].x  =  333349
Address of p[3].x  =  333357
Address of p[4].x  =  333365

Address of p[0].y  =  333337
Address of p[1].y  =  333345
Address of p[2].y  =  333353
Address of p[3].y  =  333361
Address of p[4].y  =  333369
```

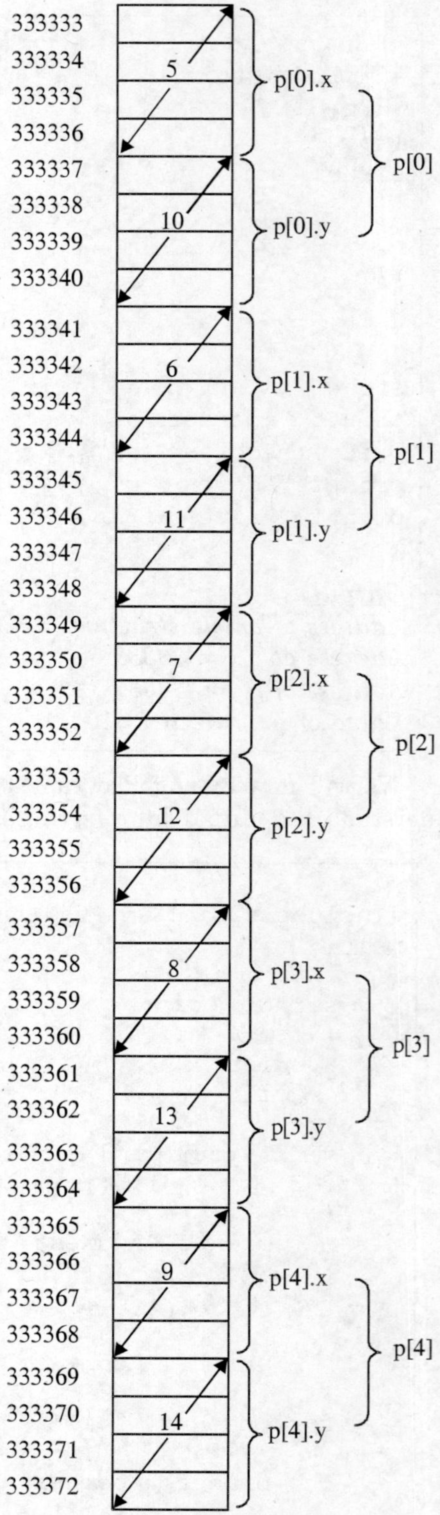

Figure 2.3 Visual representation of an array of structures in memory.

In the next program 2.4 structure inside a structure is considered which is nested structures.

Program 2.4

```
#include <stdio.h>
main( )
{
    struct  address
    {
        char  phone[8];
        char  city[5];
        long  int  pin;
    };

    struct  emp
    {
        char  name[8];
        struct  address  a;
    }
    struct emp e={“Praveen”, “2533328”,
    “QLN”,691584};

    printf(“Name : %s Phone : %s”, e.name,
    e.a.phone);
    printf(City : %s Pin : %ld”, e.a.city,
    e.apin);
    }
```

365502	‘P’
365503	‘r’
365504	‘a’
365505	‘v’
365506	‘e’
365507	‘e’
365508	‘n’
365509	
365510	‘2’
365511	‘5’
365512	‘3’
365513	‘3’
365514	‘3’
365515	‘2’
365516	‘8’
365517	
365518	‘Q’
365519	‘L’
365520	‘N’
365521	
365522	
365523	
365524	691584
365525	
365526	

Output:

Name : Praveen   Phone : 2533328
City : QLN   Pin : 691584

Here is another program which uses array of structures. You do not need to draw the memory diagram like in the previous examples. But the previous examples are expected to make you more confident in handling arrays of structures.

Example

```
#include <stdio.h>
main( )
{
      int  i;
      struct  vehicle
      {
          char  color[3];
          float  price;
          char  type[3];
      };
```

```
    struct vehicle car[] = {"Bl", 300000.5, "XX",
                            "Rd", 170000.3, "YY",
                            "Bk", 700000.67, "DD"};
    for(i=0;i<3;i++)
    {
        printf("%s %0.2f %s\n",car[i].color,car[i].price,
        car[i].type);
    }
}
```

Exercise 2.2

1. Predict the output of the following program segments

Sl. No.	Program segment	Output

1	struct date{
	int month; int day; int year;};
	struct account{
	int acct_no; char name[10];
	float bal;
	struct date lastpayment;
	}customer;
	printf("%d\n", sizeof (customer));
	printf("%d",sizeof (struct account));	

2	int x[]={7,20,1,36,18},i, j, temp,n=5;
	for(i=0;i<n-1;i++)
	{
	for(j=i+1;j<n;j++)
	if(x[j]<x[i])
	{
	temp=x[i];
	x[i]=x[j];
	x[j]=temp;
	}
	}
	printf("%d %d %d %d %d", x[0], x[1],
	x[2], x[3], x[4])	

3	int n = 5;
	float list []={3, -2, 12, 4.4, 3.5};
	int count;
	float avg, d, sum = 0;
	for (count=0;count<n; count++)
	sum+=list[count];
	avg=sum/n;
	printf("The average is %5.2f ", avg);	

4	`int b[]={10,20,30,40,50};`
	`int i;`
	`for(i=0;i<5;i++)`
	`{`
	`printf("%d ", *(b+i));`
	`}`	

5	`int b[]={0, 20, 0, 40, 5}`
	`int i, *k;`
	`k=b;`
	`for(i=0;i<=4;i++)`
	`{`
	`printf("\n%d",*k);`
	`k++;`
	`}`	

6	`int a[5]={5, 1, 15, 20, 25};`
	`int i, j, k =1; m;`
	`i=++a[1];`
	`j=a[1]++;`
	`m=a[i++];`
	`printf("%d %d %d ", i, j, m);`	

2. Read id, mark and grade ('F', 'P', 'C', or 'D') of ten students and store them in an array and then:
   (a) Print out all data.
   (b) Print out data of the students in the distinction ('D') grade.
   (c) Print out the count of students with distinction.
3. The data regarding employees in a company are: employee-id, category ('A', 'B', or 'C'), salary and tax payable. Ten such data are to be stored in a structure. The id, category and salary are to be read and the tax is to be calculated as follows:

Category	**Tax**
A	10% of salary
B	20% of salary
C	30% of salary

   After storing complete data for each employee,
   (a) Print out all data.
   (b) Print out data of the employees who pay tax more than Rs. 10,000.
   (c) Print out the count of employees in category B who pay tax more than Rs. 25,000
4. The data regarding the students are: student-id, marks in English, Hindi, Mathematics and Science (each out of 100) and overall grade. The data of twenty students are to be stored in a structure. All data except grade are to be read and the grade is to be calculated as follows:

Total marks	Grade
300–400	D
240–299	C
160–239	P
0–159	F

After storing complete data for each student,

(a) Print out all data.
(b) Print out the count of students in each category of grade.
(c) Read a student id and then display the corresponding marks and grades.
(d) Read any one student id and then print out a list of all students who have lesser marks in Mathematics compared to that particular student.

5. Given the memory diagram, write the corresponding "C" array declarations and initializations.

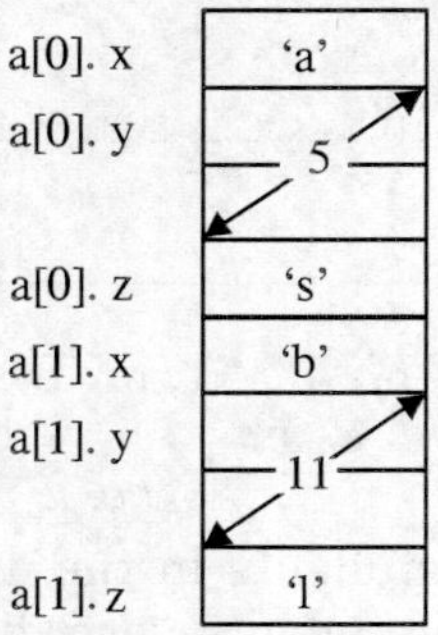

2.2.3 Two-Dimensional Arrays

Study Program 2.5, which initializes the two-dimensional array with values as shown in Table 2.1 and then prints out the addresses. Compare the output of the program, which is given below, with the memory diagram:

Table 2.1 A two-dimensional table

	Column 0	Column 1	Column 2	
Row 0	'm'	'a'	't'	**a[0]**
Row 1	's'	'a'	't'	**a[1]**
Row 2	'h'	'a'	't'	**a[2]**
Row 3	'c'	'a'	't'	**a[3]**

Output:

Address of a[0][0]= 333333, Value= m
Address of a[0][1]= 333334, Value= a
Address of a[0][2]= 333335, Value= t

Address of a[1][0]= 333336, Value= s
Address of a[1][1]= 333337, Value= a
Address of a[1][2]= 333338, Value= t

Address of a[2][0]= 333339, Value= h
Address of a[2][1]= 333340, Value= a
Address of a[2][2]= 333341, Value= t

Address of a[3][0]= 333342, Value= c
Address of a[3][1]= 333343, Value= a
Address of a[3][2]= 333344, Value= t

Program 2.5

```
#include <stdio.h>
main  ( )
{
    char  a[4][3]  =  {  {'m',  'a',  't'},  {'s',  'a',  't'},{'h',
    'a',  't'},{'c',  'a',  't'},};
    int  i,  j;
    for  (i=0;  i<4;i++)
    {
           for  (j=0;  j<3;j++)
        {
        printf("Address  of  a[%d][%d]=  %d,  Value  =  %c\n",
        i,j,  &a[i][j],  a[i][j])
        }
    }
}
```

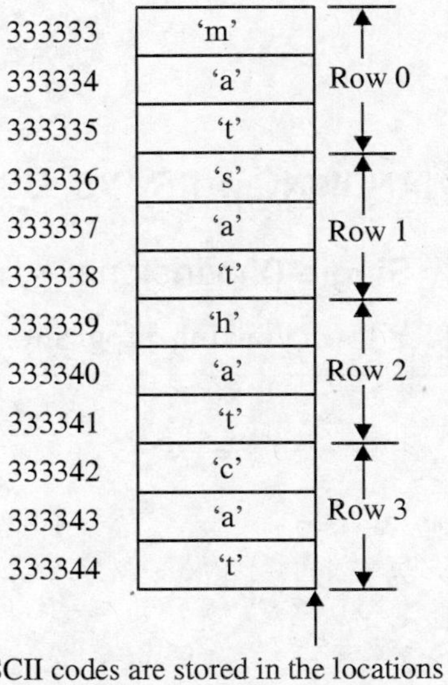

Figure 2.4 Visual representation of a 2D array in memory.

Exercise 2.3

1. For the following two-dimensional arrays, write a C program to create such an array and then to display the address and values. Also, draw the memory representation diagram assuming that the starting address is 124677.

P	H	O	N	E
M	E	R	G	E

(a)

100	20	90
10	87	34
2	65	50

(b)

2. For the given memory representation diagram, draw the matrix of size 1 by 3 and then write a C program to create and display the value.

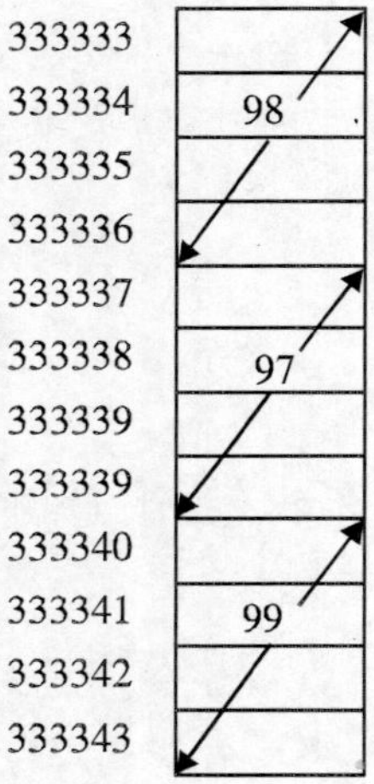

2.3 HANDLING ARRAYS USING POINTERS

2.3.1 Single-Dimensional Arrays

Consider the following program (Program 2.6).

Program 2.6

```
#include <stdio.h>
main  ( )
{
  int  a[10];
  printf("  %d",  &a[0]);
  printf("  %d",  a);
}
```

<u>Output:</u>

3316250
3316250

What do you understand from the Program 2.6? **The name of an array actually represents the address of the 0th element of the array.** What C does when we refer to the element a[i] is to get the data from address a + i. Study the following program (Program 2.7).

Program 2.7

```
#include <stdio.h>
main  ( )
{
   int  a[5]  =  {100,  200,  300  ,400,  500};
   int  i;
   for  (i=0;  i<5;i++)
   {
      printf("Address  =  %d,  value  =  %d",  &a[i],  a[i])
   }
}
```

An output that can occur for the program is given below.

Output:

Address = 276314 value = 100

Address = 276318 value = 200

Address = 276322 value = 300

Address = 276326 value = 400

Address = 276330 value = 500

Now consider the following expression: $*$ (a+1)

a → &a[0] → 276314
a+1 = 276314 + 1 = 276318

(Recall that in C pointer arithmetic is scaled. Since 276318 is an address of an integer, 276314+**1** is actually taken as 276314+ **sizeof (int)** = 276314+**4**=276318. Therefore, $*$(a+1) = $*$ (276318) = content of 276318 = 200. Thus a[1] and $*$(a+1) have the same meaning.)

Generally, **a[i] and $*$(a + i) have the same meaning**.

&a[i] is same as **a+i**
a[i] is same as **$*$(a+i)**

See below a program (Program 2.8) which reads and prints an array using this pointer equivalence. Notice that in **scanf**, the **&** sign is no longer required since we are giving the address directly.

Program 2.8

```
#include <stdio.h>
main ( )
{
int a[10];
int i;
for (i=0; i<10; i++)
   {
      scanf ("%d", (a+i));
   }
for (i=0; i<10; i++)
   {
      printf ("%d", *(a+i));
   }
}
```

Exercise 2.4

1. For the following program segments, find the output.

Sl.No.	Program segment	Output

1	`float list []={3, -2, 12, 4.4, 3.5};`
	`int j =0;`
	`while (j<=4) {`
	`printf("%0.2f, %d", list[j],`
	`&(list+j)); j++;}`	

2	`int b[]={5,10, 15, 20, 30};`
	`int j;`
	`for (j=0; j< 5; j++)`
	`{`
	`printf("%d\n", *(b+j))`
	`}`	

2.3.2 Two-Dimensional Arrays

The case of the two-dimensional array is interesting. Every two-dimensional array is stored in the memory row by row. From the row and column index (say, i and j, respectively), we can calculate exactly where an element **a[i][j]** is stored in the memory. The difference between one-dimensional and two-dimensional arrays is as follows. In the former, the name of an array is actually representing the address of the 0th element of the array (**for an array a, a → &a[0]**). In the case of the latter, the name of the array represents the address of the first row. We can cast this to a pointer to the array type, to handle it easily. Then we get (for a char array a), **(char *) a = &a[0].**

We can now use **(char *) a** to handle the array as follows. Each row is stored one after the other. Once more consider the 4 × 3 array as given in Table 2.2.

Table 2.2 A two-dimensional table

	Column 0	Column 1	Column 2	
Row 0	'm'	'a'	't'	**a[0]**
Row 1	's'	'a'	't'	**a[1]**
Row 2	'h'	'a'	't'	**a[2]**
Row 3	'c'	'a'	't'	**a[3]**

In memory, this array is stored one row after another as given in Figure 2.5.

row 0 col. 0	row 0 col. 1	row 0 col. 2	row 1 col. 0	row 1 col. 1	row 1 col. 2	row 2 col. 0	row 2 col. 1	row 2 col. 2	row 3 col. 0	row 3 col. 1	row 3 col. 2
0	1	2	3	4	5	6	7	8	9	10	11
'm'	'a'	't'	'h'	'a'	't'	's'	'a'	't'	'c'	'a'	't'

Figure 2.5 Visual representation of 2D array using pointers in memory.

If we know the first element's address, then, given the index i and j of any element, we can find its address as *i* ∗ *maximum number of columns* + *j*. You may verify this from Figure 2.5. For example, the address of a[2, 3] element of an array 4 x 3 is obtained as follows:

Assume the starting address as 0. Then address of a[2, 3] will be $2 * 4 + 3 = 11$. That is, four elements of row 0 + four elements of row 1 + 3 elements of row $2 = 4 + 4 + 3 = 11$.

Here is a program (Program 2.9) based on the above idea.

Program 2.9

```
#include <stdio.h>
main  ( )
{
    int a[4][3]  = { {'m',  'a',  't'},  {'s',  'a',  't'},{'h',
    'a',  't'},  {'c',  'a',  't'}};
    int i, j;
    for  (i=0;  i<4;i++)
    {
        for  (j=0;  j<3;j++)
        {
            printf("%c",  *  (  (char  )  a  +  i*3+j)  );
        }
        printf("\n");
    }
}
```

Exercise 2.5

1. Write a program to read a number **n** and then read **n** numbers and store them into an array of size **n**.
2. Write a program to read two numbers **m** and **n** and then read as **m** × **n** numbers and store them into an array of **m** columns and **n** rows.
3. For the following program segment, find the output.

Program segment	Output

`char p[2][3] = {'a', 'e', 'i', 'o', 'u', 'x'}, *ptr;`
`int i;`
`ptr=&p[0];`
`for (i=0; i < 6; i++)`
`{`
`printf("%c\n", *(ptr +i));`
`}`	

2.3.3 Application of Arrays

One of the important applications of the array is in the implementation of a static list. In such a list, the elements are to be stored in a sequence so that it is easy to implement the static list using one-dimensional arrays. Two operations associated with a static list are:

- Insertion of an element at a particular position
- Deletion of an element at a particular position.

The above two operations are considered in detail in the next two sections.

2.4 INSERTION

To insert an element in a particular position of an array, the elements just below the given position have to be moved downward, so as to create a vacant position at the particular place to insert the element. Such kind of movements is very expensive, both timewise and storagewise.

2.4.1 Algorithm for Insertion of an Element into Static Array

Consider a bookshelf (rack) in which there are compartments to keep individual books. The books are arranged in alphabetical order of the title of the books (Figure 2.6).

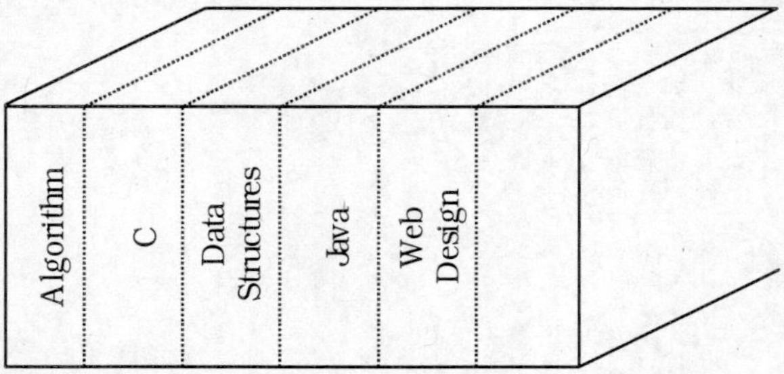

Figure 2.6 A bookshelf.

The owner of the bookshelf has bought a new book titled "COBOL". This book is to be placed in position in the bookshelf. As seen from Figure 2.6, the book is to be placed in the third compartment from the left. What steps would the owner take to accomplish this job?

Step 1: Find the empty compartment in the shelf.
Step 2: If there is no empty compartment, it means the book cannot be kept in the shelf unless one of the other books is removed or the shelf is made larger (extended). Go to step 6.
Step 3: If there is an empty compartment, move the book from the preceding left compartment to the empty right compartment.
Step 4: Repeat step 3 until the third compartment from the left is empty.
Step 5: Place the new book "COBOL" in the now empty compartment.
Step 6: End of job.

The selfsame process takes place when an element is to be inserted in an array. The process of insertion of the element in an array is accomplished only if there is at least one empty place in the array. The algorithm (2.1) for this process is given below:

Algorithm 2.1 To insert an element k at the position m of an array A of size n.

Step 1: Locate an empty position in the array after the mth position.
Step 2: If such a position (say p) is found, element k can be inserted, go to step 4.
Step 3: No empty place in the array. So cannot be inserted. STOP.
Step 4: For $i = p$ to $m + 1$ step-1.
Move $i - 1^{\text{st}}$ element to i^{th} element
End for
Step 5: Insert the element at the now empty position.
Step 6: STOP.

Example

Given an array of integers {30, 35, 45, 50, 52} arranged in ascending order (Table 2.3). It is required to insert an integer 38 into the array at position 3.

Table 2.3 Insertion of an element into an array

A[0]	A[1]	A[2]	A[3]	A[4]	A[5]	Steps
30	35	45	50	52	—	Initial
30	35	45	50	—	52	Step 7
30	35	45	—	50	52	Step 7
30	35	—	45	50	52	Step 7
30	35	38	45	50	52	Step 8

As per step 3 of the algorithm(2.1), the third position of the array is full. So as per step 5, an empty position is found in 6. Table 2.3 shows the position of the array elements when step 7 is repeatedly executed.

Exercise 2.6

1. Given in the following problems are: an array of elements, the element to be inserted and the position to be inserted. Draw a table similar to Table 2.3.
   (b) A = {'C', 'L', 'K', 'M', 'Z', ' '},
   element = 'W' at position 1
   (c) V = {'11', '12', '15', '20', ' ', '29', '0'}
   element = '7' at position 5
   (d) M = {'ten', 'twenty', 'sixty', 'fifty'}
   element = 'eight' at position 3

2.4.2 Memory Diagram of Insertion of an Element into a Static Array

Suppose a five-element character array [HLLO] is stored in the memory whose starting address is 12356. It is required to insert a new element "E" at the second position of the array. Diagrammatic representation of the insertion of an element into a static list is shown in Figure 2.7.

It is evident that to insert an element into the array, the last element of the array is moved to the empty space near the element. It is necessary to find an empty position at the second place so that the new element can be inserted. For this purpose, to create an empty position, each element is being moved. When the element at the second position is moved, an empty space will be created at the second position. To this empty position, the new element is inserted.

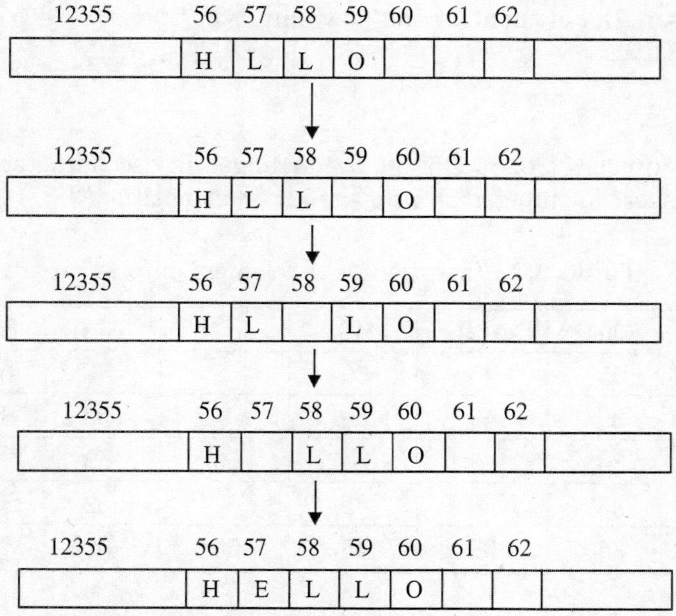

Figure 2.7 Insertion of an element in an array.

2.4.3 Program for Insertion of an Element into a Static List

Program 2.10 is the 'C' program for insertion of an element 'k' into an array A of size n at jth position.

Program 2.10

```
#include <stdio.h>
void main()
{
int a[5]={20,30,40,50},k=35,j=2,i;
for (i=5;i>=j+1;i--)
    {
    a[i]=a[i-1];
    }
a[j]=k;
printf("After Insertion..\n");
i=0;
while(i<5)
    {
    printf("%d\t",a[i]);
  i++;
  }
getch();
}
```

Output
After Insertion
20 30 35 40 50

Exercise 2.7

1. Given in the following problems are: an array of elements, the element to be inserted and the position to be inserted. Draw figures for each case similar to Figure 2.7. Also, write the steps involved when Program 2.10 is executed with these data.
   (a) A = {'C', 'L', 'K', 'M', 'Z', ' '},
   element = 'W' at position 1
   (b) V= {'11', '12', '15', '20', ' ', '29', '0'}
   element = '7' at position 5

2.5 DELETION

To delete an element from an array, the position of the element to be deleted is to be found. Once the position is found, the deletion operation is the equivalent of moving the succeeding element towards left, thus filling the empty position created by the deletion operation.

2.5.1 Algorithm for Deletion of an Element from a Static Array

The algorithm for deletion is similar to that of the insertion given in Section 2.4.1, except that the movement of the element is towards left instead of right as in the insertion case. The following example makes this idea clear.

Example

Given an array of integers {30, 35, 38, 45, 50, 52}. It is required to delete the element 45 from it. The necessary steps are given in Table 2.4.

Table 2.4 Deletion of an element from an array

A[0]	A[1]	A[2]	A[3]	A[4]	A[5]	Steps
30	35	38	45	50	52	Initial
30	35	38	50	50	52	A[3]=A[4]
30	35	38	50	52	52	A[4]=A[5]
30	35	38	50	52	–	A[5]='\0'

The element 45 is searched from the beginning of the list to find its position. It is found in 4th position. The element is deleted and all the elements to the right of it are moved to left as indicated by 3rd, 4th and 5th rows of Table 2.4.

Exercise 2.8

1. Delete the element 23 from an array of the first eight prime numbers arranged in ascending order.
2. Draw a table (similar to Table 2.4) for the above problem.
3. Write an algorithm for deletion of an element from a static array.

2.5.2 Memory Diagram of Deletion of an Element from a Static Array

Suppose a five-element character array [HELLO] is stored in the memory whose starting address is 12356. It is required to delete the element E from the array. The various steps for deleting the element E are shown in Figure 2.8.

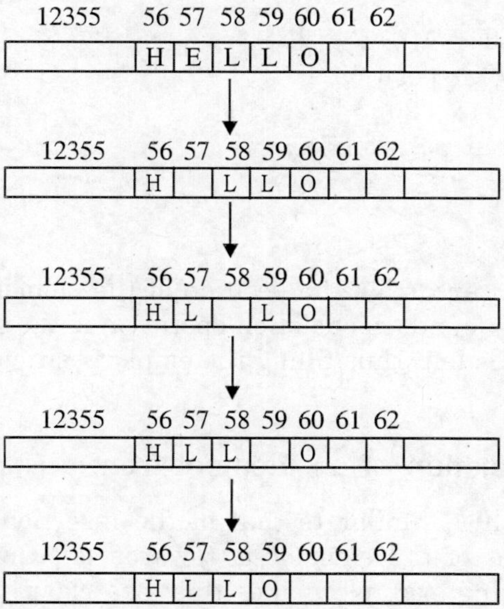

Figure 2.8 Deletion of an element from an array.

Exercise 2.9

1. Delete the element 15 from an array of the first eight multiples of three arranged in ascending order.
2. Draw a figure similar to Figure 2.8 for the above problem.

2.5.3 Program for Deletion of an Element from a Static List

Program 2.11 is the C program for the deletion of jth element from the array A.

Program 2.11

```
#include <stdio.h>
void main()
{
     int A[5]={20,30,40,50,60};
     int j=2,i,n=5;
     for(i=j;i<=n-1;i++)
     {
          A[i]=A[i+1];
     }
     A[i]='\0';
     printf("After Deletion..\n");
     for (i=0;i<n-1; i++)
     {
          printf("%d ",A[i]);
     }
getch();
}
```

Output

After Deletion

20 30 50 60

Exercise 2.10

1. Write a program to delete the element 23 from an array of the first eight prime numbers arranged in ascending order.
2. Write a program to delete the element 15 from an array of the first eight multiples of three arranged in descending order.

Chapter 3

Linked Lists

3.1 INTRODUCTION

As stated in Chapter 1, the linked list is a linear dynamic data structure. Before we study linked lists, we need to know more about dynamic memory allocation. Memory is allocated for variables in two ways:

- Static (or compile-time)
- Dynamic (or run-time)

So far, we have used static memory allocation. In a program which declares an integer variable **x,** memory locations of size enough for an integer (four locations since size of an int is four bytes) are reserved for **x** at compile time itself. Arrays are also known as static data structures since they also get their required memory allocated during compile time. The problem with static memory allocation is that the memory usage may not be efficient. Consider an array **marks,** to store the marks of students in a course which is conducted semesterwise. The maximum input of the course is, say, 100. The number of students can vary in each semester. Hence in a semester even if there are only 75 students, 100 locations will still be reserved and 25 of them wasted. (We can rewrite the program each time with the array declaration exactly matching the number of students; but then the program is no longer a general one.)

Dynamic memory allocation is in sharp contrast with static memory allocation. Memory gets allocated at the time of running the program and hence we can use memory to exactly meet our needs. We shall learn how to do this in C. Before that, an analogy may be very helpful. Static memory allocation is like reserving rooms in a hotel in advance for a picnic. At the time of the picnic, we may have lesser number of people turning up, but we will still have to pay for the rooms booked. But look at the good aspect: you are assured of rooms and it is very likely that (if you demand) you will get adjacent rooms. Consider going to the same hotel without booking. The bad things are obvious—you may end up not having enough rooms, and even if you get them, they may not be adjacent. Just imagine if you want to pass a message to all! Here are a few concepts that are easy to appreciate from the above analogy:

- Contiguous memory allocation: allocation of adjacent memory locations.
- Non-contiguous memory allocation: allocation of non-adjacent memory locations.

- Heap: collection of all free memory locations available for allocation.
- De-allocation: releasing of allocated memory after use, to be added back to the heap.

3.1.1 The malloc Function

The C language provides the **malloc** function which can be used for dynamic allocation of memory. The syntax of malloc function is:

malloc (sizeof (data type))

You should include <**malloc.h**> to use the function. The function returns a void pointer (the address of the first location, but it is not yet specified as address of a particular data type like int, char, etc.). Usually, we cast it as a pointer to the data type we desire. Here is a small Program 3.1, which dynamically allocates memory for an integer.

Program 3.1

```
#include <stdio.h>
#include <malloc.h>
void main()
    {
        int *p;
        p=(int *) malloc(sizeof(int));
        printf("Memory allocated at %d\n",p);
    }
```

We can now use the memory location obtained in Programs 3.1 to store the value of an integer (Program 3.2).

Program 3.2

```
#include <stdio.h>
#include <malloc.h>
void main()
    {
        int *p;
        p=(int *)malloc(sizeof(int));
        *p=56;
        printf("Integer in memory=%d\n",*p);
    }
```

See one more example with data type int replaced by struct pair (Program 3.3).

Program 3.3

```
#include<stdio.h>
#include<malloc.h>
void main()
    {
        struct pair
        {
        int x;
        int y;
        };
        struct pair *p;
        p=(struct pair *) malloc(sizeof (struct pair));
        (*p).x=56;
        (*p).y=47;
    }
```

The brackets around *p is required to control the precedence between * and . operators. However, this situation is so common that C has a short-hand notation for this:

(*p).x p->x
(*p).y p->y

We will be using this notation very often in learning linked lists.

Let us see how memory is allocated in Programs 3.1,3.2 and 3.3. In Program 3.1, **p** contains an address (say, 3586 which is that of an integer). So, the size of **p** is 2 bytes (assume that the size of the address data is 2 bytes) and *p is 4 bytes (since it is an integer). See Figure 3.1.

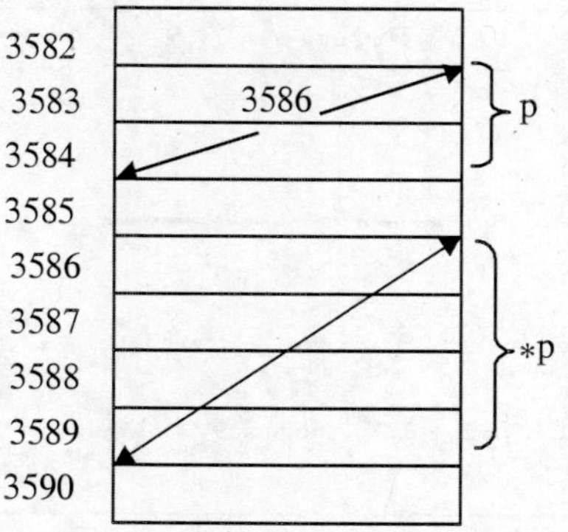

Figure 3.1 Visual representation of variables of Program 3.1 in memory.

In the same manner, the memory allocated for the variables in programs 3.2 and 3.3 is given in Figures 3.2 and 3.3.

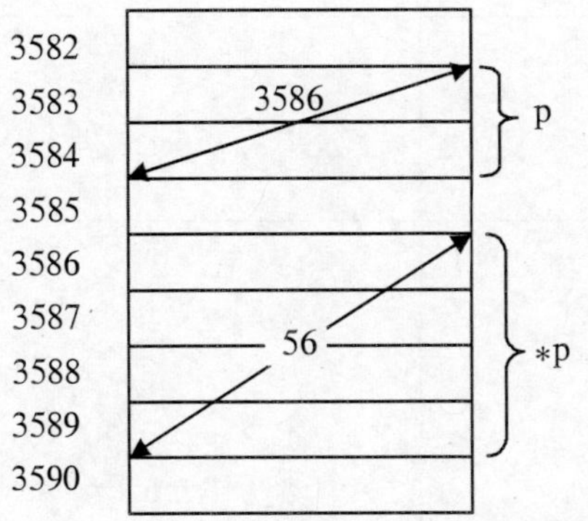

Figure 3.2 Memory representation of variables of Program 3.2.

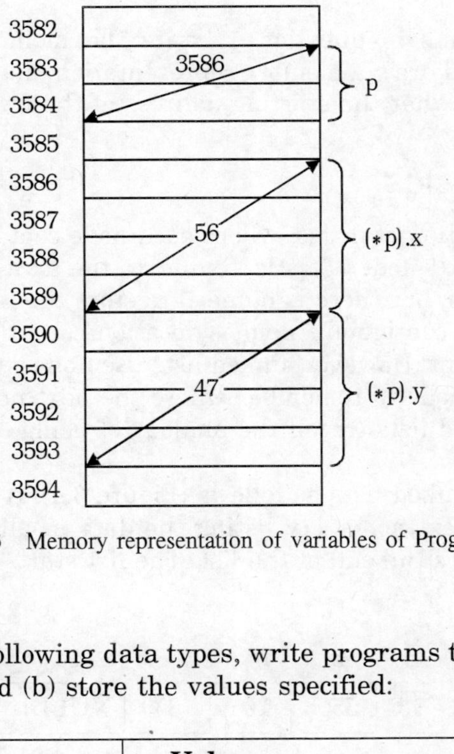

Figure 3.3 Memory representation of variables of Program 3.3.

Exercise 3.1

1. For each of the following data types, write programs to (a) declare a pointer to the data type and (b) store the values specified:

Data type	**Value**
`float`	`345.23`

`char`
`struct pair`
`{ int x;`
`int y;`
`};`
	`'U'`
	
	`{{5,9}, {33,44}}`

`struct point`
`{ struct pair a;`
`struct pair b;`
`};`
	`{2347, 89.78, 'D'};`

`struct person`
`{ char name[25];`
`int age;`
`char sex;`
`float height;`
`float weight;`
`char nationality[10];`
`};`
	`{"Ali", 25, 'M', 175.3,`
	`78.9, "Indonesian"}`

2. For the programs in question 1, state the memory allocated for each of the variables and draw a memory representation diagram similar to Figure 3.1. You can assume that the starting address of the free space available is 4925.

3.2 LINKED LIST BASICS

The linked list is a collection of nodes, where each node contains some data along with information about the next node. This is similar to the array in some ways. An array is a collection of elements, but there is no need to store the information about the next element since arrays use contiguous memory locations and the next element is always the physically next element. However, linked lists use non-contiguous memory locations and hence require each node to remember where the next node is, if we are to handle all the nodes of the linked lists (recall the analogy of using adjacent and non-adjacent hotel rooms).

Let us picture the linked lists as follows (Figure 3.4). A node has an integer data and the address of the next node. Try listing the data in all the nodes of the list. An address of NULL indicates the end of the list. The list starts from the node at location 4 (shown in grey).

	1	2	3	4	5	6	7	8	9	10	11	12	13	14
		750	8	350	10	550	12	850	NULL	450	6	650	2	

Figure 3.4 Visual representation of a linked list.

You may verify that the numbers in the linked list in Figure 3.4 are: 350, 450, 550, 650, 750 and 850.

The first node starts at address 4. Its content in the next field is 10. That means the next node is at address location 10. Hence, the succeeding node has data value 450 with the next field value 6. Proceeding in this manner, we can enumerate the succeeding data values in the linked list as 550, 650, 750 and 850.

Since each node has two fields, the size of each node is 8 bytes (4 bytes for integer data value and 4 bytes for address). The memory representation diagram for the linked list is given in Figure 3.5. The starting address is at 1. The next element starts at the location specified at location 5. In this diagram, address occupies 4 bytes.

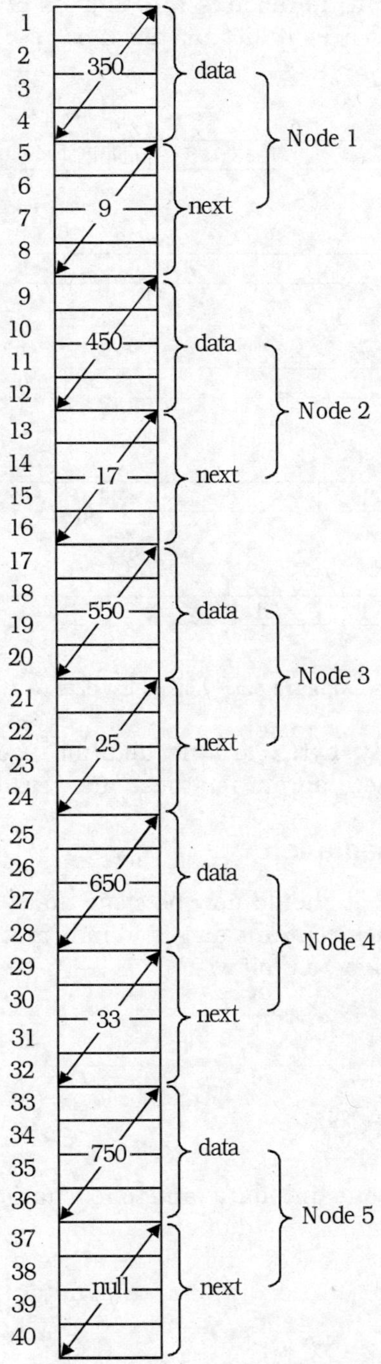

Figure 3.5 Visual representation of a linked list in memory.

Exercise 3.2

1. List the data stored in each of the linked list. The starting node is shown in grey. The last item in the node is the address of the next node. The address of locations are shown in italics on the top.

(a)

1	*2*	*3*	*4*	*5*	*6*	*7*	*8*	*9*	*10*	*11*	*12*	*13*	*14*
A	9	B	13	L	7	C	Null	L	3	**M**	**1**	I	5

(b)

1	*2*	*3*	*4*	*5*	*6*	*7*	*8*	*9*	*10*	*11*	*12*	*13*	*14*
1	3	3	5	5	9			9	Null	**11**	**13**	13	1

(c)

1	*2*	*3*	*4*	*5*	*6*	*7*	*8*	*9*	*10*	*11*	*12*	*13*	*14*
I	**3**	O	5	U	9			9	Null	A	13	E	1

(d)

1	*2*	*3*	*4*	*5*	*6*	*7*	*8*	*9*	*10*	*11*	*12*	*13*	*14*
K	5	N	1	U	9	T	11	C	7	A	Null	**I**	**3**

(e)

1	*2*	*3*	*4*	*5*	*6*	*7*	*8*	*9*	*10*	*11*	*12*	*13*	*14*
8	B	10	4	F	Null	**9**	**A**	**1**	7	C	4		

Figure 3.6 Linked list data.

2. Find out how many bytes are needed for each node given in question 1 (a) –1(e). Draw the diagram for these answers as given in Figure 3.5

3.2.1 Linked List Representation

From the foregoing examples, it should now be clear that each node of a linked list can be defined as a structure, which contains data and information about the next node. For single int data, this can be done as follows:

```
struct node
  {
     int data;
     struct node *next;
  };
```

If each node contains one int data and one character data, then the **struct** definition is as follows:

```
struct node
  { int data;
     char type;
     struct node *next;
  };
```

Let us now write a program (Program 3.4) to create a linked list of a single node with int data 55. Let us call the first node address as head.

Note that NULL is a keyword used in C to indicate a null pointer, a pointer which is pointing to nothing. Except for the last two lines in the program, all the remaining parts are common for all the linked list programs. The first few lines are **include** statements, followed by structure declaration. For a linked list structure, there has to be at least 2 fields — one for the data field and the other to store the information regarding position of the next element. The latter field must be a pointer field since it contains the address of the next element.

Program 3.4

```
#include  <stdio.h>
#include<malloc.h>
void  main( )
{    struct  node
     {    int  data;
          struct  node  *next;
     };
     struct  node  *head;
     head=(struct  node  *)malloc  (sizeof(struct  node));
     head->data55;
     head->next=NULL;
}
```

We now expand Program 3.4 to create two nodes containing data 55 and 66, respectively as given in Program 3.5. The size of the variables declared in Program 3.5 is given below:

head = 2 bytes
*head = 6 bytes

Program 3.5

```
#include<stdio.h>
#include<malloc.h>
void  main( )
{    struct  node
     {    int  data;
          struct  node  *next;
     };
     struct  node  *head;
     head=(struct  node  *)malloc(sizeof(struct  node));
     head->data=55;
     head->next=(struct  node  *)malloc  (sizeof  (struct  node));
     head->next->>data=66;
     head->next->next=NULL;
}
```

Exercise 3.3

1. Write a program similar to Programs 3.4 and 3.5 to create a linked list with three nodes, storing the values 55, 66 and 77, respectively.
2. Modify the above program to read the data for each node from the keyboard.
3. For each of the following cases, the head pointer is the address of the node shown in grey. Give the value of each of the expressions specified.

(a) char data:
head->data=.......
head->next=.........
head->next->data=........
head->next->next=...........
head->data->>next=............(valid?)

1	2	3	4	5	6	7	8	9	10	11	12	13	14
A	9	A	13	L	7	A	Null	L	3	M	1	I	7

(b) int data
head->next=......
head->next->data=......
head->next->next=.........
head->next->next->data=.............
head0>data->data->data=.........(valid?)

1	2	3	4	5	6	7	8	9	10	11	12	13	14
1	3	3	5	5	9			9	Null	**11**	**13**	13	1

(c) int dat1 ; char data2
head->data1=......
head->data2=.........
head->next=..........
head->next->data1=.........
head->next->data1=.........
head->next->next->data2=............

1	2	3	4	5	6	7	8	9	10	11	12	13	14
8	B	10	4	F	Null	**9**	**A**	**1**	7	C	4		

4. State the size of each node in question 3(a) – 3(c).

3.3 GENERAL PROGRAM FOR LINKED LISTS

The earlier examples for creating linked lists of 2 or 3 nodes are obviously not useful for a large number of nodes. Here is a program (Program 3.6) that reads integer data and stores it in a linked list until the data is entered as 0, which indicates the end of the data. Please note that the part of the program shown in bold is likely to appear in all linked list programs.

Program 3.6

```
#include <stdio.h>
#include <malloc.h>
void main( )
{
    struct node
    {
        int data;
        struct node *next;
    };
    struct node *head, *temp;
    int x;
    head= (struct node *)malloc (sizeof(struct node));
    temp=head;
    while(temp!=NULL)
    {
        scanf("%d",&x);
        temp->data=x;
        if(x==0)
        {
            temp->next=NULL;
        }
        else
        {
            temp->next=(struct node *)malloc(sizeof(struct
            node));
        }
        temp=temp->next;
    }
}
```

Exercise 3.4

1. Write a program to create a linked list with nodes containing character data. Data should be read from the keyboard until the data 'z' is entered.
2. For the above program, assume that the heap has free locations between 333330 to 333365, 333355. Also assume that the data entered are: 'f', 't', 'm', 's', 'z'. Draw the memory diagram of the linked list.
3. Write a program to create a linked list with nodes containing one integer and one character data. Data should be read from the keyboard until the integer data is entered 0.

3.4 PROCESSING OF LIST OF NODES

Like in arrays, we might need to process each node of the linked list. Typical cases are:

- Print out data of all nodes
- Print out selectively data of nodes
- Print out count of nodes
- Print out selectively count of nodes
- Reset selectively data of nodes
- Search for a particular data

Consider the case where it is needed to print out data of all nodes. Then in Program 3.6, the following program segment (Program 3.7) is to be included to get the output.

Program 3.7

```
temp=head;
while(temp!=NULL)
{
    printf("%d"\n", temp->data);
    temp=temp->next;
}
```

Some more cases are given in the following sections. We are only giving the relevant part of the program. If any new variables are included (like sum, count, etc.), they have to be declared in the beginning.

3.4.1 Printing Selectively

Print all data greater than 50 (Program 3.8).

Program 3.8

```
temp=head;
while(temp!=NULL)
{
    if (temp->data>50)
        printf("%d\n", temp->data);
    temp=temp->next;
}
```

3.4.2 Finding Sum

Calculate and print out the sum of all data in the nodes (Program 3.9).

Program 3.9

```
sum=0;
temp=head;
while(temp!=NULL)
{
    sum=sum+temp->data;
    temp=temp->next;
}
printf("Sum=%d\n", sum);
```

3.4.3 Finding Count

Calculate and print out the count of nodes (Program 3.10).

Program 3.10

```
count =0;
temp=head;
while(temp!=NULL)
{
    count++;
    temp=temp=temp->next;
}
printf("Count=%d\n",count);
```

3.4.4 Combination of Programs 3.8, 3.9, 3.10

Calculate and print out the sum and count of nodes with data values greater than 50 (Program 3.11).

Program 3.11

```
sum=0;  count=0;
temp=head;
while(temp!=NULL)
{
    if  (temp->data>50)
    {
        sum=sum  +  temp->data;  count++;
    }
    temp=temp->next;
}
printf("There are %d nodes with data greater than 50\n", count);
printf("The sum of data values greater than 50=%d\n", sum);
```

Exercise 3.5

1. Write a program to create a linked list with nodes containing character data. The data should be read from the keyboard until the data 'z' is entered. The program should also:
   (a) Print out all data.
   (b) Print out all upper case alphabets.
   (c) Print out the count of all upper case alphabets.
   (d) Print out if the data 'k' is present in the linked list.
2. Write a program to create a linked list with nodes containing one integer and one character data. The data should be read from the keyboard until the integer data is entered as 0. The program should also:
   (a) Print out all data.
   (b) Print out data of all nodes which store upper case alphabets.
   (c) Print out the count of nodes with int data greater than 50 and the char data 'A'.

3. Write a program to store the name, id, age, sex, mark (total out of 100) and grade ('F', 'P', 'C', or 'D') of students in a linked list. The data should be read from the keyboard until the student id is entered as 0. The grade is not to be read, but is to be calculated from the marks as: 0–39: Fail, 40–59: Pass, 60–74: Credit, 75–100: Distinction. The program should also:
   (a) Print out a list of students (name and id alone) with their marks.
   (b) Find the count of students who have credit/distinction.
   (c) Find the average marks.
   (d) Read a moderation mark and then increase all marks by this value.
   (e) Read a student id and then display the corresponding details from the linked list.
4. Printing out a linked list can be done in so many different ways, some of which can be very helpful in analysing the internal details of the list. Try out the following (for an integer linked list):

```
temp=head;
while(temp!=NULL)
{
     rintf("[%d  |  %d]→", temp->data, temp->next);
     emp=temp->next;
}
```

Note: The above program can produce an output like the following:

[44 |333333]→[55|33337]→[66|333356]→[77|333380]→etc.

3.5 INSERTION AND DELETION

There are two operations which might be required to maintain data in a linked list: insertion and deletion. While creating the linked list, we were inserting data at the end of the linked list always. If we need to insert a data between existing nodes, this needs to be done in a special way. Similarly, deletion also has to be handled separately. Let us discuss these one by one.

Here, we assume two simplifications: (i) the node we are trying to delete or insert before is present in the list, (ii) insertion or deletion is not at the beginning of the list. We will, towards the end of this section tackle these cases also.

3.5.1 Deletion

Let us consider the case of a linked list with int data in each node. Suppose we want to delete the node with data 55. Let us first look at the situation pictorially (Figure 3.7). Here is the original list with head = 4.

1	2	3	4	5	6	7	8	9	10	11	12	13	14
	75	Null	**35**	**10**	55	**12**			45	6	65	2	

Figure 3.7 Deletion from a linked list—Step 1.

If we write out the nodes in their current order, we have 35, 45, 55, 65, 75. Let us look at the node to be deleted and its previous and succeeding nodes alone. The previous node of 55 is 45, and the succeeding node is 65. That is, 45 → 55 → 65. When 55 is deleted, 45 and 65 will be the two consecutive nodes. So, the change is to be made in the next filed of 45. That is, by making the next node of (45) as 12, we will in effect exclude the node (55) from the list. This can be written as

prev->next=temp->next; (see Figure 3.8)

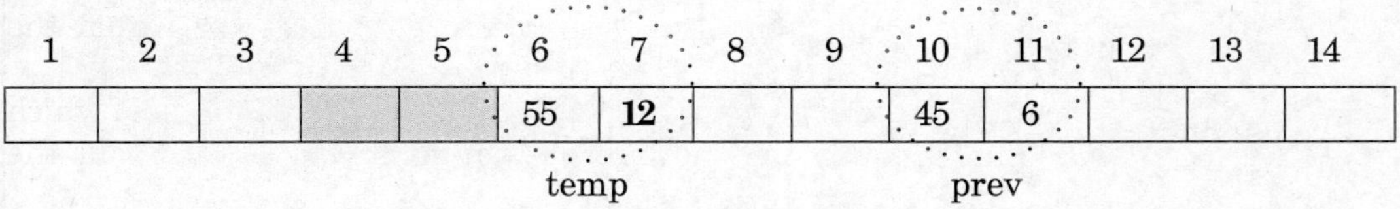

Figure 3.8 Deletion from a linked list—Step 2.

Here is the complete list after the operation (Figure 3.9). The node (55) is still there in memory, but it is out of the list. (You can use dealloc() function to remove the node from the memory also.)

1	2	3	4	5	6	7	8	9	10	11	12	13	14
	75	Null	**35**	**10**	55	**12**			45	12	65	2	

Figure 3.9 Deletion from a linked list—Step 3.

Try writing out the elements in the linked list and verify that that they are: 35, 45, 65, 75.

Let us now consider the program for deletion. The first task is to locate the previous node of the node to be deleted. We have to declare a pointer struct node *prev in addition to head and temp. The previous node is located as follows:

```
temp=head;
while  (temp!=NULL&&temp->data!=55)
{
    prev=temp;
    temp=temp->next;
}
Now the pointers are adjusted to effect the deletion:
    prev->next=temp->next;
```

Here is the complete program (Program 3.12), which has been made more general by reading the data to be deleted. (You should include a if (temp!=NULL) before the above statement to handle the case of the node to be deleted being absent).

Program 3.12

```
#include <stdio.h>
#include <malloc.h>
void main()
{
    struct node
    {
        int data;
        struct node *next;
    };
    stouct node *head, *temp, *prev;
    int x;
int a,. b,;
head=(struct node) malloc (sizeof(struct node));
temp=head;
while(temp!=NULL)
{
    scanf("%d",&x);
    temp->data=x;
    if (x==0)       {temp->next= NULL;}
    else {temp-> next=(struct node *) malloc (sizeof(struct node));}
    temp=temp->next;
}
printf("Enter data to be deleted >>");
scanf("%d", &a);
temp=head;
while(temp!=NULL && temp->data!=a)
{
    prev=temp;
    temp=temp->next;
}
if (temp!=NULL)
{
    prev->next= temp->next;
}
temp= head; //Printing the list after deletion
while (temp!=NULL)
{
    printf("%d\n", temp->data);
    temp=temp->next;
}
}
```

Exercise 3.6

1. For each of the linked list shown below:
   (a) List the data stored.
   (b) Delete the data indicated (circle the temp and previous nodes, then apply prev->next = temp->next).
   (c) Redraw the linked list.
   (d) List the data stored after the deletion.

The starting node is shown in grey. The last item in the node is the address of the next node. The addresses of locations are shown in italics on top of these nodes.

(a) Data to be deleted: 'S'

1	*2*	*3*	*4*	*5*	*6*	*7*	*8*	*9*	*10*	*11*	*12*	*13*	*14*
B	9	C	13	L	7	A	Null	L	3	**M**	**1**	I	7

Answer:

1	*2*	*3*	*4*	*5*	*6*	*7*	*8*	*9*	*10*	*11*	*12*	*13*	*14*

(b) Data to be deleted: 1

1	*2*	*3*	*4*	*5*	*6*	*7*	*8*	*9*	*10*	*11*	*12*	*13*	*14*
1	3	3	5	5	9			**9**	Null	11	13	13	1

Answer:

1	*2*	*3*	*4*	*5*	*6*	*7*	*8*	*9*	*10*	*11*	*12*	*13*	*14*

(c) Data to be deleted: A (first one)

1	*2*	*3*	*4*	*5*	*6*	*7*	*8*	*9*	*10*	*11*	*12*	*13*	*14*
M	**3**	A	5	L	7	A	9	A	11	S	13	I	Null

Answer:

1	*2*	*3*	*4*	*5*	*6*	*7*	*8*	*9*	*10*	*11*	*12*	*13*	*14*

(d) Data to be deleted: 55

1	*2*	*3*	*4*	*5*	*6*	*7*	*8*	*9*	*10*	*11*	*12*	*13*	*14*
99	Null	88	1	77	3	66	5	55	7	44	9	**33**	**11**

Answer:

1	*2*	*3*	*4*	*5*	*6*	*7*	*8*	*9*	*10*	*11*	*12*	*13*	*14*

(e) Data to be deleted: (7, C)

1	2	3	4	5	6	7	8	9	10	11	12	13	14
8	B	10	4	F	Null	**9**	**A**	**1**	7	C	4		

Answer:

1	2	3	4	5	6	7	8	9	10	11	12	13	14

2. Write a program to create a linked list with nodes containing one integer and one character data. The data should be read from the keyboard until the integer data is entered as 0. Then: (a) Read a char **a** and delete the node with char data equal to **a:** (b) Modify (a) to ensure that all nodes with char data = = **a** are deleted.
3. Write a program to store the name, id, age, sex, mark (total out of 100) and grade ('F', 'P', 'C', or 'D') of students in a linked list. The data should be read from the keyboard until the student id is entered as 0. The grade is not to be read, but is to be calculated from the marks (0–39: Fail, 40–59: Pass, 60–74: Credit, 75–100: Distinction). The program should also read a student id and then delete the corresponding details of the student.

3.5.2 Insertion

Insertion can be specified as before or after a node which has specific data. For example, let us consider the case of a linked list with int data in each node. Suppose we want to insert a node with data 50 before the node with data 55. Let us first look at the situation pictorially (Figure 3.10). Here is the original list with head = 4.

1	2	3	4	5	6	7	8	9	10	11	12	13	14
	75	Null	**35**	**10**	55	12			45	6	65	2	

Figure 3.10 Insertion into a linked list—Step 1.

If we write out the nodes in their current order, we have 35, 45, 55, 65, 75. Now, let us create a new node with data = 50, to be inserted in the linked list between 45 and 55. We can use any of the free locations. Let us select 8 (see Figure 3.11).

1	2	3	4	5	6	7	8	9	10	11	12	13	14
	75	Null	**35**	**10**	55	12	50	....	45	6	65	2	

Figure 3.11 Insertion into a linked list—Step 2.

The new node with value 50 should come between the nodes with values 45 and 55. Let us look at these nodes alone. The next node of (45) is 6. This should become 8. And to maintain the continuity, the next node of the new node (50) should be made 6 (see Figure 3.12).

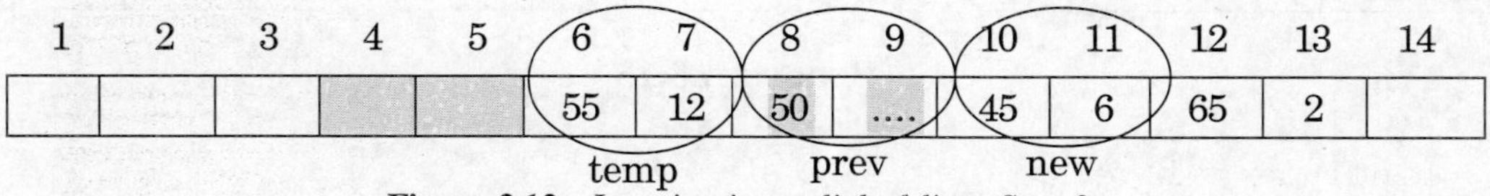

Figure 3.12 Insertion into a linked list—Step 3.

This can be written as

new->next=temp; prev->next=new, (see Figure 3.13). The steps required to insert a node can be written as:

1	2	3	4	5	6	7	8	9	10	11	12	13	14
					55	12	50	6	45	8			

Figure 3.13 Insertion into a linked list—Step 4.

We give below the complete linked list (Figure 3.14):

1	2	3	4	5	6	7	8	9	10	11	12	13	14
	75	Null	**35**	**10**	55	12	50	6	45	8	65	2	

Figure 3.14 Insertion into a linked list—Step 5.

If we write out the nodes now, we have 35, 45, 50, 55, 65, 75.

Let us now consider the program for insertion. The first task is to locate the previous node. We have to declare a pointer struct node *prev in addition to head and temp. The node before the insertion point is located as follows:

```
temp=head;
while(temp!=NULL&&temp->data!=55)
{
    prev=temp;
    temp=temp->next;
}
Now create the new node:
    new=(struct node *)malloc(sizeof(struct node));
    new->data=50;
Now the next pointers are adjusted to effect the insertion:
    new->next=temp;
    prev->next=new;
```

You should add an if (temp!=NULL) to take care of the situation of the data 55 being not found in the list. Here is the complete program (Program 3.13) which has been made more general by reading the data& position to be inserted.

Program 3.13

```
#include<stdio.h>
#include<malloc.h>
void main()
    {
    struct node
    {
        int data;
        struct node *next;
    };
    struct node *head, *temp, *prev, *newnode;
    int x;
    int a,b;
    head=(struct node *)malloc(sizeof(struct node));
    temp=head;
    while(temp!=NULL)
    {
        scanf("%d", &x);
        temp->data=x;
        if (x==0)
        {temp->next=NULL;}
        else
        {temp->next=(struct node *)malloc(sizeof(struct node));}
        temp=temp->next;
    }
    printf("Enter data to be inserted in the new node and the
    data of the node after which new node is to be inserted>>");
    scanf("%d %d", &a, &b);
    temp=head;
    while(temp!=NULL&&temp->data!=b)
    {
        prev=temp;
        temp=temp->next;
    }
    if(temp!=NULL)
    {
        newnode=(struct node *)malloc(sizeof(struct node));}
        newnode->data=a;
        newnode->next=temp;
        prev->next=newnode;
    }
    temp=head; //Printing list after insertion
    while(temp!=NULL)
    {
        printf("%d\n", temp->data);
        temp=temp->next;
    }
}
```

Exercise 3.7

1. Answer the following questions for each of the linked list given in Figure 3.15:
   (a) List the data stored.
   (b) Insert the data indicated (circle new, temp and prev, then apply new->next=temp; prev->next=new; Also, for new, select, redraw the linked list the first free location from left).
   (c) List the data stored after the insertion.

The starting node is shown in grey. The last item in the node is the address of the next node. The addresses of locations are shown in italics on the top. For creating new nodes, use the first free memory location available from the left.

(a) Data to be inserted: 88 before node with data 99

1	*2*	*3*	*4*	*5*	*6*	*7*	*8*	*9*	*10*	*11*	*12*	*13*	*14*
99	Null									**55**	**13**	66	1

Answer:

1	*2*	*3*	*4*	*5*	*6*	*7*	*8*	*9*	*10*	*11*	*12*	*13*	*14*

(b) Data to be inserted: A before node with data L

1	*2*	*3*	*4*	*5*	*6*	*7*	*8*	*9*	*10*	*11*	*12*	*13*	*14*
				A	Null	I	5	S	7	**M**	**13**	L	9

Answer:

1	*2*	*3*	*4*	*5*	*6*	*7*	*8*	*9*	*10*	*11*	*12*	*13*	*14*

(c) Data to be inserted: 7, C before node with data 6,D

1	*2*	*3*	*4*	*5*	*6*	*7*	*8*	*9*	*10*	*11*	*12*	*13*	*14*	*15*
8	B	13	4	F	Null	**9**	**A**	**1**				6	D	4

Answer:

1	*2*	*3*	*4*	*5*	*6*	*7*	*8*	*9*	*10*	*11*	*12*	*13*	*14*

Figure 3.15 Linked list data.

2. Write a program to create a linked list with nodes containing one integer and one character data. The data should be read from the keyboard until the integer data is entered as 0. Then: (a) Read two chars **a** and **b** and insert a new

node with data **a** before the node with data **b**, (b) Modify to ensure that insertion is done before all nodes with data **b.**

3. Write a program to store the student name, id, age, sex, mark (0–100) and grade ('F', 'P', 'C', or 'D') of students in a linked list. The data should be read from the keyboard until the student id is entered as 0. The grade is not to be read, but is to be calculated from the marks (0–39: Fail, 40–59: Pass, 60–74: Credit, 75–100: Distinction). The program should also read details of a new student and also an existing student id (x) and then insert the new details before the node with student id x.

3.6 THE SPECIAL CASE OF HEAD NODE

Suppose we want to delete the head node, or we want to insert a new node before the head node. There are two things to take note here. The head pointer, once assigned, is usually not changed. Also, for the head node, there is no previous node. Thus, the case of the head node is to be handled especially.

3.6.1 Deletion

For deleting the head node, we simply copy the contents of the second node to the head node:

```
head->data=head->next->data;
head->next=head->next->next;
```

Exercise 3.8

1. Modify the program in Exercise 3.6 to handle the case of the head node deletion.
2. For each of the linked list shown below:

   (a) List the data stored.
   (b) Delete the data indicated.
   (c) Redraw the linked list.
   (d) List the data stored after the deletion.

The starting node is shown in grey. The last item in the node is the address of the next node. The addresses of locations are shown in italics on top of these nodes.

(a) Data to be deleted: 'M'

1	*2*	*3*	*4*	*5*	*6*	*7*	*8*	*9*	*10*	*11*	*12*	*13*	*14*
A	9	A	13	L	7	A	Null	L	3	**M**	**1**	I	7

Answer:

1	*2*	*3*	*4*	*5*	*6*	*7*	*8*	*9*	*10*	*11*	*12*	*13*	*14*

(b) Data to be deleted: 11

1	*2*	*3*	*4*	*5*	*6*	*7*	*8*	*9*	*10*	*11*	*12*	*13*	*14*
1	3	3	5	5	9			9	Null	**11**	**13**	13	1

Answer:

1	*2*	*3*	*4*	*5*	*6*	*7*	*8*	*9*	*10*	*11*	*12*	*13*	*14*

(c) Data to be deleted: M

1	*2*	*3*	*4*	*5*	*6*	*7*	*8*	*9*	*10*	*11*	*12*	*13*	*14*
M	**3**	A	5	L	7	A	9	A	11	S	13	I	Null

Answer:

1	*2*	*3*	*4*	*5*	*6*	*7*	*8*	*9*	*10*	*11*	*12*	*13*	*14*

Figure 3.16 Linked list for deletion.

3.6.2 Insertion

For inserting before the head node, we first create a temp node in which we copy the head node data. Then write the new data into the head node and insert the temp node after the head node. Suppose the data to be inserted is x; then the following program segment will achieve the required result:

```
new=(struct node *)malloc(sizeof(struct node));
new->data=head->data;
new->next=head->next;
head->data=x;
head->next=new;
```

Exercise 3.9

1. Modify the program in Section 3.5 to handle insertion before the head node.
2. For each of the linked list shown below:
   (a) List the data stored.
   (b) Insert the data indicated.
   (c) Redraw the linked list.
   (d) List the data stored after the insertion.

The starting node is shown in grey. The last item in the node is the address of the next node. The addresses of locations are shown in italics on the top.

(a) Data to be inserted: 44 before node with data 55

1	2	3	4	5	6	7	8	9	10	11	12	13	14
99	Null									**55**	**13**	66	1

Answer:

1	2	3	4	5	6	7	8	9	10	11	12	13	14

(b) Data to be inserted: **M** before node with data **A**

1	2	3	4	5	6	7	8	9	10	11	12	13	14
				A	Null	I	5	S	7	**A**	**13**	L	9

Answer:

1	2	3	4	5	6	7	8	9	10	11	12	13	14

3.7 ARRAYS VERSUS LINKED LISTS

ARRAY	LINKED LIST
Static data structure: Number of elements of array to be declared at compile time, memory allocated at compile time	Dynamic data structure: Number of nodes need not be declared, memory allocated at run-time
Random data structure: Any element can be directly accessed by referring to its index. Time taken to access any element is independent of its position. Can be used for both sequential and random access applications (e.g. mark processing or bank balance enquiry)	Sequential data structure: Each node can be accessed only after traversing through all previous nodes. Time taken to access a node depends on its position (Max time for last node, minimum time for first one). Suitable only for sequential access applications (e.g. mark processing)
No memory overhead Array of 10 int takes 10∗4=40 bytes Array of 10 char takes 10∗1=10 bytes	Memory overhead (one pointer per node) Linked list of 10 int takes 10∗(4 + 4) = 80 bytes Linked list of 10 char takes 10∗(1 + 4) = 50 bytes
Contiguous memory required	Can work with non-contiguous memory
Insertion and deletion of array elements requires all succeeding elements to be shifted down or up.	Insertion and deletion of list nodes requires only the preceding and succeeding nodes to be modified

Arrays are comparatively easy to program. They can be handled efficiently using **for** loops	Linked list programming is comparatively difficult involving pointers. They are usually processed with the following **do while** loop:
	do
	{ .....
	    .....
	    temp=temp=temp->next;
	} while (temp!=NULL);

Exercise 3.10

1. Refer back to Exercise 1.1. For each of the data type mentioned there, assume that we are creating arrays with ten elements and linked lists with ten nodes. Prepare a comparison of memory required for each, in each case.
2. In our programs so far, we had created linked lists by adding new nodes to the end of the linked list. A sorted linked list can be created by always entering the new node in the proper position. You need to check from the first node for deciding the correct position for each new node and then insert the new node accordingly. Modify the program in Section 3.3, to create a sorted linked list.
3. Proper programming practice requires all memory that is allocated to be freed after use. (In our programs so far, when the program finishes running, the operating system frees all memory allocated.) There is a **dealloc**() function for memory allocation. Study the syntax of this function and modify your node deletion program using **dealloc**().
4. Develop the following functions for linked lists of int data. Please note that you will have to cut and paste your struct node definition outside the main, since the functions also need to refer to it.
   (a) int is Empty (struct node *h)—returns if the linked list is empty, 0 otherwise.
   (b) int search (struct node *h, int x)—returns if the data x is present in the linked list.
   (c) int count (struct node *h)—returns the count of the nodes in the linked list.
   (d) void delete (struct node *h, int x)—deletes the node with data x.
   (e) void insert (struct node *h, int x, int y)—inserts a node with data x before a node with data y.
   (f) void print list (struct node *h)—print out the data of all nodes.
5. Using the functions developed in question 4 above, write a menu-based program for the following operations on an integer linked list:
   - Create
   - Delete node
   - Insert node
   - Print out nodes
   - Count nodes
6. Instead of setting the next pointer of the last node to NULL, set it to head and we can get the circular linked list. With a circular linked list, you do not have to start from the head node always. From any value of temp, you can traverse forward to visit all the nodes and come back to the node you started with. You need to write your **while** loop for processing the nodes carefully, otherwise you will end up with an infinite loop.
   (a) Write a program to create a circular linked list of integers, reading integer data until 0 is encountered and then print out all node data.
   (b) Modify the sorted linked list program using the circular linked list.
7. Develop functions to (a) copy linked lists and (b) concatenate two linked lists.
8. Implement the linked list using arrays.

9. The size of integers always has an upper limit in all computers if you use the basic data types. Using a linked list, you can read huge numbers (say, over 50 digits) and store each digit as character in a linked list. Write a program to read two numbers this way and add them.
10. Study the **vi editor** in Unix/Linux. Develop a miniature text editing program with similar functionalities.

3.8 DOUBLY LINKED LIST

In the linked list structure so far seen, the link is pointed towards one direction only. Hence using the link, only the next element can be found. That is, using this type of structure, given a node of the list, it is very difficult to find the previous node. So, another type of structure, which is very useful in finding both the next node and the previous node of a current node, is given by the doubly linked list technique. In this list, a typical node contains at least three fields in which two of them contain information about the address of the previous node and the next node. A diagrammatic representation of the doubly linked list is given in Figure 3.17.

Previous	Data	Next
28	10	35

Figure 3.17 Visual representation of doubley linked list.

For example, consider the doubly linked list given in Figure 3.18a. Each node contains three fields. The node marked in grey is the starting node of the list.

1	2	3	4	5	6	7	8	9	10	11	12	13	14	15	16	17	18	19	20	21
13	36	19	19	60	10	10	20	null	4	30	7	null	10	1				1	28	4

Figure 3.18(a) Visual representation of a doubly linked list in memory.

In the starting node, which has address 13, the first field of the node is NULL. This is the previous field of the starting node. Since there are no nodes before the starting node, its value is NULL. The second field is the data field, whose value is 10. The third field is the next field which gives information about the next node. The value in this field is 1, which means that the next node starts at address 1. The data of the second node is 36. In this manner, members of the linked list are obtained as 10, 36, 28, 60, 30, 20.

Given any node, it is easy to find the next node and the previous node. For example, in the above figure (Figure 3.18), if data of the current node is 28 (whose address starts at 19) then the previous node and the next node are as follows (Figure 3.18b):

1	2	3	4	5	6	7	8	9	10	11	12	13	14	15	16	17	18	19	20	21
13	36	19	19	60	10	10	20	null	4	30	7	null	10	1				1	28	4
	Prev			next															current	

Figure 3.18(b) Visual representation of a doubly linked list in memory.

Exercise 3.11

1. For the lists given below, write the elements of the list in order.

(a)

1	*2*	*3*	*4*	*5*	*6*	*7*	*8*	*9*	*10*	*11*	*12*	*13*	*14*	*15*	*16*	*17*	*18*	*19*	*20*	*21*
13	B	19	19	D	10	10	F	null	4	E	7	null	A	1				1	C	4

(b)

1	*2*	*3*	*4*	*5*	*6*	*7*	*8*	*9*	*10*	*11*	*12*	*13*	*14*	*15*	*16*	*17*	*18*	*19*	*20*	*21*
7	36	13	19	60	10	10	20	1	4	30	7	1	10	Null				Null	28	4

3.8.1 Doubly Linked List Representation

From the examples given before it must be clear that each node of a doubly linked list can be defined as a structure, which contains data, information about the previous node and the next node. For single int data, a doubly linked list can be defined as follows:

```
struct node
  {
     struct node *prev;
     int data;
     struct node *next;
  };
```

If each node contains one int data and one character data, then the struct definition is as follows:

```
struct node
  {
     struct node *prev;
     int data;
     char type;
     struct node *next;
  };
```

If we write a program to create a doubly linked list of a single node with int data 55, it will be very similar to Program 3.4 except that the struct is to be defined as above and NULL value is assigned to next and prev fields. Let us call the first node address as head. Program 3.14 does this creation.

Program 3.14

```
#include<stdio.h>
#include<malloc.h>
void main()
{
     struct node
     {
          struct node *prev;
          int data;
          struct node *next;
     };
     struct node *head;
     head=(struct node *)malloc (sizeof(struct node));
     head->data55;
     head->prev=NULL;
     head->next=NULL;
}
```

We now expand Program 3.14 to create two nodes containing data 55 and 66 respectively as given in Program 3.15. Remember that for each node, two link fields are there. So, these fields have to be filled up properly.

Program 3.15

```
#include<stdio.h>
#include<malloc.h>
void main()
     {
     struct node
     {    struct node *prev;
          int data;
          struct node *next;
     };
     struct node *head;
     head=(struct node *)malloc(sizeof(struct node));
     head->prev = NULL;
     head->data=55;
     head->next=(struct node *)malloc (sizeof(struct node));
     head->next->>data=66;
     head->next->next=NULL;
     head->next->prev=head;
     }
```

Exercise 3.12

1. Write a program similar to Program 3.15 to create a doubly linked list with three nodes, storing the values 55, 66 and 77, respectively.
2. Modify the above program to read the data for each node from the keyboard.

3. For each of the following cases, the head pointer is the address of the node shown in grey. Give the value of each of the expressions specified.

char data:
head->data=........
head->next=..........
head->next->prev=........
head->next->data=.........
head->prev=.........
head->next->next=...........
head->data->next=.............(valid?)

(a)

1	2	3	4	5	6	7	8	9	10	11	12	13	14	15	16	17	18	19	20	21
13	B	19	19	D	10	10	F	Null	4	E	7	Null	A	1				1	C	4

(b)

1	2	3	4	5	6	7	8	9	10	11	12	13	14	15	16	17	18	19	20	21
7	36	13	19	60	10	10	20	1	4	30	7	1	10	Null				Null	28	4

3.8.2 General Program for Doubly Linked Lists

The earlier examples for creating linked lists of two or three nodes are obviously not useful for a large number of nodes. Here is a program (3.16) that reads integer data and stores it in a linked list until the data is entered as 0, which indicates the end of data. Please note that the part of the program shown in bold is likely to appear in all linked list programs.

Program 3.16

```
#include <stdio.h>
#include <malloc.h>
void main( )
{   struct node
      {
         struct node *prev;
         int data;
         struct node *next;
      };
    struct node *head, *temp;
    int x;
    head= (struct node *)malloc (sizeof(struct node));
    head->prev = NULL;
    temp=head;
    while(temp!=NULL)
    {
         scanf("%d",&x);
         temp->data=x;
```

```
        if(x==0)
                temp->next=NULL;
    else
      {       temp->next=(struct  node *)malloc(sizeof(struct  node));
                temp->next->prev=temp;
                temp=temp->next;
      }
    }
}
```

Exercise 3.13

1. Write a program to create a doubly linked list with nodes containing character data. The data should be read from the keyboard until the data 'z' is entered.
2. For the above program, assume that the heap has free locations between 333330 to 333365. Also assume that the data entered are: 'f', 't', 'm', 's', 'z'. Draw the memory diagram of the doubly linked list.
3. Write a program to create a linked list with nodes containing one integer and one character data. The data should be read from the keyboard until the integer data is entered 0.

3.8.3 Processing of Doubly Linked List of Nodes

All kinds of processes specified in Section 3.4 are applicable in the case of doubly linked list also. Moreover, some additional processes are very easy in the case of the doubly linked list when compared to the single list. One such process is to print the data in the list in reverse order. That is, data is to be printed from the last element to the first. For this, using the **next** field information, we can traverse to the end of the list and then, using **prev** field information, we can traverse back to the front of the list. Program 3.17 gives the relevant details of this process.

Program 3.17

```
temp=head;
while(temp->next!=NULL)
{
    temp=temp->next;
}
while  (temp!=NULL)
{
    printf("%d  /n",  temp->data);
    temp  =  temp->prev
}
```

Exercise 3.14

1. Write a program to create a doubly linked list with nodes containing character data. The data should be read from the keyboard until the data 'z' is entered. The program should also:
   (a) Print out all data.

(b) Print out all data in reverse order.
(c) Print out all upper case alphabets.
(d) Print out the count of all upper case alphabets.
(e) Print out if the data 'k' is present in the linked list.

2. Write a program to create a doubly linked list with nodes containing one integer and one character data. The data should be read from the keyboard until the integer data is entered as 0. The program should also:
   (a) Print out all data.
   (b) Print out data of all nodes which store upper case alphabets.
   (c) Print out the count of nodes with int data greater than 50 and the char data 'A'.
   (d) Reverse the link of nodes.
3. Write a program to store the name, id, age, sex, mark (total out of 100) and grade ('F', 'P', 'C', or 'D') of students in a doubly linked list. The data should be read from the keyboard until student id is entered as 0. The grade is not to be read, but is to be calculated from the marks as :0–39: Fail, 40–59: Pass, 60–74: Credit, 75–100: Distinction. The program should also:
   (a) Print out a list of students (name and id alone) with their marks.
   (b) Find the count of students who have credit/distinction.
   (c) Find the average marks.
   (d) Read a moderation mark and then increase all marks by this value.
   (e) Read a student id and then display the corresponding details from the linked list. Also, display the details of the previous and next students.

3.8.4 Doubly Linked List Insertion

Consider a doubly linked list given in Figure 3.19.

1	2	3	4	5	6	7	8	9	10	11	12	13	14	15	16	17	18	19	20	21
7	36	13	19	60	10	10	42	1	4	30	7	1	61	Null				Null	28	4

Figure 3.19 A doubly linked list.

The elements in the list are 28, 60, 30, 42, 36, 61 whose addresses are 19, 4, 10, 7, 1, 13. Suppose it is required to insert a node p with data 121 after the node q having data 42. Then the following changes have to be made to make the insertion operation successful:

- Previous (next of q) = Address of p
- Next of p = Next of q
- Next of q = Address of p
- Previous of p = Address of q

The address of node q is 7. Suppose the address of node p is 16. The following figures show the changes to be made in the link fields.

1	2	3	4	5	6	7	8	9	10	11	12	13	14	15	16	17	18	19	20	21
7	36	13				10	42	1							Null	121	Null	Null	28	4
							q									p				

Figure 3.20(a) Insertion into a doubly linked list—Step 1.

Step 1: Previous (next of q) = Address of p

1	2	3	4	5	6	7	8	9	10	11	12	13	14	15	16	17	18	19	20	21
16	36	13				10	42	1							Null	121	Null	Null	28	4
															q	p				

Figure 3.20(b) Insertion into a doubly linked list—Step 2.

Step 2: Next of p = Next of q

1	2	3	4	5	6	7	8	9	10	11	12	13	14	15	16	17	18	19	20	21
16	36	13				10	42	1							Null	121	1	Null	28	4
							q									p				

Figure 3.20(c) Insertion into a doubly linked list—Step 3.

Step 3: Next of q = Address of p

1	2	3	4	5	6	7	8	9	10	11	12	13	14	15	16	17	18	19	20	21
16	36	13				10	42	16							Null	121	1	Null	28	4
							q									p				

Figure 3.20(d) Insertion into a doubly linked list—Step 4.

Step 4: Previous of p = Address of q

1	2	3	4	5	6	7	8	9	10	11	12	13	14	15	16	17	18	19	20	21
16	36	13				10	42	16							7	121	1	Null	28	4
							q									p				

Figure 3.20(e) Insertion into a doubly linked list—Step 5.

Final list after insertion:

1	2	3	4	5	6	7	8	9	10	11	12	13	14	15	16	17	18	19	20	21
16	36	13	19	60	10	10	42	16	4	30	7	1	61	Null	7	121	1	Null	28	4
							q									p				

Figure 3.20(f) Insertion into a doubly linked list—Step 6.

If we write out the nodes now, we have 28, 60, 30, 42, 121, 36, 61.

Let us now consider the program for insertion. The first task is to locate the node with data, say, 'a'. Once the node is located, then the four steps mentioned above have to be repeated in that order. The node can be located as follows:

```
q=head;
while(q!=NULL && q->data!=42)
{
    q=q->next;
}
```

Now, create the new node:

```
    p=(struct node *)malloc(sizeof(struct node));
    p->data=121;
```

Now, the remaining fields are adjusted to effect the insertion:

```
    q->next->prev = p
    p->next= q->next
    q->next = p
    p->prev = q
```

You should add an if (q!=NULL) to take care of the situation of the data 42 being not found in the list. Consider the program to insert a node after a position specified by the user. The first part of this program is same as Program 3.16. The remaining portion of it is given as Program 3.18.

Program 3.18

```
q=head;
printf("Enter data to be inserted in the new node and the data
of the node after which new node is to be inserted>>");
scanf("%d %d",&a, &b);
while(q!=NULL)
{
    if(q->data==b)
    {
        p=(node *)malloc(sizeof(node));
        p->data = a;
        q->next->prev = p
        p->next = q->next
        q->next = p
        p->prev = q
        break;
    }
        q=q->next;
}
q=head;
printf("\nPRINTING AFTER INSERTION");
while(q!=NULL)
```

```
{
    printf("\n%d",q->data);
    q=q->next;
}
getch();
}
```

In the previous program, an element is to be inserted after the given element. Let us consider the case of insertion of an element before the given element. The solution is very similar to Program 3.18 except where the actual insertion takes place. The change to be incorporated is given by Program 3.19, in which p represents the new node to be inserted before the node q.

Program 3.19

```
while(q!=NULL)
{
    if(q->data==b)
    {
        p=(node  *)malloc(sizeof(node));
        q->prev->next  =  p;
        p->next=q;
        p->prev=q->prev;
        q->prev=p;
        p->data=a;
        break;
    }
    q=q->next;
}
```

Exercise 3.15

1. For the following doubly linked list, insert a node with value 100:
   (b) Before the node with data 1.
   (c) Before the node with data 28 (remember this will be the first node).
   (d) After the node with data 36.
   (e) After the node with data 61 (note that this is the last node of the list).

1	*2*	*3*	*4*	*5*	*6*	*7*	*8*	*9*	*10*	*11*	*12*	*13*	*14*	*15*	*16*	*17*	*18*	*19*	*20*	*21*
7	36	13	19	60	10	10	42	1	4	30	7	1	61	Null				Null	28	4

   For each case, draw the sequence of memory representation diagrams similar to Figure 3.20.
2. Write a program to create a doubly linked list with nodes containing one integer and one character data. The data should be read from the keyboard until the integer data is entered as 0. Then: (i) Read two chars **a** and **b** and insert a new node with data **a** before the node with data **b**, (b) Modify part

(a) to ensure that insertion is done before all nodes with data **b**, (ii) Modify part (a) to ensure that insertion is done after all nodes with data **b.**

3. Write a program to store the name, id, age, sex, mark (0–100) and grade ('F', 'P', 'C', or 'D') of students in a doubly linked list. The data should be read from the keyboard until student id is entered as 0. The grade is not to be read, but is to be calculated from the marks (0–39: Fail, 40–59: Pass, 60–74: Credit, 75–100: Distinction). The program should also read details of a new student and also an existing student id (x) and then (a) insert the new details before the node with student id x, and (b) insert the new details after the node with student id x .

3.8.5 Doubly Linked List Deletion

Consider a doubly linked list given in Figure 3.21.

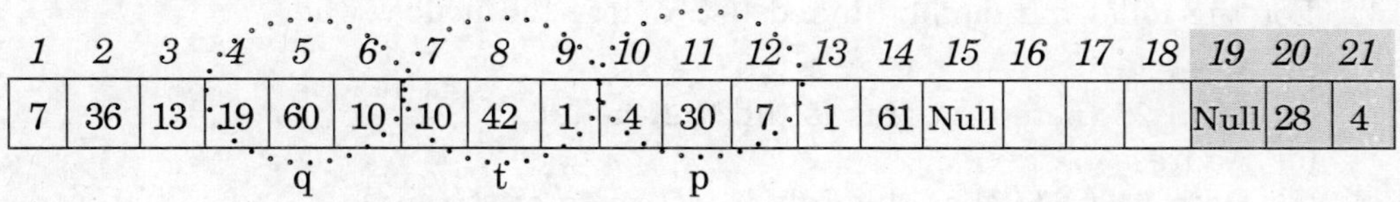

Figure 3.21 Deletion into a doubly linked list.

Consider the case of deletion of node p with data 30 in Figure 3.21. The nodes before and after this node have data 60 and 42, respectively. Denote these nodes by q and t, respectively. The following changes have to be made to make the deletion operation successful:

```
q->next=p->next
t->prev=p->prev
```

You can see in Figure 3.22, these changes have been made. Now the sequence of the elements in the list is 28, 60, 42, 36, 61. So, the node has been deleted. But, physically, it is in the list.

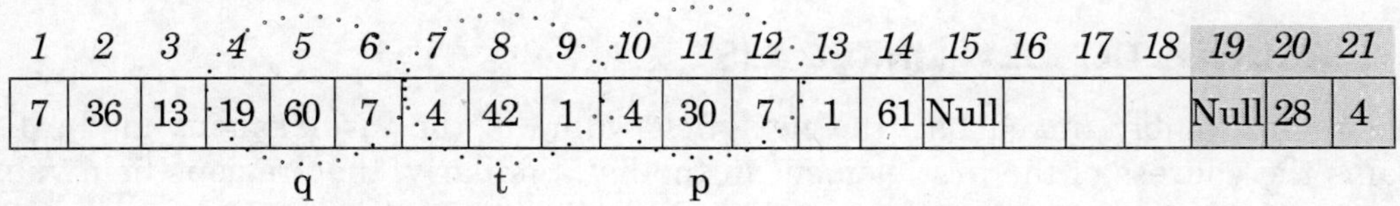

Figure 3.22 Deletion into a doubly linked list.

We cannot access that node. That is why it is said to be deleted. The above two changes can be done in another way also. The prev of p contains q and the next of p contains t. So, the above two statements can be written as follows:

```
p->prev->next  = p->next
p->next->prev=p->prev
```

Program 3.20 gives the relevant portion of the statements that will achieve the above said result.

Program 3.20

```
while(p!=NULL)
{
    if(p->no==b)
    {
        p->prev->next  =  p->next
        p->next->prev=p->prev
        break;
    }
    p=p->next;
}
```

Exercise 3.16

1. For the following doubly linked list, delete the node with:
   (a) Data 36.
   (b) Data 28 (note that this is the first node).
   (c) Address 4.
   (d) Data 61 (note that this is the last node of the list).

1	2	3	4	5	6	7	8	9	10	11	12	13	14	15	16	17	18	19	20	21
7	36	13	19	60	10	10	42	1	4	30	7	1	61	Null				Null	28	4

   For each case, draw the sequence of memory representation diagrams similar to Figure 3.22.
2. Write a program to create a doubly linked list with nodes containing one integer and one character data. The data should be read from the keyboard until the integer data is entered as 0. Then: (a) Read a char **a,** delete the node with data **a**, (b) Modify part (a) to ensure that deletion is done for all nodes with data **a.**

3.9 CIRCULAR DOUBLY LINKED LIST

In a circular doubly linked list, the next field value of the last element in the list contains the address of the first element in the list. Similarly, the previous field value of the first node contains the address of the last element in the list. Hence the name circular. So, in this case, it is very easy to access the starting element from the last element. As an example, consider the list given in Figure 3.23. The starting node, say p, is at address 19. The last node, say q, is at address 13. So, assign p to the next field of q and q to prev field of p. These changes are incorporated in Figure 3.24.

1	*2*	*3*	*4*	*5*	*6*	*7*	*8*	*9*	*10*	*11*	*12*	*13*	*14*	*15*	*16*	*17*	*18*	*19*	*20*	*21*
7	36	13	19	60	10	10	42	1	4	30	7	1	61	Null				Null	28	4

Figure 3.23 A doubly linked list.

1	2	3	4	5	6	7	8	9	10	11	12	13	14	15	16	17	18	19	20	21
7	36	13	19	60	10	10	42	1	4	30	7	1	61	19				13	28	4

Figure 3.24 A circular doubly linked list.

So, in the creation program, instead of assigning null values, proper field values are to be given. If we write a program to create a circular doubly linked list of a single node with int data 55, it will be very similar to Program 3.14 except that the values have to be assigned to prev field of the first node and the next field of the last node. Note that the struct declaration of circular linked list is similar to the doubly linked list. Let us call the first node address as head. Program 3.21 does this creation.

Program 3.21

```
#include<stdio.h>
#include<malloc.h>
void main()
{
    struct node
    {
        struct node *prev;
        int data;
        struct node *next;
    };
    struct node *head;
    head=(struct node *)malloc (sizeof(struct node));
    head->data55;
    head->prev=head;
    head->next=head; }
}
```

We now expand Program 3.21 to create two nodes containing data 55 and 66, respectively, as given in Program 3.22. Remember that for each node, there are two link fields. So, these fields have to be filled up properly.

Program 3.22

```
#include<stdio.h>
#include<malloc.h>
void main()
{
    struct node
    {
        struct node *prev;
        int data;
        struct node *next;
    };
    struct node *head, temp;
    head=temp=(struct node *)malloc(sizeof(struct node));
```

```
        head->prev  =  NULL;
        head->data=55;
        temp->next=(struct  node  *)malloc  (sizeof(struct  node));
        temp=temp->next
        temp->data=66;
        temp->next=head;
        temp->prev=head;
        head->prev=temp;
    }
```

The process of insertion and deletion of the circular doubly linked list is similar to that of the doubly linked list. The main difference is in finding the end of the list. In all the previous programs, the checking was based on NULL value of the next field of the last node. But in this case, we have to check for the equivalence of the next field value of a node with head. Whenever these are equal, it means that the end of the list has been reached. As an example, consider Program 3.23 where it is required to print data selectively, say, data > 50. Look how the condition is given in **while** loop.

Program 3.23

```
temp=head;
while(temp->next!=head)
{   if  (temp->data>50)
    {
        printf("%d\n",  temp->data);
    }
    temp=temp->next;
}
```

Exercise 3.17

1. Make the following doubly linked list as circular. Then do the following operations and find the resultant doubly linked circular linked list in each case.
   (a) Delete node with data 36.
   (b) Insert node with data 44 after the node with data 28.
   (c) Insert node with data 66 before the node with data 61.
   (d) Print all nodes with odd data values.
   (e) Insert node with data 44 before the node with data 28.
   (f) Insert node with data 66 after the node with data 61.

1	2	3	4	5	6	7	8	9	10	11	12	13	14	15	16	17	18	19	20	21
7	36	13	19	60	10	10	42	1	4	30	7	1	61	Null				Null	28	4

2. Write a program to create a circular doubly linked list with nodes containing one integer and one character data. The data should be read from the keyboard until the integer data is entered as 0. Then: (a) Read a char **a,** delete the node with data **a,** (b) Modify (a) to ensure that deletion is done for all nodes with data **a,** (c) Print all nodes with data > 100.

Chapter 4

Stacks and Queues

4.1 INTRODUCTION

The stack is a sequence of items, which can be added and removed from one end only. It is a concept known to every one. We make stacks of books, plates and many other things. What goes into a stack first, comes out last and what goes in last, comes out first. Hence, a stack is often known as a LIFO (last-in, first-out) list. Both array and linked list can be made to work as stacks. We consider both the array implementation and the linked list implementation.

The stack is a very useful and popular data structure. The operating system and other system programs use it extensively. Whenever nested function calls are made, the programs keep track of the location to return to, by storing it in stacks. Complex arithmetic expressions like (2 + 3/7*8 + 24/9*5 – 8) can be calculated easily by using stacks.

4.2 STACK USING ARRAYS

Stacks can be implemented easily using arrays by defining a structure containing an array and a variable to indicate the position of the top of stack. Consider a stack that is used to store integer data items. In such a case, its structure is given as follows:

```
struct stack
{
    int data[10];
    int top;
}
```

Now we can create a stack by declaring **struct stack s1**.

By convention, **top** is initialized to **–1,** which indicates an empty stack. When top equals the maximum index of the array (9 in this case), the stack is full. Any data added to the stack is done at the top position. Any data removed from the stack is also from the top position. These operations are known as **push** and **pop**. The value of top is changed with each push/pop. What happens during these operations are given in the box below. Figure 4.1 depicts an example of pushing and poping an integer data as indicated by the commands in the last column.

PUSH – Add data x to stack:
increment top and then set data[top]=x

POP – Remove and return data from stack:
return data[top] *and then decrement top*

data[0]	data[1]	data[2]	data[3]	data[4]	data[5]	data[6]	data[7]	data[8]	data[9]	**top**	Remarks
										–1	Empty
100										0	Push(& s1,100)
100	200									1	Push(&s1,200)
100	200	300								2	Push(&s1,300)
100	200	300	400							3	Push(&s1,400)
100	200	300	400	500						4	Push(&s1,500)
100	200	300	400	500	600					5	Push(&s1,600)
100	200	300	400	500	600	700				6	Push(&s1,700)
100	200	300	400	500	600	700	800			7	Push(&s1,800)
100	200	300	400	500	600	700	800	900		8	Push(&s1,900)
100	200	300	400	500	600	700	800	900	999	9	Push(&s1,999) *Stack is full*
100	200	300	400	500	600	700	800	900	999	8	Pop(&s1)
100	200	300	400	500	600	700	800	900	999	7	Pop(&s1)
100	200	300	400	500	600	700	800	900	999	6	Pop(&s1)
100	200	300	400	500	600	700	800	900	999	5	Pop(&s1)
100	200	300	400	500	600	700	800	900	999	4	Pop(&s1)
100	200	300	400	500	600	700	800	900	999	3	Pop(&s1)
100	200	300	400	500	600	700	800	900	999	2	Pop(&s1)
100	200	300	400	500	600	700	800	900	999	1	Pop(&s1)
100	200	300	400	500	600	700	800	900	999	0	Pop(&s1)
100	200	300	400	500	600	700	800	900	999	–1	Empty

Figure 4.1 Pushing and popping of integer data in a stack.

Exercise 4.1

1. For each of the stacks specified below, draw the diagram of the stack similar to Figure 4.1, for the operations specified.

(a)
```
struct stack
{    char data[10];
     int top;
};
struct stack s1;
```

data[0]	data[1]	data[2]	data[3]	data[4]	data[5]	data[6]	data[7]	data[8]	data[9]	**top**	Remarks
										–1	Empty
											Push(&s1,m)
											Push(&s1, a)
											Push(&s1, l)
											Push(&s1, a)
											Push(&s1, y)
											Push(&s1, s)
											Push(&s1, i)
											Push(&s1, a)
											Pop(&s1)
											Pop(&s1)
											Pop(&s1)
											Pop(&s1)
											Pop(&s1)
											Pop(&s1)
											Pop(&s1)

(b)
```
struct stack
    {
        char data[10];
        int top;
    };
    struct stack s2;
```

data[0]	data[1]	data[2]	data[3]	data[4]	data[5]	data[6]	data[7]	data[8]	data[9]	**top**	Remarks
										–1	Empty
											Push(&s2, 'a')
											Pop(&s2);
											Push(&s2, 'b')
											Push(&s2, 'c')
											Pop(&s2);
											Push(&s2, 'd')
											Push(&s2, 'e')
											Push(&s2, 'f')
											Push(&s2, 'g')
											Pop(&s2)
											Pop(&s2)
											Pop(&s2)
											Push(&s2, 'h')
											Push(&s2, 'i')
											Pop(&s2)

(c)
```
struct student
{  int id;
   int mark;
   char grade;
};
struct student john={2569, 5, 'F'};
struct student mary={3556, 65, 'C'};
struct student krishna={3457, 85,'D'};
struct student ali={3476, 45, 'P'};
struct stack
{   struct student data[5];
    int top;
};
struct stack s3;
```

data[0]	data[1]	data[2]	data[3]	data[4]	**top**	Remarks
					–1	
						Push(&s3, john);
						Push(&s3, mary);
						Pop(&s3);
						Push(&s3, krishna);
						Push(&s3, ali);
						Pop(&s3);
						Pop(&s3);

4.3 STACK IMPLEMENTATION

The operations PUSH and POP involve a series of commands to be executed, which are given in the box shown below. Here is a program (Program 4.1) that reads integer data until 0 is entered (or stack is full), pushes them to a stack and, finally, pops out and prints the data. The push and pop operations can be concisely programmed in the C language using the ++ and --operators. Please note that using pre/post is to be done carefully.

PUSH – Add data x to stack:

increment top and then data[top]=x

data[++top]=x

POP – Remove and return data from stack:

return data[top] and then decrement top

return data[top—]

Program 4.1

```
#include<stdio.h>
struct stack
{   int data[100];
    int top;
};
void push(struct stack *s, int x)
{   s->data[++s->top]=x;
} //Increment top and set data[top]=x
int pop(struct stack *s)
{
    return (s->data[s->top--]);
} //Return data[top] and then decrement top
void main( )
{   struct stack s1;
    int x;
    s1.top=-1;
    do
    {
        scanf("%d", &x);   // Push until x==0 or stack is full
        push(&s1, x);
    }while(x!=0 && s1.top <99);
    while(s1.top!=-1)   //Pop and print until stack is empty
    {
        x=pop(&s1);
        printf("data = %d\n", x);
    }
}
```

Exercise 4.2

1. Write a program to read character until 'z' is input and push them one by one into a stack. Finally, pop out data one by one and print them out.
2. Write a program to read student data (id, mark and grade—refer to Exercise 4.1, question 1(c)), until student data with id = 0 is input and push each into a stack. Finally, pop out data and print them.
3. What are the conditions for a stack to be (a) full and (b) empty? Assume the data array to be of size **N**.
4. In push and pop function, two conditions should be checked. For push, the stack should not be full. For pop, the stack should not be empty. Modify the program given in Section 4.3 to incorporate this.
   Hint: For the integer stack with array size of 100, push and pop will have to be modified in the following way.
   ```
   (a) if (s->top ==100) {printf("Stack full");}
       else {s->data++s->top=x;}
   (b) if (s->top=-1) {printf("Stack Empty"); return 0;}
       else {return (s->data[s->top--]);}
   ```

5. Write the following functions for stacks:
   int **stackFull**(struct stack ∗ s)—*return 0 if the stack is not full and returns 1 if the stack is full*
   int **stackEmpty**(struct stack ∗ s)—*return 0 if the stack is not empty and returns 1 if the stack is empty*
   int **stackTop**(struct stack ∗ s)—*return the current value of the stack top*
   int **intialiseStack**(struct stack ∗ s)—*sets the value of the stack top to –1*
6. Given a stack and new variables 'Red' and 'Black'. Write an algorithm 'change' which replaces all the occurrences of 'Red' in the stack by 'Black'.

4.4 APPLICATIONS OF STACK

The stack is a powerful data structure and is used in many applications. Some such applications are given in the following sections.

4.4.1 Checking Palindromes

A palindrome is a word/sentence that is the same if read both ways. Here are some palindromes:

MALAYALAM	DENNIS SINNED
GOD SAW I WAS DOG	DAD
RATS LIVE ON NO EVIL STAR	DID
DEED	POP
RAW SEXES WAR	RADAR
STEP ON NO PETS	REDIVIDER

You might have noticed that if you push some characters into a stack and pop them out, they will appear in **reverse order**. This technique can be used to check if a string is a palindrome. Program 4.2 reads a string and checks if it is a palindrome or not.

Program 4.2

```
#include<stdio.h>
#include<string.h>
struct stack
{
    char data[100];
    int top;
};
void push(struct stack * s, char x) {s->data[++s->top]=x;}
char pop(struct stack * s){return (s->data[s->top—]);}

void main( )
{
    struct stack s;
    char string[] = "RATS LIVE ON NO EVIL STAR";
    int palin=1, i;
```

```
    s.top=-1;
    if(strlen(string)==1)
        palin=1; // All strings with 1 character are palindromes
    else
      {
        i=0;
        while  (string[i]!='\0')  //Push  the  string  into  stack
        {
            push(&s,  string[i]);
            i++;
        }
    i=0;
    while(string[i]!='\0') // Pop the string and compare with original
      {
        if(string[i]!=pop(&s))
        {
            palin=0;
            break;
        }
        i++;
      }
    }
   if(palin==0)   {printf("Not  Palindrome\n");}
   else            {printf("Palindrome\n");}
}
```

Note: To read a string that contains spaces like "GOD SAW I WAS DOG", format %s will not work. For these cases, instead of **scanf()**, **gets()** should be used.

Exercise 4.3

1. Write a C program to check whether a given number is palindrome or not.
2. Modify Program 4.2 to accept a string from the user and to find if it is a palindrome or not.

4.4.2 Checking if Brackets are Balanced

There are various situations in which it is needed to check if a string contains equal number of '(' and ')'. Such a situation arises in compiler software written for any kind of language. To check this, first of all, the string must be traversed from left to right (or from right to left). As each '(' is encountered, it should be remembered. So '(' is pushed into a stack. Whenever a ')' is encountered, the top element of the stack containing ')' must be popped out. This process is repeated till the end of the string is reached. At end if the stack is empty, then the string is a palindrome. An algorithm for this problem is given below:

Algorithm

```
while (not at the end of the string)
{   if (the next character is a '(' )
                {push '(' to stack; }
    else if (the character is a ')' )

    {
        if the stack is empty display 'Not balanced'
        else
                  pop from stack;
    }
    if (the stack is empty) display balanced
    else display not balanced
}
```

Note that this algorithm assumes the string contains "(" and ")" brackets only.

The C program for checking of brackets is given in Program 4.3. Here the stack is implemented as an array. In this program, three types of brackets are considered, viz. (, { and [.

Program 4.3

```
#include <string.h>
#include <alloc.h>
# include <stdio.h>
int arr[10];
int top=-1;
struct stack
{
    char data[100];
    int top;
};
void push(struct stack * s, char x) {s->data[++s->top]=x;}
char pop(struct stack * s){return (s->data[s->top-]);}
void main()
{
    struct stack s;
    int i, val =0;
    char exp[]="(a+b) * c";
    char symbol;
for(i=0;exp[i]!='\0';i++)
{
    if(exp[i]=='('||exp[i]=='[' ||exp[i]=='{')
    {
        push(&s, exp[i]);
    }
```

```
    else
      {
            if(exp[i]==')'  ||exp[i]==']'  ||  exp[i]=='}')
            {
                if  (top!=-1)
                    symbol=pop(&s);
                    switch  (symbol)
                    {
                        case  '(': if  (exp[i]==')')
                        val=1;
                        case  '[': if  (exp[i]==']')
                        val=1;
                        case  '{': if  (exp[i]=='}')
                        val=1;
                    }
                    }
                if(!val)
                    break;
            }
  }
  if(!val  ||  top!=-1)
  {
      printf("\n Not correct");
  }
  else
  {
      printf("\n Correct");
  }
      getch();
  }
```

Figure 4.2 shows the execution of the algorithm for checking balanced brackets of input string (a(b)c).

data[0]	data[1]	top	Remarks
		–1	Empty
(		0	Push "("
(	(	1	Push "("
(		0	Pop
		–1	Pop

Figure 4.2 Execution of algorithm for checking of balanced brackets of (a(b)c).

Figure 4.3 shows the execution of the algorithm for checking balanced brackets of input string (a(bc)).

data[0]	data[1]	top	Remarks
		–1	Empty
(		0	Push
(	(	1	Push
(		0	Pop, Stack not empty

Figure 4.3 Execution of algorithm for checking of balanced brackets of (a(bc)).

Figure 4.4 shows the execution of the algorithm for checking balanced brackets of input string (ab)c).

data[0]	top	Remarks
	–1	Empty
(	0	Push
	–1	Pop
		Stack empty but there is a ")"

Figure 4.4 Execution of algorithm for checking of balanced brackets of ((ab)c).

Exercise 4.4

1. Write a program to read a mathematical expression ((2 + 3) ∗ (5 + 8)) as a string and check if it has balanced brackets using Program 4.3.

4.4.3 Evaluation of Expressions

Expressions that we normally use, where the operator comes between the operands, are known as *infix expression*. There is a great deal of ambiguity in finding the value of infix expression. For example, the expression 5 + 6 ∗ 7 – 8/4 can be evaluated in at least two ways as follows:

(a) $5 + 6 * 7 - 8/4 = (5 + 6) * 7 - (8/4) = 11 * 7 - 2 = 77 - 2 = 75$
(b) $5 + 6 + 7 - 8/4 = 5 + (6 * 7) - (8/4) = 5 + 42 - 2 = 5 + 40 = 45$

Manually, these expressions are evaluated using the precedence rules. In computers, to overcome these difficulties, expressions are evaluated in one of the two forms: (a) Postfix expression, and (b) Prefix expression. The fundamental property of these two expressions is that the order in which the operations are to be performed is completely determined by the positions of the operands and operators in the expression.

In the postfix expression, operators are written after the operands and in the case of the prefix expression, operators are written before the operands. A very simple example is given below:

Infix expression	Postfix expression	Prefix expression
A + B	AB+	+AB

In the postfix expression, the operator + comes after the operands A and B, and in the prefix expression, it comes before the operands. Let us look at another example.

A + B + C

As per the precedence rule, the evaluation of the expression takes place as follows:

((A + B) + C)

To obtain the postfix expression of A + B + C, replace each right parenthesis with the operator just preceding it (find the operator which has not been replaced by the right parenthesis). This process is very clear from the following expression:

((A + B) + C = AB + C +

Similarly, to obtain the prefix expression of A + B + C, replace the most included left parenthesis with the succeeding operator. This process is very clear from the following expression:

((A + B) + C) = ++ABC

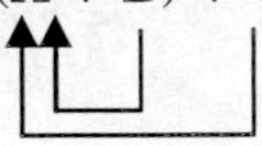

Example 4.1

1.

Infix expression	Bracketed expression as per precedence rule	Postfix	Prefix
7 x 8 + 5	((7 x 8) + 5)	7 8 x 5 +	+ x 7 8 5
A + B / C	(A + (B/C))	A B C/ +	+ A/B C
A x (B + C)	(A x (B + C))	A B C + x	x A + B C

We will also look into the conversion of these three forms from one type to another.

4.4.3.1 Evaluation of postfix expressions

As explained earlier, in a postfix expression, the operators succeed the operands. So, given a postfix expression, its general evaluation rule is to apply an operator to two operands that immediately precede it. Look at the following examples which are self-evident:

Postfix	Infix	Value
2 3 +	2 + 3	5
7 8 5 + *	7 * (8 + 5)	91

Using stack, it is very easy to implement the postfix evaluation. Whenever the program encounters an integer, it is pushed into the stack. Whenever an operator is encountered, two elements from the top of the stack are popped off, the operation is applied, and then pushed onto the stack. This process is repeated until the input expression string is empty.

Algorithm

Let P be an arithmetic expression written in the postfix notation. A stack is used to hold operands while evaluating the expression.

Step 1: Scan P from left to right and repeat steps 2 and 3 for each element of P until the end of P is encountered.

Step 2: If an operand is encountered, push it onto the stack.

Step 3: If an operator X is encountered, then:

(a) Remove the top two elements, a and b, from the stack where 'a' is the top element of the stack and 'b' is the next top element.

(b) Evaluate b X a.

(c) Push the result onto the stack.

End if

End of Step 1

Step 4: Set result = top element on the stack.

Step 5: Exit.

Let us see how a postfix expression (for example, 2 3 + 5 *) is evaluated using the above algorithm. The input is scanned from left to right to read character by character. The first character is an operand, so it is pushed onto the stack. The next character is also an operand. So, it is also pushed onto the stack. Next, an operator is encountered. So, two elements from the stack are popped out. These two elements are the operands of the current operator. The operation is applied and the result is pushed back to the stack, and the process is repeated until the end of string is reached. The final result is the top element of the stack. These steps are represented in Figure 4.5. Program 4.4 gives the postfix evaluation, using an array.

S1	S2	C	Stack	Remarks
		2	2	Operand, push
		3	3	Operand, push
3	2	+	5	Pop, evaluate, push
		5	5	Operand, push
5	5	*	25	Pop, evaluate, push

Figure 4.5 Evaluation of postfix expression.

Program 4.4

```
#include<ctype.h>
#include<stdio.h>
#include<string.h>
struct stack
{
    char data[100];
    int top;
};
void push(struct stack * s, char x) {s->data[++s->top]=x;}
char pop(struct stack * s){return (s->data[s->top-]);}

void main( )
{
    int i, k, l,res;
    char post[]='785+*';
    struct stack s;
    s.top=-1;
    for(i=0;post[i]!='\0';i++)
    {
        if (isdigit(post[i]))
            push(&s, post[i]-'0');
        else
        {
        k=pop(&s);
        l=pop(&s);
        switch(post[i])
          {
            case '+': res = k+l; break;
            case '-' : res = k-l; break;
            case '*' : res = k*l; break;
            case '/' : res= k/l; break;
            case '$':
                    res=1;
                    for(i=0;i<l;i++)
                         res=res*k;
                    break;
          }
        push(&s, res);
      }
    }
    k=pop(&s);
    printf("\nResult = %d",k);
    getch( );
}
```

Exercise 4.5

1. Write the postfix and prefix form of the given infix expressions after bracketing the expression as per the precedence rule.

Infix expression	Bracketed expression	Postfix	Prefix
A + B + C + D			
A x B + C – D			
A/B x C			
A x B + C			
A/(B x C)			

2. Evaluate the following postfix expressions by using the algorithm given in Section 4.4.3. Show the status of the stack after each step of the algorithm. Assume the following values for the identifiers: A = 7; B = 3; C = 12; D = –5; E = 1.

(a) ABC+–   (b) ABC-D*+   (c) AB+C-DE*+

4.4.3.2 Evaluation of prefix expressions

In a prefix expression, operators precede the operands. In the evaluation of a prefix expression, an operator is applied to two operands that succeed the operator. Look at the following examples which are self-evident:

Prefix	Infix	Value
+ 2 3	2 + 3	5
* + 7 8 5	(7 + 8)*5	91

Prefix expressions can also be evaluated using a stack. It is exactly similar to postfix expression evaluation, except that the input string should be read from right to left. Whenever an operand is encountered, it is pushed onto the stack. When an operator is encountered, two elements are popped off the stack, do the operation and push the result onto the stack. This process is repeated till the beginning of the string. Remember, we are scanning the input form right to left. Given below is the algorithm for prefix evaluation. Program 4.5 gives the prefix evaluation where the stack is implemented using an array.

Algorithm

Step 1: Input a prefix string 'P'.

Step 2: Declare the stacktop.

Step 3: For each element 'C' of 'P' do [read elements from the end of P].

Step 4: If 'C' is an operand
  Push C to stack.

Step 5: Else
  Pop top two elements S_1, S_2 off the stack.

Step 6: Evaluate k = S_1 C S_2.

Step 7: Push k onto the stack.

Stop 8: Endfor [Until the beginning of P].

An example is worked out below (Figure 4.6) for P = **∗5∗76.**

S1	S2	C	Stack	Remarks
		6	6	Operand, push
		7	7	Operand, push
7	6	∗	42	Pop, evaluate, push
		5	5	Operand, push
5	42	∗	210	Pop, evaluate, push

Figure 4.6 Evaluation of prefix expression.

Program 4.5

```
#include<ctype.h>
#include<stdio.h>
#include<string.h>
struct stack
{
    int item[100];
    int top;
};
void push(struct stack * s, int x) {s->item[++s->top]=x;}
int pop(struct stack * s){return (s->item[s->top—]);}

void main( )
{
    int i,k,l, res;
    char pref[] = '*5*76';
    struct stack s;
    s.top=-1;
    for(i=strlen(pref)-1;i>=0;i--)
{
    if (isdigit(pref[i]))
        push(&s, pref[i]-'0');
    else
      {
        k=pop(&s);
        l=pop(&s);
        switch(pref[i])
            {
```

```
                case '+': res = k+l; break;
                case '-': res = k-l; break;
                case '*': res = k*l; break;
                case '/': res = k/l; break;
                case '$': res = 1;
                    for(i=0;i<l;i++)
                        res=res*k;
                    break;
            }
        push(&s, res);
        }
    }
k=pop(&s);
printf("\nResult = %d",k);
getch( );
}

eval(int x, int y, char op)
{
int res, i;
switch(op)
{
case '+': res = x+y; break;
case '-': res = x-y; break;
case '*': res = x*y; break;
case '/': res = x/y; break;
case '$':
res=1;
for(i=0;i<y;i++,res*=x;break;}
return(res);
}
```

Exercise 4.6

1. Evaluate the following prefix expressions by using the algorithm given in Section 4.3.3.2. Show the status of the stack after each step of the algorithm. Assume the following values for the identifiers: a= 7; b = 3; c = 12; d = –5.

   (a) – + abc
   (b) + a–bc
   (c) *+ab–cd

4.4.3.3 Postfix to infix

We have seen how to evaluate an expression given in its postfix or prefix form. Now we will see how to derive the infix form from a postfix form. The input string postfix P is scanned from left to right to read character by character. If the scanned character is an operand, it is pushed onto the stack. If it is an operator, say X, two elements, say S2 and S1, are popped off the stack to form a "operand-operator-operand" string and is again pushed onto the stack. As stated earlier, an infix expression gives rise to ambiguity. This is avoided by using brackets in the expression. So, the infix that is obtained from the postfix needs brackets to avoid ambiguity. For this, it is necessary to remember the previous operator, say, F. If the precedence of X is higher than that of F, then brackets are to be added to S2 and S1 (provided the length of S1 and S2 is greater than one). The algorithm for the above-described procedure is given below. Program 4.6 takes as input a postfix expression and returns the corresponding infix expression.

Algorithm

Step 1: Enter the postfix string, say P.
Declare an empty character 'F' {to remember the previous operator}.
Step 2: For each character 'X' in 'P'.
Step 3: If X is an alphanumeric character – Push onto the stack.
Else
{
Step 4: Pop off the top elements, say S_2, S_1, from the stack.
Step 5: Check if the new operator 'X' has higher precedence than the previous operator 'F'.
Step 6: If true
{If length of S_1 >1 – Add brackets to S_1 {S_1 > 1 then (S_1)}
Assign 'X' to 'F'.
Step 7: If length of S_2 >1 – Add brackets to S_2 {S_2 > 1 then (S_2)}
}
Step 8: Concatenate S_1 X S_2
Step 9 Push onto the stack (Push concatenated string)
}
Step 10: End for (Until end of string P).

Example 4.2

Suppose it is required to convert the postfix expression P = AB + C * into infix expression. Figure 4.7 illustrates the various steps of this process.

S1	S2	**C**	Stack	Remarks
		A	A	Operand, push
		B	B	Operand, push
A	B	+	A+B	Pop, concatenate, push
		C	C	Operand, push
A+B	C	*		Pop
(A+B)	C		(A+B)*C	Length of S1 > 1 so (S1)

Figure 4.7 Conversion of postfix to infix.

Program 4.6

```
#include<ctype.h>
#include<stdio.h>
#include<string.h>
#include<conio.h>
#include<alloc.h>
typedef struct stack
{
    char data[20][20];
    int top;
}st;
void push(st *stack, char ch[])
{
    strcpy(stack->data[++(stack->top)],ch);
}
char* pop(st *stack)
{
    return(stack->data[(stack->top)-]);
}
int check(char c)
{
    switch( c)
    {
      case '+':return 1;
      case '-':return 1;
      case '*':return 3;
      case '/':return 3;
      case '%':return 3;
      case '^':return 7;
    }
return 0;
}
int precedence(char c, char d)
{
    if (check(c) == check(d))
      return 2;
    if (check(c) < check(d))
      return 1;
    else return 0;
}
void convert(char ch[])
{ char temp[10];
    strcpy(temp, "(");
    strcat(temp, ch);
    strcat(temp, ")");
```

```
    strcpy(ch, temp);
  }
  void main()
  {
    char f=' ',post[20]="AB+C*DE-+",*k,*l,inf[20]="\0";
    int i,x;
    st stack;
    clrscr();
    l=(char*)malloc(20);
    k=(char*)malloc(20);
    stack.top=-1;
    for(i=0;post[i]!=0;i++)
    {
        if(isalnum(post[i]))
        {
            *k =post[i]; *(k+1)='\0';
            push(&stack,k);
        }
        else
        {
            strcpy(k,pop(&stack));
            strcpy(l,pop(&stack));
            x=precedence(f,post[i]);
            if(x==1)
            {   if(strlen(l)>1)
                  convert(l);
            }
            else
            if(x==2)
            {   if(strlen(k)>1)
                  convert(k);
            }
            strcpy(inf,l);
            *l=post[i];
            *(l+1)='\0';
            strcat(inf,l);
            strcat(inf,k);
            f=post[i];
            push(&stack, inf);
        }
    }
    strcpy(k,pop(&stack));
    printf("result %s",k);
    getch();
  }
```

Exercise 4.7

1. Convert the following postfix expressions to infix expressions using the algorithm given in Section 4.4.3.3. Show the status of the stack after each step of the algorithm.

   (a) ABC+ –   (b) ABC–D*+   (c) AB+C–DE*+

2. The conversion of prefix to infix is almost similar to the algorithm described in Section 4.4.3.3 except that the input string should be scanned from right to left. Write an algorithm to do this conversion. Work out the algorithm on the following prefix expressions:

   (a) – + abc
   (b) + a – bc
   (c) *+ab – cd

3. Write a program for the algorithm implemented in question 2.

4.4.3.4 Infix to postfix

In this section, we discuss how to convert an expression in infix form to its postfix form. The input infix string is scanned from left to right, character by character. Whenever an operand is encountered, it, is added to the output string denoted by, say, postfix. If the character, say C, being scanned is an operator, we have to compare the priority of C with that of the top element of the stack, say f. If f has a higher priority than C, then pop f and add it to the postfix string. Repeat it till an f is reached whose priority is less than C. Now push C to the stack. Once the end of the string is reached, pop all the elements from the stack and add it to postfix string. The following algorithm and Program 4.7 implement this procedure.

Algorithm

Step 1: Declare an array 'Postfix'.
Read an infix expression, say 'S'.

Step 2: Create an empty stack and declare Stacktop.

Step 3: For each character 'C' in string S Do.

Step 4: if C = Operand, then Add to 'Postfix'
Else

Step 5: {

Step 6: While (Precedence of operator on the stacktop > precedence of C) and stack not empty
{ Pop and add to Postfix }

Step 7: Push C to stack
}

Step 8: Endfor {Until the end of string 'S'}

Step 9: while stack ! empty
{
Pop from Stack
Add it to Postfix
}

Step 10: print postfix
Example: Infix = A+B∗C

The various steps of the algorithm with this example are given in Figure 4.8. The final postfix is ABC∗+.

f	C	Stack	Postfix	Remarks
	A		A	Add operand to postfix
+	+	+	A	Push operator
	B		B	Add operand to postfix
	*	*		Priority of the operand on the stack top is less than C, so push.
	C		C	Add operand to postfix
	\0		*	Pop and add to postfix
			+	Pop and add to postfix

Figure 4.8 Conversion of infix to postfix.

Program 4.7

```
#include<ctype.h>
#include<stdio.h>
#include<string.h>
#include<conio.h>
#include<alloc.h>

typedef struct stack
{
    char data[20];
    int top;
}st;
void push(st *stack, char ch)
{   stack->data[++(stack->top)]=ch;
}
char pop(st *stack)
{
    return(stack->data[(stack->top)—]);
}
int precedence(char c)
{   switch(c)
    {
```

```
        case  '+':return  1;
        case  '-':return  1;
        case  '*':return  3;
        case  '/':return  3;
        case  '%':return  3;
        case  '^':return  7;
    }
return  0;
}
void  main()
{  char  post[20],inf[20]="A+B*C";
    int  i,j=0;
    st  stack;
    clrscr();
    stack.top=-1;
    for(i=0;inf[i]!=0;i++)
    {
      if(isalnum(inf[i]))
      {
        post[j++]=inf[i];
      }
    else
    {   while(stack.top!=-1  &&  (precedence(stack.data[stack.
        top])>  =  precedence(inf[i])))
        {
            post[j++]=pop(&stack);
        }
        push(&stack,inf[i]);
    }
    }
    while(stack.top!=-1)
    post[j++]=pop(&stack);
    post[j]='\0';
    printf("result  %s",post);
    getch();
}
```

Exercise 4.8

1. Convert the following infix expressions to the postfix form. Your answer should be accompanied by a table as given in Figure 4.8.
   (a) a + b − c
   (b) a + (b − c)
   (c) (a + b)∗(c − d)
   (d) (a − b)/(c∗d$e)

2. The algorithm and program to convert an infix expression to a prefix expression is similar to what was discussed in this section, except that the output string is to be reversed at the end. Try to write an algorithm to do this operation. Also, write a program to implement it. Work out the algorithm on the infix expression given in question 1.

4.5 IMPLEMENTATION OF STACK USING LINKED LIST

All the programs using stack seen so far was implemented as arrays. Here, the array size should be known beforehand or huge storage space has to be allocated for the program. This difficulty can be overcome by implementing stack as a linked list.

Consider a stack consisting of a single integer data field. A stack, when implemented as a linked list, is similar to the single linked list considered in the previous chapters. Thus, it can be defined as follows:

```
sruct stack
  {
    int data;
    struct stack *next;
  }
```

When a stack is implemented as a linked list, the push operation process consists of the following steps:

Step 1: Allocation of a new node.

Step 2: Fill the data field of a new node.

Step 3: Add the new node to the top of the stack (now implemented as a linked list).

The allocation of the new node in step 1 is done using **malloc** function as follows:

new_node = (struct stack *) malloc (sizeof(struct stack));

The information to be assigned in the data field of the new_node can be obtained from the user, say it is x. Then step 2 can be written as follows:

new_node --> data = x

In step 3, it is required to add the new_node to the top of the list. Suppose top is the variable that contains information about the present top node of the list. Then the insertion of the new_node can be achieved using the following steps:

new_node --> next = top
top = new_node

Note that the new_node added will be the top element since it is required so in a stack. **Push** function is given in Program 4.8.

Program 4.8

```
struct stack *top, *new_node;
void push(int x)
{   new_node = (struct stack *) malloc (sizeof(struct stack));
    new_node->data=x;
    new_node->next = top;
    top = new_node;
}
```

The pop operation involves assigning the value of the top element to the next element. The pop function is given in Program 4.9.

Program 4.9

```
int pop()
{   if(top==NULL)
    {
        printf("Stack Empty");
        return 0;
    }
    else
      { datavalue = top->data;
        top = top ->next;
        return(datavalue);
      }
}
```

Here is a program 4.10 that reads integer data until 0 is entered and pushes them to a stack and, finally, pops out and prints the data. The push and pop function described in Programs 4.8 and 4.9 are not given completely in Program 4.10.

Program 4.10

```
#include "stdio.h"
#include "alloc.h"
#include "ctype.h"
#include "conio.h"
struct stack
{
    int data;
    struct stack *next;
};
struct stack *top, *new_node;
int datavalue;
main()
{
```

```
    top=NULL;
    scanf("%d", &datavalue);
    while(datavalue!=0)
    {   push(datavalue); // Push until x==0
        scanf("%d", &datavalue);
    }
    while(top!=NULL) // Pop and print until stack empty
    {
        datavalue=pop();
        printf("data = %d\n", datavalue);
    }
}
```

Exercise 4.9

1. Implement Program 4.2 using the linked list.
2. Implement Program 4.5 using the linked list.

4.6 INTRODUCTION TO QUEUE

A queue is a sequence of items, to which new items can be added at one end and removed from the other end only. Queuing is a concept known to every one. We queue up in banks, shops, and so on. What goes into a queue first, comes out first and what goes in last, comes out last. Hence, a queue is often known as a FIFO (first-in, first-out) list. Both array and linked list can be made to work as queues.

Whenever tasks are to be scheduled, queues are useful. Queues are very common in the everyday functions of computers. The most obvious is printing queues. When you send multiple print jobs to a printer, each printing job is inserted at the rear of the print queue in the order it was sent. Each job is then printed in the order sent to the printer. Any type of stream throughput of I/O will use a queue. Processes waiting to be executed by a CPU are also usually in the form of a "ready" queue. When priority is assigned to each task being queued, queues are known as *priority queues*, which are however, not covered here.

4.7 QUEUE USING ARRAYS

A queue can be implemented easily using arrays by defining a structure containing an array and two variables to indicate the position of the **front** and **rear** of the queue. The following example is for int data:

```
struct queue
{   int data[10];
    int front;
    int rear;
};
```

Now, we can create a queue by declaring **struct queue q1**. By convention, front and rear are initialized to **–1,** which indicates an empty queue (later, we will see that whenever front==rear, the queue is empty). When rear equals the maximum index of the array (9 in this case), the queue is full. Any data added to the queue is done at the rear position. Any data removed from the queue is from the front position. These operations are known as **add,** and **delete**. The value of rear is changed with each add, and the value of front is changed with each delete.

You may note the difference between a real-life queue and the queue data structure implementation. Whereas people move forward in queues when the queue progresses, this does not happen in computer queues. Hence, we may have this strange situation of the array having position free, but the queue is considered full. You may, however, modify the implementation to change this. Let us look at add and delete operations using an example. It is shown in Figure 4.9.

data [0]	data [1]	data [2]	data [3]	data [4]	data [5]	data [6]	data [7]	data [8]	data [9]	front	rear	Remarks
										–1	–1	Empty
100										–1	0	Add(&q1,100)
100	200									–1	1	Add(&q1,200)
100	200	300								–1	2	Add(&q1,300)
100	200	300	400							–1	3	Add(&q1,400)
100	200	300	400	500						–1	4	Add(&q1,500)
100	200	300	400	500	600					–1	5	Add(&q1,600)
100	200	300	400	500	600	700				–1	6	Add(&q1,700)
100	200	300	400	500	600	700	800			–1	7	Add(&q1,800)
100	200	300	400	500	600	700	800	900		–1	8	Add(&q1,900)
100	200	300	400	500	600	700	800	900	999	–1	9	Add(&q1,999) *Queue is full*
100	200	300	400	500	600	700	800	900	999	0	9	Delete(&q1)
100	200	300	400	500	600	700	800	900	999	1	9	Delete(&q1)
100	200	300	400	500	600	700	800	900	999	2	9	Delete(&q1)
100	200	300	400	500	600	700	800	900	999	3	9	Delete(&q1)
100	200	300	400	500	600	700	800	900	999	4	9	Delete(&q1)
100	200	300	400	500	600	700	800	900	999	5	9	Delete(&q1)
100	200	300	400	500	600	700	800	900	999	6	9	Delete(&q1)
100	200	300	400	500	600	700	800	900	999	7	9	Delete(&q1)
100	200	300	400	500	600	700	800	900	999	8	9	Delete(&q1)
100	200	300	400	500	600	700	800	900	999	9	9	Empty

Figure 4.9 Insertion and deletion of integer data in a queue.

Note: At the beginning and the end, the queue is empty. Note that the condition is front==rear. For the queue to be full, the condition is rear==9.

Exercise 4.10

1. For each of the queue specified below, draw the diagram of the queue similar to Figure 4.9, for the operations specified.

(a
```
struct queue
{
    char data[10];
    int front;
    int rear;
};
struct queue q1;
```

data [0]	data [1]	data [2]	data [3]	data [4]	data [5]	data [6]	data [7]	data [8]	data [9]	front	rear	Remarks
										–1	–1	Empty
												Add(&q1, m)
												Add(&q1, a)
												Add(&q1, l)
												Add(&q1, a)
												Add(&q1, y)
												Add(&q1, s)
												Add(&q1, i)
												Add(&q1, a)
												Delete(&q1)
												Delete(&q1)
												Delete(&q1)
												Delete(&q1)
												Delete(&q1)
												Delete(&q1)
												Delete(&q1)

(b)
```
struct queue
{   char data[10];
    int front;
    int rear;
};  struct queue q2;
```

data [0]	data [1]	data [2]	data [3]	data [4]	data [5]	data [6]	data [7]	data [8]	data [9]	front	rear	Remarks
											–1	Empty
												Add(&q2,'a')
												Delete(&q2)
												Add(&q2,'b')
												Add(&q2,'c')
												Delete(&q2)
												Add(&q2,'d')
												Add(&q2,'e')
												Delete(&q2)
												Add(&q2,'g')
												Delete(&q2)
												Delete(&q2)
												Add(&q2,'h')
												Add(&q2,'i')
												Delete(&q2)

```
(c) struct student
{
    int id;
    int mark;
    char grade;
};
 struct student john = {2569, 5, 'F'};
 struct student mary = {3556, 65, 'C'};
 struct student krishna = {3457, 85,'D'};
 struct student ali = {3476, 45, 'P'};
 struct queue
 {
        struct student data[5];
        int front;
        int rear;
 };
struct queue q3;
```

data [0]	data [1]	data [2]	data [3]	data [4]	front	rear	Remarks
					–1	–1	
							Add(&q3, john);
							Add(&q3, mary);
							Delete(&q3);
							Add(&q3, krishna);
							Add(&q3, ali);
							Delete(&q3);
							Delete(&q3);

4.8 IMPLEMENTATION OF QUEUES USING ARRAY

Here is a program that reads integer data until 0 is entered (or queue is full) and adds them to a queue and, finally, deletes them and prints the data. The add and delete operations can be concisely programmed in the C language using the ++ and – operators. Please note that using pre/post is to be done carefully.

ADD – Add data x to the queue:
increment rear and then set data[rear]=x

DELETE – Remove and return data from queue:
increment front and return data[front]

Program 4.11

```
#include<stdio.h>
struct queue
{
    int data[100];
    int front, rear;
};
  void add(struct queue *q, int x) {q->data[++q->rear]=x;}
  int del(struct queue *q) {return q->data[++q->front];}
  void main()
{
    struct queue q;
    q.front=-1;
    q.rear=-1;
    int x;
      do
    {          // Adding to queue
        scanf("%d", &x);
          add( &q, x);
```

```
    }while(x!=0  &&  q.rear<99);
    while  (q.rear  !=  q.front)
    {   //Delete  from  queue
        x=del(&q);
        printf("%d  \n",  x);
    };
}
```

Exercise 4.11

1. Write a program to read characters until 'z' is input and add them one by one into a queue. Finally, delete data one by one and print them out.
2. Write a program to read student data (id, mark and grade – refer to Exercise 4.1, question 1(c)), until student data with id=0 is input and add each to a queue. Finally, delete data one by one and print them.
3. What are the conditions for a queue to be (a) full and (b) empty ? Assume the data array to be of size **N**.
4. In add and delete function, two conditions should be checked. For add, the queue should not be full. For delete, the queue should not be empty. Modify the program given in Section 4.6 to incorporate this.
5. Write the following functions for queues:
   int **queueFull**(struct queue ∗q) — *return 0 if the queue is not full and return 1 if the queue is full*
   int **queueEmpty**(struct queue ∗q) — *return 0 if the queue is not empty and return 1 if the queue is empty*
   int **queueFront**(struct queue ∗q) — *return the current value of queue front*
   int **queueRear**(struct queue ∗q) — *return the current value of queue rear*
   int **intializeQueue**(struct queue ∗q) — *sets the value of queue front and rear to –1*

4.9 QUEUE USING LINKED LIST

Queues can also be implemented using the linked list just like in the case of stacks. In this case, the queue structure will be dynamic in nature. The structure is as follows:

```
struct  queue
{
    int  data;
    struct  queue  *next;
};
struct  queue  *rear,  *front;
```

The rear and front are pointers which contain the information regarding the starting and ending element of the queue, respectively. This is necessary because to insert an element in the queue, it has to be inserted in the rear. To delete an element from the queue, it is to be deleted from the front.

The insertion process involves the following steps:

Step 1: Allocate a new node.
Step 2: Assign data value to a new node.
Step 3: Insert the new node in the queue.

Step 1 involves the **malloc** function which you already know. Step 2 is also familiar to you. In step 3, the insertion of the new node can be done as follows:

rear—>next = new_node;

rear = new_node;

The insertion function of the queue is given in Program 4.12.

Program 4.12

```
struct queue *rear,*front, *new_node;
void queue_insert(int x)
{
    new_node = (struct queue *) malloc (sizeof(struct queue));
    new_node->data=x;
    new_node->next =NULL;
    rear->next= new_node;
    rear=new_node;
    if(front==NULL)
        front=rear;
}
```

Deletion of a node from the queue involves returning the data value of the node and updating the front pointer. This can be done as follows:

datavalue = front->data;
front = front->next;

The deletion function of the queue is given in Program 4.13.

Program 4.13

```
int queue_delete()
{   datavalue = front->data;
    front = front->next;
    return datavalue;
}
```

The following is a program (Program 4.14) that reads integer data until 0 is entered and inserts them to a queue and, finally, deletes and prints the data. The insertion function and the deletion function are given in Programs 4.12 and 4.13.

Program 4.14

```
#include "stdio.h"
#include "alloc.h"
#include "ctype.h"
#include "conio.h"
struct queue
{
    int data;
    struct queue *next;
};
struct queue *rear,*front, *new_node;
int datavalue;
void main()
{
    rear=NULL; front = NULL;
    scanf("%d", &datavalue);
    while(datavalue !=0)
    {
        queue_insert(datavalue); // Push until datavalue=0
        scanf("%d", &datavalue);
    }
while(front!=NULL) //Pop and print until stack empty
    {
        datavalue=queue_delete();
        intf("data = %d\n", datavalue);
    }
}
```

Exercise 4.12

For all the programs given below, use the linked list representation of the queue.

1. Write a program to read characters until 'z' is input and add them one by one into a queue. Finally, delete data one by one and print them out.
2. Write a program to read student data (id, mark and grade – refer to Exercise 4.1, question 1(c)), until student data with id=0 is input and add each to a queue. Finally, delete data one by one and print them.

Chapter 5

Binary Trees

5.1 TREES

Trees are an important type of data structure. They are very useful on a number of occasions. In some ways, a tree is similar to the linked list. A tree is a *hierarchical* collection of *nodes*, where each node contains data as well as information about successor nodes. Pictorially, trees are represented as shown in Figure 5.1.

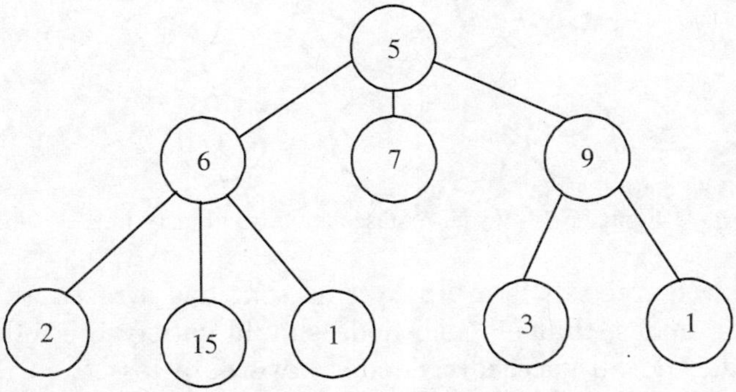

Figure 5.1 Visual representation of a tree.

The following are the important terminologies:

- Child node: A node coming under another node (e.g.: 7, 6, 15), (Figure 5.1).
- Parent node: A node coming above another node. In a tree, every node will have only a single parent (e.g.: 5, 6, 9, Figure 5.1). (If there are more than one parent for any node, there will be *closed loops* or *cycles* in the structure and it is known as a graph.)
- Root node: A special node which has no parent node (e.g.: 5, Figure 5.1).
- Leaf node: A special node which has no child nodes (e.g.: 2, 7, 15, Figure 5.1).

There are four kinds of trees we need to consider:

1. Ordinary trees: No restriction on the number of children or in the order of data in nodes. Example: (See Figure 5.2).

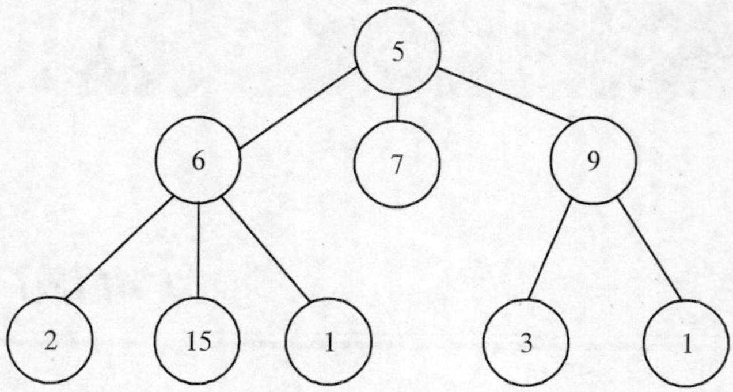

Figure 5.2 Visual representation of a tree.

2. Binary trees: Each node has a maximum of 2 child nodes (0, 1 or 2). When there are two child nodes, one is designated the left node and the other, the right node. Example: (See Figure 5.3).

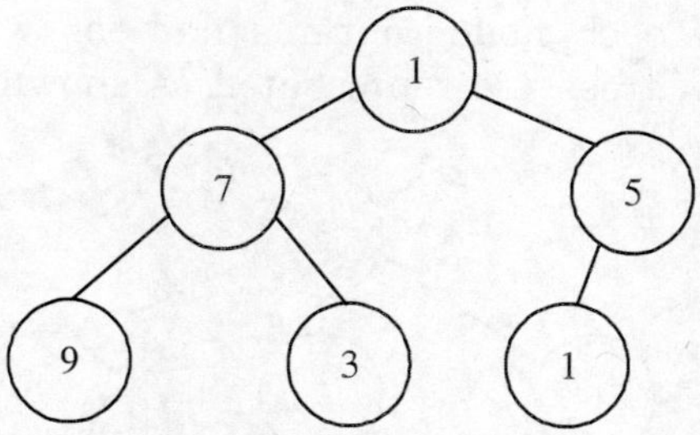

Figure 5.3 Visual representation of a binary tree.

3. Binary search trees: It is a binary tree that has a restriction on the order of data in the nodes, that is, each node should satisfy the following criteria:
   - Left node and all succeeding nodes have data less than the current node.
   - Right node and all succeeding nodes have data greater than the current node.

   Example: (See Figure 5.4).

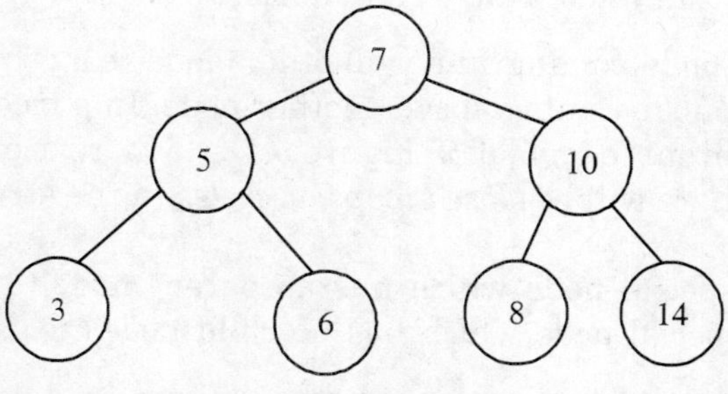

Figure 5.4 Visual representation of a binary search tree.

The binary tree given in Figure 5.5 is not a binary search tree because the node containing data 9 is the left sub tree of the node containing data 8. Thus, it cannot be a binary search tree.

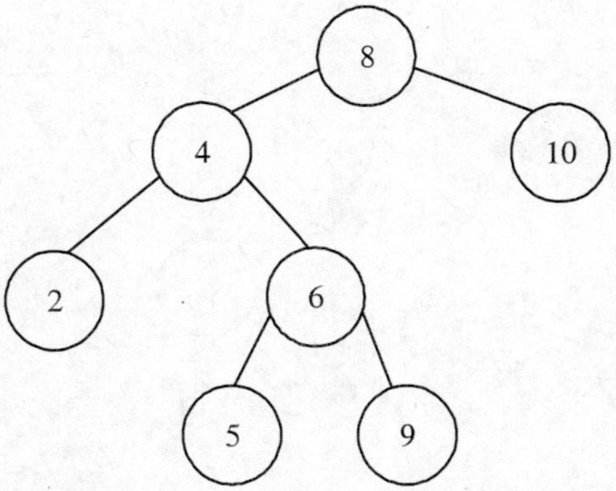

Figure 5.5 Visual representation of a binary tree not a BST.

4. Heaps: A tree in which all nodes have data greater than their child nodes. Example: (Figure 5.6).

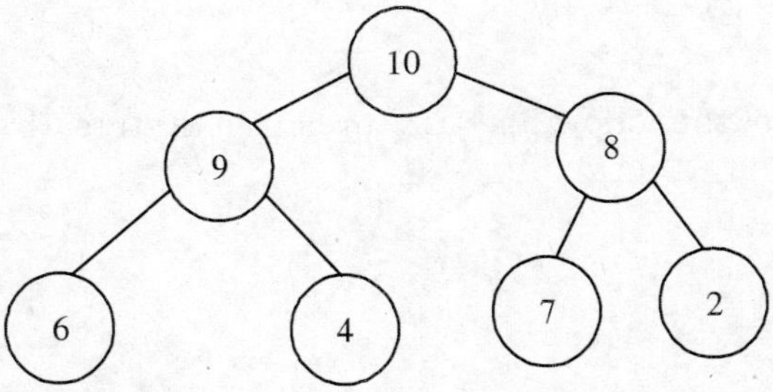

Figure 5.6 Visual representation of a heap.

Some other associated terminologies are:

- Forest: A forest is a set of disjointed trees.
- Ordered tree: A rooted tree is a tree in which one node has a special property that it has no parent. Such a node is called the root of the tree. An ordered tree is a rooted tree in which there is an order among the children of the node.
- Orchard: An orchard is an ordered set of ordered trees.

Exercise 5.1

1. For each of the following trees, identify the following:

   (a) Child node(s) of each node.
   (b) Parent node(s) of each node.
   (c) Root node(s).
   (d) Leaf node(s).

(a)

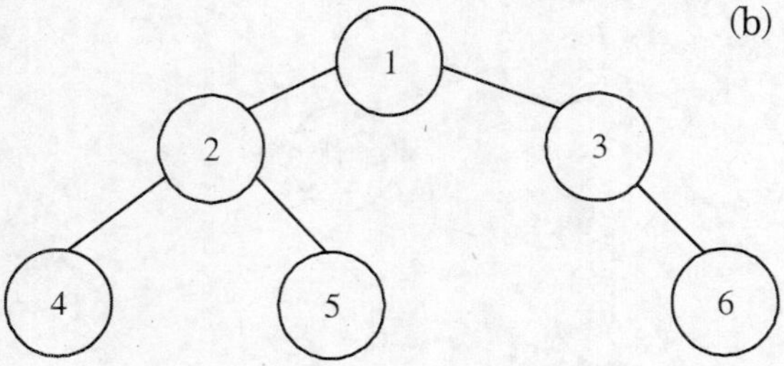

(b)

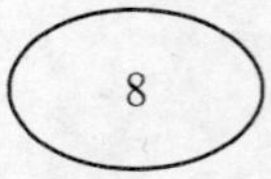

(c)

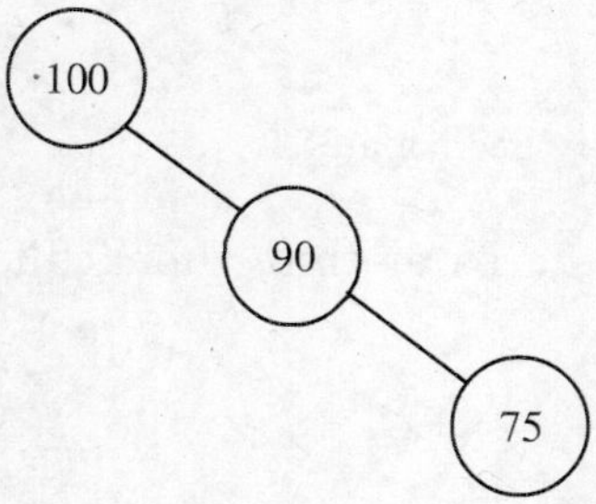

(d)

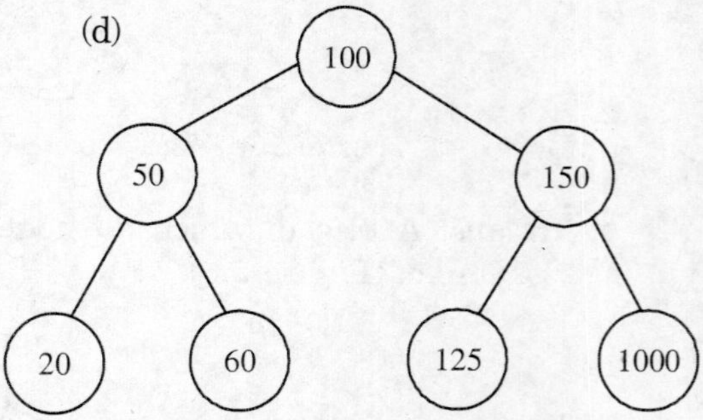

2. Classify each of the following structures into (a) tree, (b) binary tree, (c) binary search tree, and (d) graph:

(a)

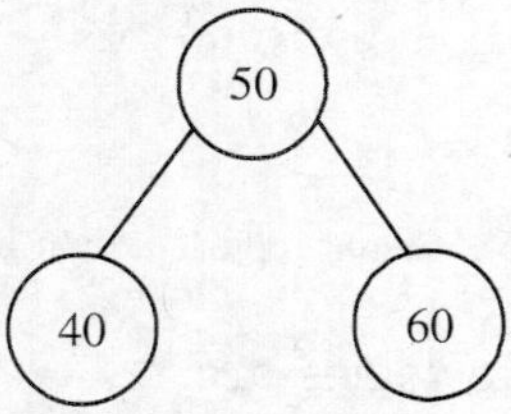

(b)

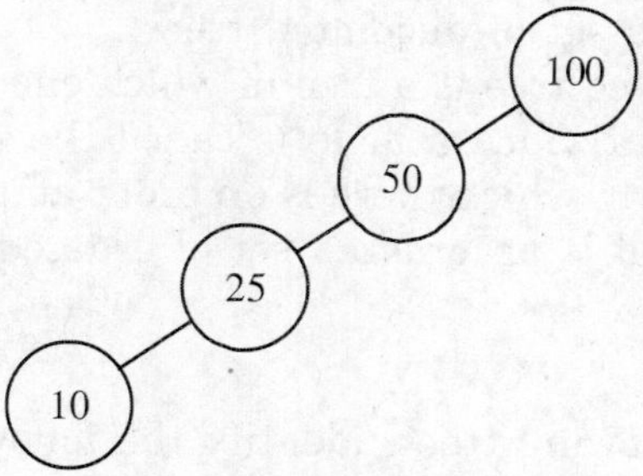

(c)

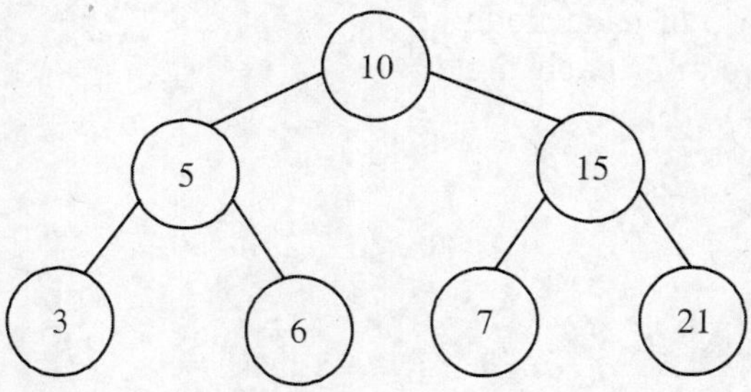

(d)

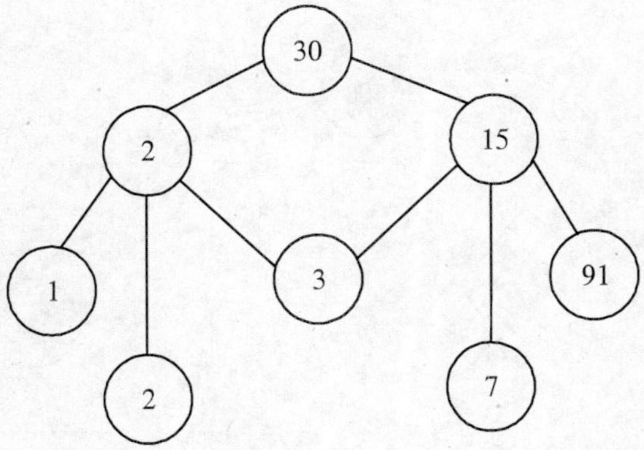

3. For the following binary tree, find whether they are binary search tree or not. If not, state reasons.

(a)

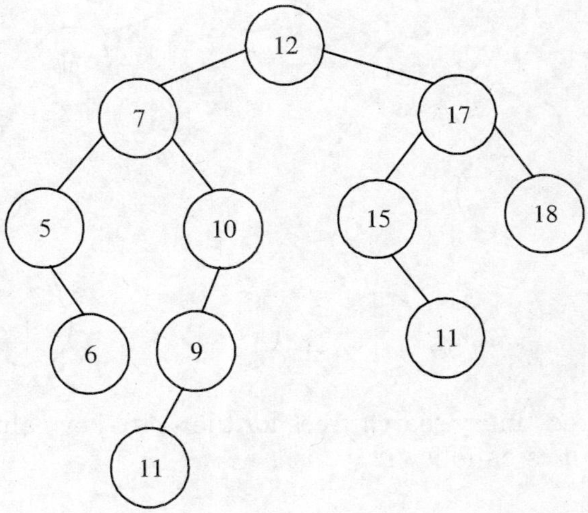

(b)

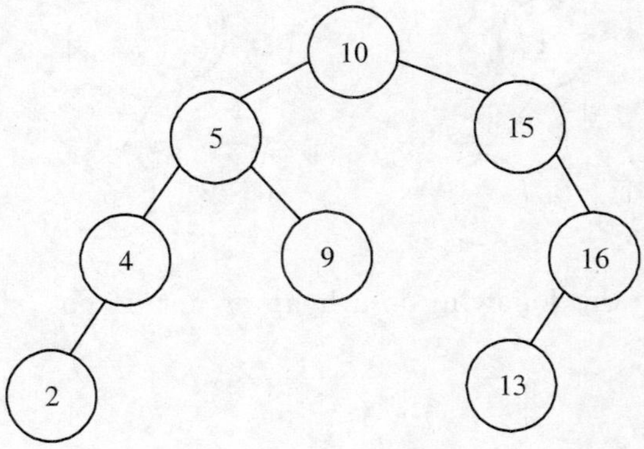

(c)

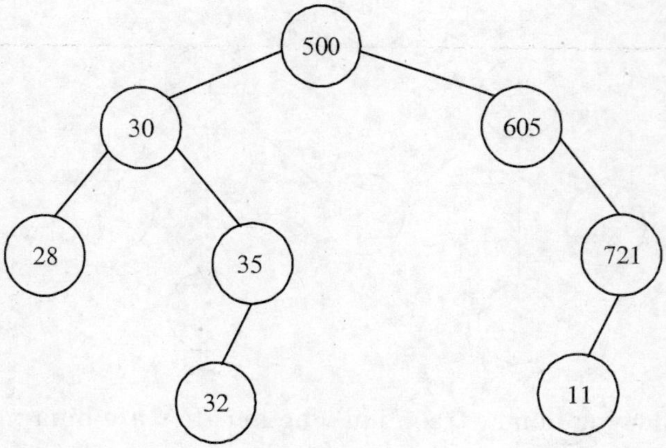

(d)

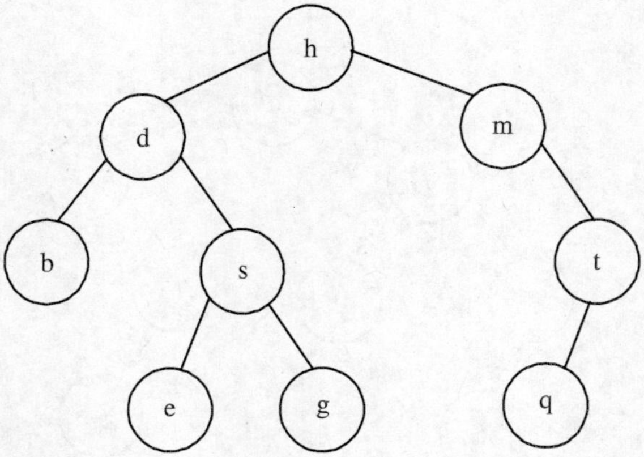

4. Draw three binary search trees for the set of key values {1, 2, 3, 4, 5}. One way of doing it is as follows:

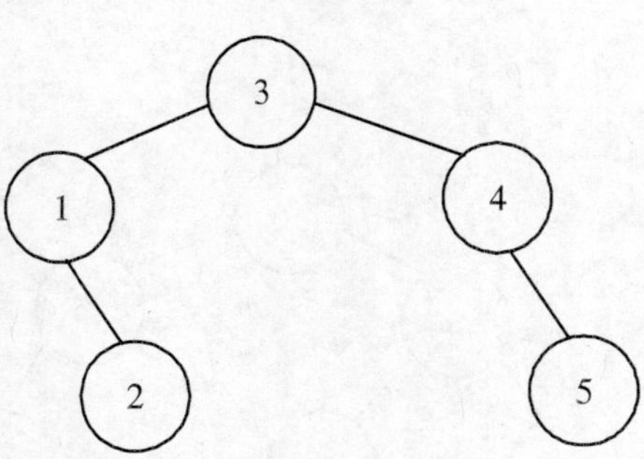

5. State whether the following is a heap or not. If not, state the reasons.

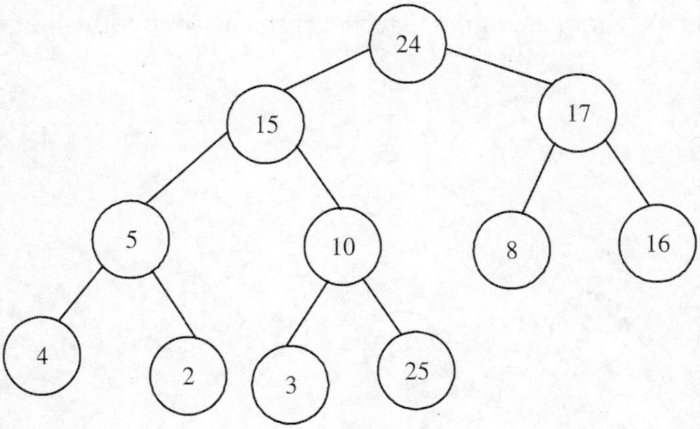

5.1.1 Application of Trees

General applications of trees are in the following areas:

- Implementation of the file system in several operating systems.
- Evaluation of arithmetic expressions.
- In search operations, the time taken for the data stored in the tree structure is less than the other search techniques.
- Symbol tables: A symbol table is a data structure created during compilation process to store the information about the attributes of the variables used in the program. Each node of the table contains the name of the variable and a list of attributes of the variable. A symbol table can be static or dynamic. The binary search tree method is generally used to search for an element of the symbol table.

5.2 BASICS OF BINARY TREE

Recall that a binary tree is a collection of *nodes,* where each node contains some data along with information about the succeeding left and right nodes. Let us picture the binary tree as a set of nodes, each node having 3 fields – an integer data and address of the left and right nodes. Let us try drawing the binary tree given in Figure 5.7. The root node is at location 8 (shown in grey) in this figure.

1	2	3	4	5	6	7	8	9	10	11	12	13	14	15	16	17	18	19	20	21	22	23	24
35	11	NULL	45	19	14		25	1	4	55	NULL	NULL	65	NULL	22			50	NULL	NULL	75	NULL	NULL

Figure 5.7 Visual representation of a binary tree in memory.

Pictorially, a node of a tree can be represented as shown in Figure 5.8.

Data	Left	Right
25	**1**	**4**

A node

Figure 5.8 Visual representation of a node.

You may verify that the binary tree represented by the above is as follows (see Figure 5.9):

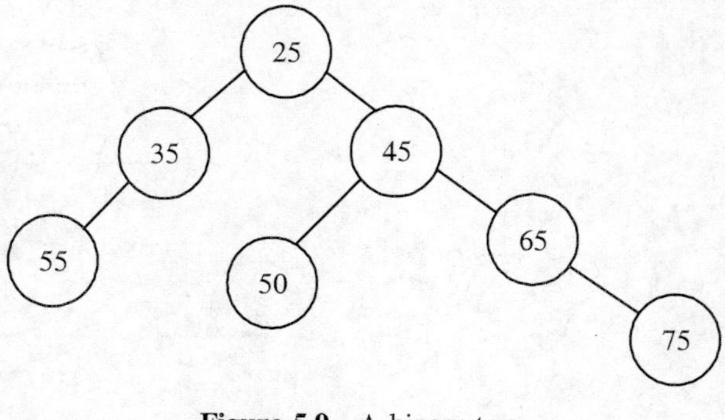

Figure 5.9 A binary tree.

Exercise 5.2

1. Draw the binary tree corresponding to each memory diagram given below. The root node is shown in grey. The last two items in the node are the address of the left and right nodes, respectively. The addresses of locations are shown in italics on the top.

(a)

1	*2*	*3*	*4*	*5*	*6*	*7*	*8*	*9*	*10*	*11*	*12*	*13*	*14*	*15*	*16*	*17*	*18*	*19*	*20*	*21*	*22*	*23*	*24*
6	19	10	7	16	22	1	1	4	10	NULL	NULL	29	NULL	NULL	12	NULL	NULL	9	NULL	NULL	14	NULL	13

(b)

1	*2*	*3*	*4*	*5*	*6*	*7*	*8*	*9*	*10*	*11*	*12*	*13*	*14*	*15*	*16*	*17*	*18*	*19*	*20*	*21*	*22*	*23*	*24*
90	7	10	91	NULL	NULL	80	13	16	95	4	19	75	NULL	NULL	85	NULL	NULL	97	NULL	NULL	100	1	NULL

(c)

1	*2*	*3*	*4*	*5*	*6*	*7*	*8*	*9*	*10*	*11*	*12*	*13*	*14*	*15*	*16*	*17*	*18*	*19*	*20*	*21*	*22*	*23*	*24*
60	10	22	10	19	NULL	20	4	NULL	40	7	NULL	93	NULL	NULL	85	NULL	13	8	NULL	NULL	74	NULL	16

(d)

1	*2*	*3*	*4*	*5*	*6*	*7*	*8*	*9*	*10*	*11*	*12*	*13*	*14*	*15*	*16*	*17*	*18*	*19*	*20*	*21*	*22*	*23*	*24*
97	22	NULL	8	NULL	NULL	45	NULL	19	88	1	NULL	28	NULL	4	77	NULL	13	20	NULL	16	54	7	NULL

(e)

1	2	3	4	5	6	7	8	9	10	11	12	13	14	15	16	17	18	19	20	21	22	23	24
75	16	10	33	NULL	22	50	19	13	77	NULL	NULL	100	1	NULL	60	NULL	NULL	49	4	NULL	36	NULL	NULL

2. Draw the memory diagrams of the following binary trees. The addresses are written on the top of the node.

(a)

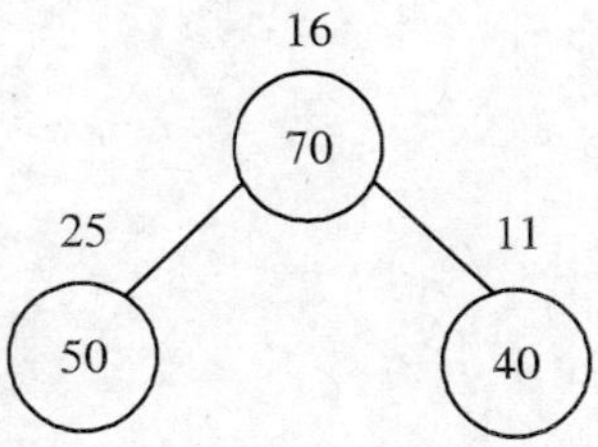

(b)

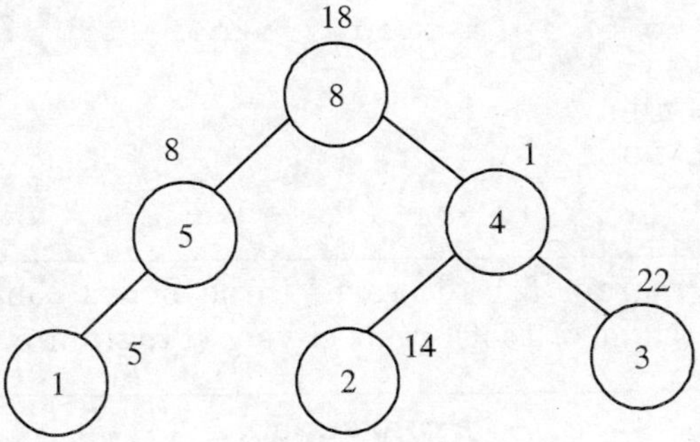

5.2.1 Binary Tree Implementation

From Section 5.2, it must be clear that each node of a tree can be defined as a structure, which contains data and information about the left and right child nodes. For single int data, this can be done as follows:

```
struct node
{
    int data;
    struct node *left;
    struct node *right;
};
```

If each node contains one int data and one character data, then the struct definition is as follows:

```
struct node
{
    int data1;
```

```
    char data2;
    struct node *left;
    struct node *right;
};
```

Let us now write a program (Program 5.1) to create a tree with a single node with int data 55. Let us call the first node address root.

Program 5.1

```
#include<stdio.h>
#include<malloc.h>
void main( )
{
struct node
{
    int data;
    struct node *left;
    struct node *right;
};
struct node *root;
root=` (struct node *) malloc (sizeof(struct node));
    root->data=55;
    root->left=NULL;
    root->right=NULL;
}
```

We now expand Program 5.1 to create three nodes containing data 44 (root), 55 (left of root) and 66 (right of root), respectively (Program 5.2).

Program 5.2

```
#include<stdio.h>
void main( )
{   struct node
    {
        int data;
        struct node *left;
        struct node *right;
    };
    struct node *root;
    root= (struct node *) malloc (sizeof(struct node));
    root->data=45;
    root->left=(struct node *) malloc (sizeof(struct node));
    root->right=(struct node *) malloc (sizeof(struct node));
    root->left->data=55;
    root->left->left=NULL;
    root->left->right=NULL;
    root->right->data=65;
    root->right->left=NULL;
    root->right->right=NULL;
}
```

Exercise 5.3

1. For each of the following cases, the root pointer is the address of the node shown in grey. Give the value of each of the expressions specified.

(a) int data:
root->data=................
root->left=................
root->left->data=..............
root->right->left=..............
root->left->right->data=..............

1	2	3	4	5	6	7	8	9	10	11	12	13	14	15	16
6	NULL	NULL	8	NULL	NULL		30	NULL	NULL	10	14	8	20	1	4

(b) char data
root->data=................
root->left=................
root->left->data=..............
root->right->left=..............
root->left->right->data=..............

1	2	3	4	5	6	7	8	9	10	11	12	13	14	15	16
L	NULL	4	A	7	NULL	S	NULL	NULL	M	13	1	A	NULL	NULL	

(c) int data1 + char data2
root->data1=................
root->data2=................
root->left=..................
root->left->data1=..............
root->left->right=..............
root->left->right->data2=.............. (invalid ?)

1	2	3	4	5	6	7	8	9	10	11	12	13	14	15	16	17	18	19	20	21	22	23	24
20	B	NULL	NULL			10	A	1	11	30	C	15	19	40	D	NULL	NULL	50	E	NULL	NULL		

5.2.2 Construction of Binary Search Tree

Before discussing the general program for creating binary search trees, we need to practice the process of creating binary search trees by hand. Assume that we have the following data: 25, 7, 43, 12 [see Figure 5.10(a) – (d)].

1. First we create a root node and enter the first data

Figure 5.10(a) Construction of a BST—Step 1.

2. The second data (7) is compared with the root node data. It is less than the root node data (25) and is put in a new node on the left of the root node as this position is not occupied.

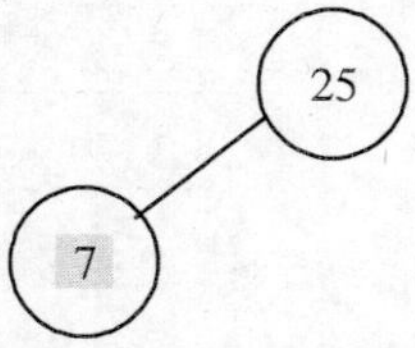

Figure 5.10(b) Construction of a BST—Step 2.

3. The third data (43) is compared with the root node data. It is greater than the root data (25) and is put in a new node on the right of the root node since that position is not occupied.

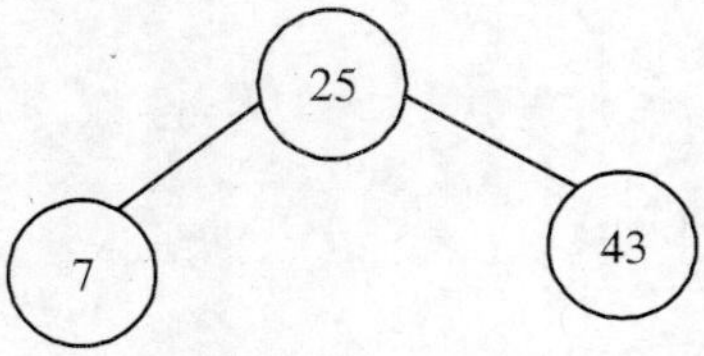

Figure 5.10(c) Construction of a BST—Step 3.

4. The fourth data (12) is compared with the root node data. It is less than the root data (25) and hence should be put in a new node on the left of the root node. However, since that position is already occupied, we again compare 12 with the data in that node (7). Since the new data is greater than this, it is put in a new node on the right of the this node because that position is not occupied.

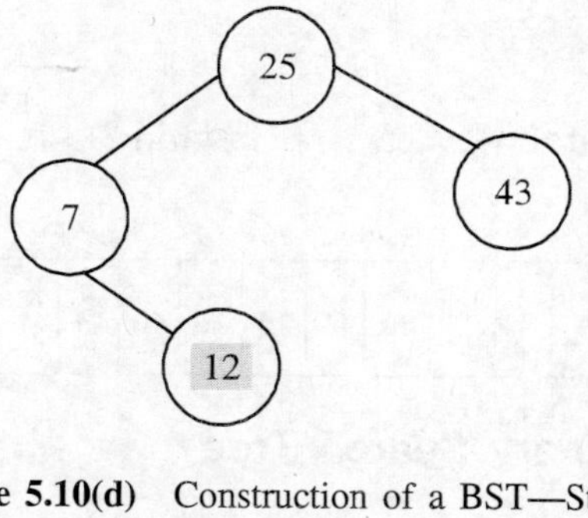

Figure 5.10(d) Construction of a BST—Step 4.

Exercise 5.4

1. For each of the following cases, draw the binary search tree. Take special care to observe the process so that it is easy to understand the program in the next section.

(a) 100, 5, 107, 7, 6.
(b) 100, 200, 300, 400, 105, 205, 55, 50.
(c) 100, 50, 25, 30, 35, 40.
(d) 1, 2, 3, 4, 5, 50, 10, 9, 8, 7.
(e) 56, 58, 13, 45, 37, 80, 63, 95.
(f) 50, 75, 25, 60, 85, 15, 30, 12, 18, 28, 32, 82, 87, 58, 63.

2. Given below are some binary search trees and a new node to be inserted in that tree. State where they are to be inserted.

(a)

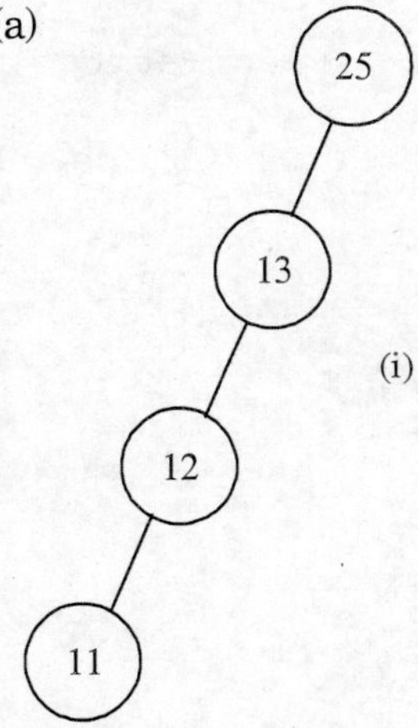

(i) new node = 14

(b)

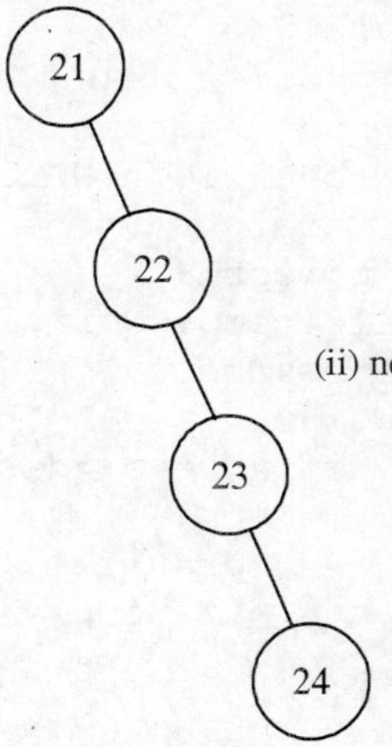

(ii) new node = 25

(c) In (a), after adding node 14, insert node = 28
(d) In (c), after adding node 28, insert node = 25
(e) In (b), after adding node 25, insert node = 10

5.3 GENERAL PROGRAM FOR CREATING BINARY SEARCH TREES

The earlier examples for creating trees of one or three nodes are obviously not useful for a large number of nodes. Here is a program that reads integer data and stores it in a binary search tree until the data is entered as 0, which indicates the end of data. If you have already observed the process of inserting nodes into a binary search tree during Exercise 5.4, Program 5.3 will be easy to understand. Please note that the part of the program shown in bold is likely to appear in all binary tree programs.

Program 5.3

```
#include<stdio.h>
#include<malloc.h>
void main( )
{
    struct node
{
    int data;
    struct node *left;
    struct node *right;
};
```

```
struct node *root, *temp, *prev, *newnode;
int x;
root= (struct node *) malloc (sizeof(struct node));
scanf("%d", &x); //root node created outside loop
root->data=x;
root->left=NULL;
root->right=NULL;
while(x!=0) //For each data
{
    scanf("%d", &x);
    newnode= (struct node *) malloc (sizeof(struct node));
    newnode->data=x;
    newnode->left=NULL;newnode->right=NULL; // get ready
        the new node
    temp=root;
    while(temp!=NULL) // This loops locates the place for
        newnode
    {
        if(x<temp->data)
        {
            prev=temp; temp=temp->left;
            if(temp==NULL)
                prev->left=newnode;
        }
        else
        {
            prev=temp; temp=temp->right;
            if(temp==NULL)
                prev->right=newnode;
        }
    }
}
```

Exercise 5.5

1. Write a program to create a binary search tree with nodes containing character data. The data should be read from the keyboard until the data 'z' is entered.
2. For the above program, assume that the heap has free locations between 333330 to 333390 ready for allocation in the following order: 333335, 333365, 333345, 333355, 333375. Also, assume that data entered are: 'f', 't', 'm', 's', 'z'. Draw the memory diagram of the tree.
3. Write a program to create a binary search tree with nodes containing one integer and one character data (*take integer data as the key data).* The data should be read from the keyboard until the integer data is entered as 0.

5.4 PROCESSING OF TREE NODES

We can process each node of a linked list by traversing the list from the first to the last node. In a binary tree, however, there are three (actually more) ways of traversing all the nodes. They are:

- ♦ In-order (LEFT, CURRENT, RIGHT)
- ♦ Pre-order (CURRENT, LEFT, RIGHT)
- ♦ Post-order (LEFT, RIGHT, CURRENT)

Consider the following tree (Figure 5.11).

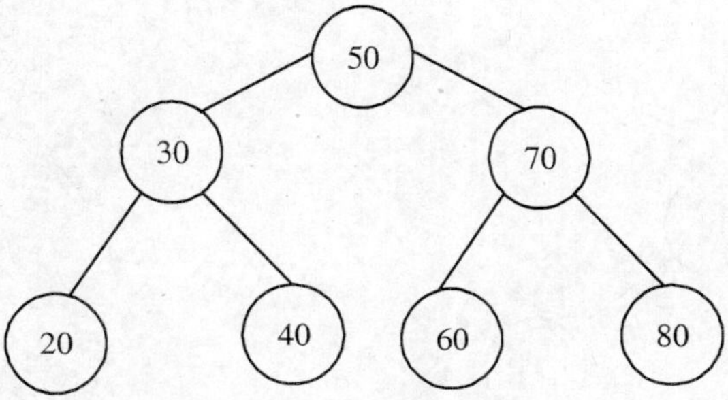

Figure 5.11 A binary tree.

Traversing the nodes using in-order traversal works as follows (Figure 5.12):

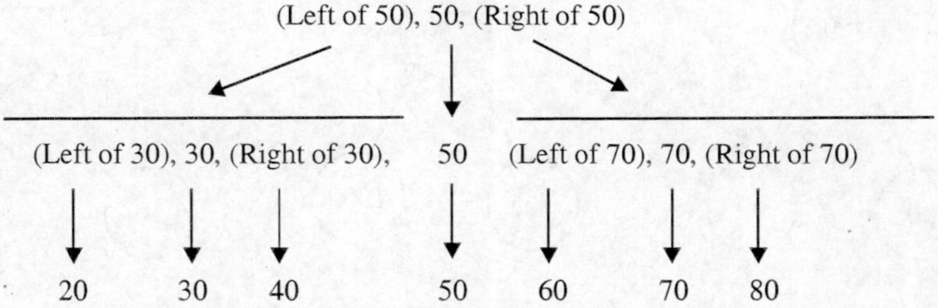

Figure 5.12 In-order traversal of a binary tree.

Similarly, you may verify that the other traversals give the following result:

Pre-order: 50, 30, 20, 40, 70, 60, 80
Post-order: 20, 40, 30, 60, 80, 70, 50

You may have noted that an in-order traversal of a binary search tree will return the data in sorted order.

Exercise 5.6

1. For each of the following trees, print out the data in the nodes using (a) in-order, (b) pre-order and (c) post-order traversals:

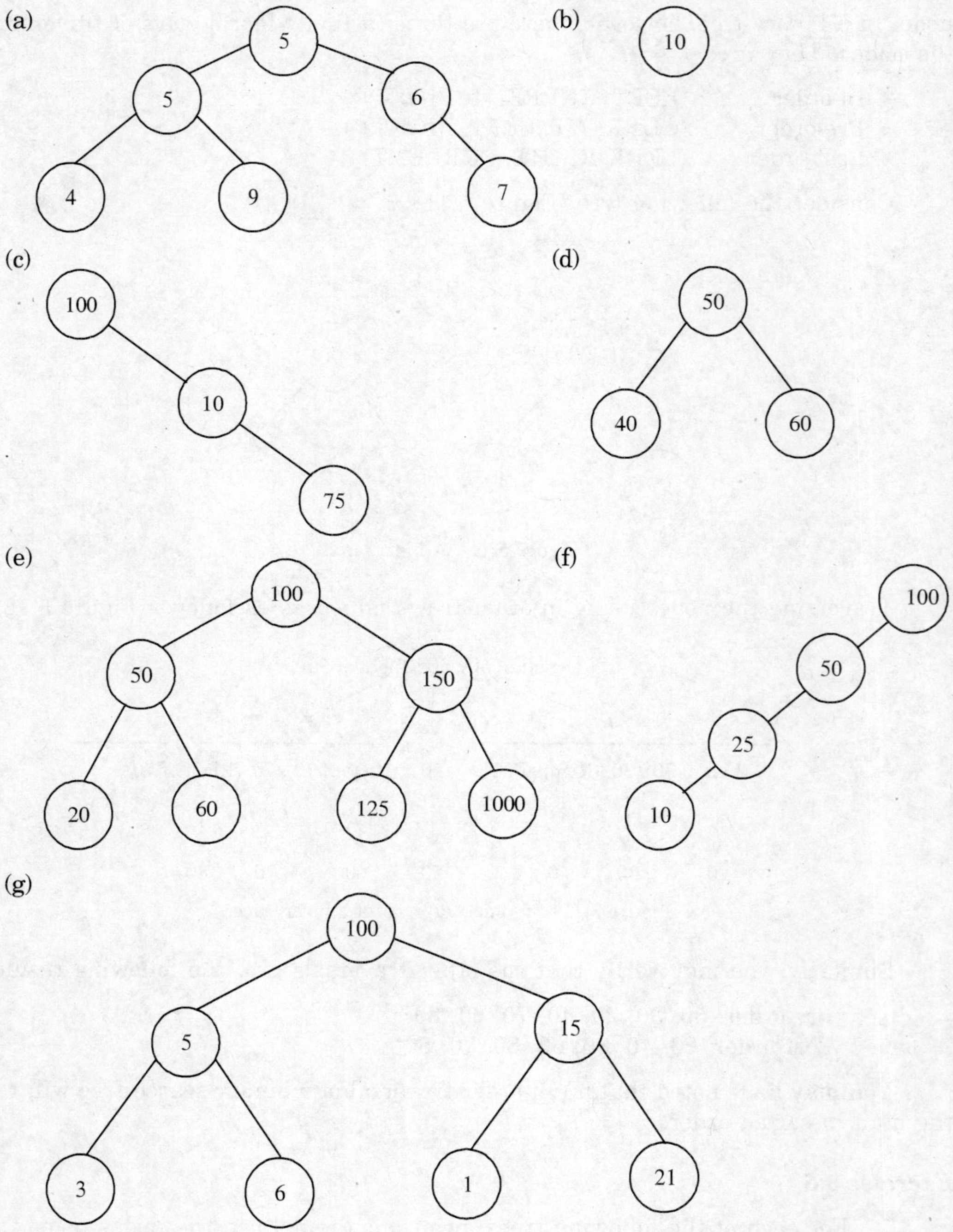

5.4.1 Programs of Tree Traversals

You can write the tree traversals as recursive functions. The three functions Inorder, Preorder and Postorder are given in Programs 5.4, 5.5 and 5.6 respectively.

Program 5.4

```
void printInorder(struct node *r)
{
    if (r!=NULL)
    {
        printInorder(r->left);
        printf("%d", r->data);
        printInorder(r->right);
    }
}
```

Program 5.5

```
void printPreorder(struct node *r)
{
    if (r!=NULL)
    {   printf("%d", r->data);
        printPreorder(r->left);
        printPreorder(r->right);
    }
}
```

Program 5.6

```
void printPostorder(struct node *r)
{
    if (r!=NULL)
    {   printPostorder(r->left);
        printPostorder(r->right);
        printf("%d", r->data);
    }
}
```

When you use these functions, you should declare struct node outside the main( ) as a global variable so that the functions can also use struct node variables. The following program (Program 5.7) shows the use of printInorder( ) function:

Program 5.7

```
#include<stdio.h>
#include<malloc.h>
struct node
{       //Struct node is now global
    int data;
    struct node *left;
    struct node *right;
};
void printInorder(struct node *h) //Function definition
{   if(h!=NULL)
    {   printInorder(h->left);
```

```
        printf("%d",  h->data);
        printInorder(h->right);
    }
}
void main( )
{   ....... // No change here, except removing struct declaration
    from program 5.3
    printInorder(root);
}
```

Other processing of nodes would include the following, each of which can be done using any one of the three traversals:

- Print out data of all nodes.
- Print out selectively data of nodes.
- Print out count of nodes.
- Print out selectively by count of nodes.
- Reset selectively data of nodes.
- Search for a particular data.

Some examples, are given in the following sections which use in-order traversal only.

5.4.2 Printing Selectively

For example, print all data greater than 50 (Program 5.8).

Program 5.8

```
void printInorder(struct node *r)
{   if(r!=NULL)
    {   printInorder(r->left);
        if (r->data >50)
            printf("%d",  r->data);
        printInorder(r->right);
    }
}
```

5.4.3 Finding Count

For example, return the count of nodes (Program 5.9).

Program 5.9

```
int countNodes(struct node *r)
{   int c=0;
      if(r!=NULL){c=1+countNodes(r->left)+countNodes(r->right);}
      return c;
}
```

5.4.4 Finding Sum

For example, return the sum of all data in the nodes (Program 5.10).

Program 5.10

```
int  sumNodes(struct  node  *r)
{   int  s=0;
    if(r!=NULL){s=r->data+sumNodes(r->left)+sumNodes(r->right);}
    return  s;
}
```

5.4.5 Selective Sum

For example, return the sum of data greater than 50 (Program 5.11).

Program 5.11

```
int  sumNodes(struct  node  *r)
{   int  s=0;
    if(r!=NULL)
    {
        if  (r->data  >50)
            {s=r->data+sumNodes(r->left)+sumNodes(r->right);
    else
        {s=  sumNodes(r->left)+sumNodes(r->right);}
    }
    return  s;
}
```

5.4.6 Searching

Program 5.12

```
int  Search(struct  node  *r,  int  k)
{
    if(r!=NULL)
    {   if  (r->data==k)  {return  1;}
        return  Search(r->left,  k);
        return  Search(r->right,  k);
    }   return  0;
}
```

Exercise 5.7

Use in-order traversal for all the questions:

1. Write a program to create a binary search tree with nodes containing character data. The data should be read from the keyboard until the data 'z' is entered. The program should also:
   (a) Print out all data.
   (b) Print out all upper case alphabets.
   (c) Print out the count of all upper case alphabets.
   (d) Print out if the data 'P' is present in the linked list.
2. Write a program to create a binary search tree with nodes containing one integer and one character data. The data should be read from the keyboard until the integer data is entered as 0. The program should also:
   (a) Print out all data.
   (b) Print out data of all nodes which store upper case alphabets.
   (c) Print out the count of nodes with int data greater than 50 and the char data 'A'.
3. Write a program to store the id, name, age, sex, mark (total out of 100) and grade ('F', 'P', 'C', or 'D') of students in a binary search tree. The data should be read from the keyboard until student id is entered as 0. Assume student id to be the *key* data. The grade is not to be read, but is to be calculated from the marks (0–39: Fail, 40–59: Pass, 60–74: Credit, 75–100: Distinction. The program should also:
   (a) Print out a list of students (name and id alone) with credit marks.
   (b) Find the count of students who have credit/distinction.
   (c) Find the average marks.
   (d) Read a moderation marks and then increase all marks by this value.
   (e) Read a student id and then display the corresponding details from the binary search tree.

5.5 AVL TREES

AVL trees are height balanced binary trees. Adelson–Velskii and Landis introduced this binary structure in 1962. Hence the name AVL trees. In AVL trees, the height of both left and right sub tree is either same or their difference in heights is 1. This helps the searching to be completed in much less time than the binary search tree. The balance factor (BF) of a node is defined as height of the left sub tree - height of the right sub tree. A binary search tree will be an AVL tree if the balance factor of each node of the binary search tree is either 0, 1 or –1.

Consider the binary search tree given in Figure 5.13.

BF of 1 = 0 – 4 = –4
BF of 2 = 0 – 3 = –3
BF of 3 = 0 – 2 = –2
BF of 4 = 0 – 1 = –1
BF of 5 = 0 – 0 = 0

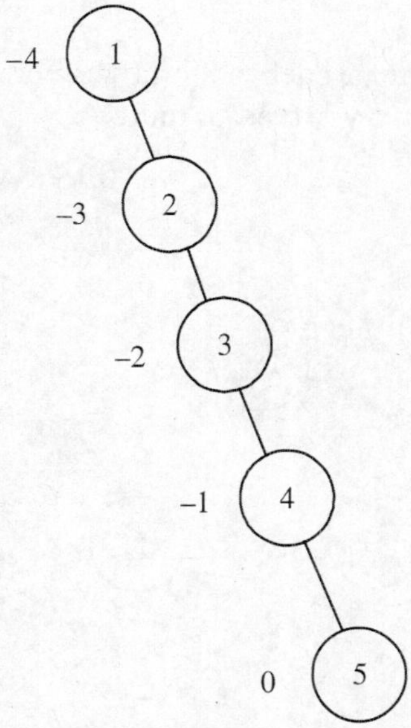

Figure 5.13 A binary search tree.

In this search tree to find node 5, we have to do five comparisons to find the result. The binary search tree of Figure 5.13 has right sub tree of height 4 whereas left sub tree of height 0. The same binary search tree can be reconstructed as in Figure 5.14, which makes it an AVL tree.

BF 3 = 2 – 2 = 0
BF 2 = 1 – 0 = 1
BF 4 = 0 – 1 = –1
BF 1 = 0 – 0 = 0
BF 5 = 0 – 0 = 0

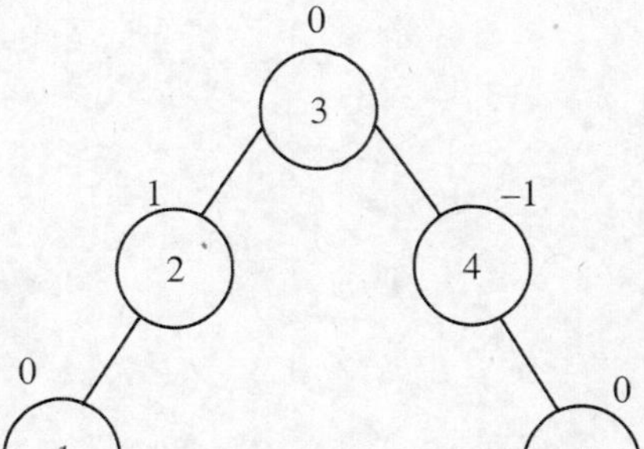

Figure 5.14 AVL tree.

Now the searching of node 5 needs only two comparisons.

Exercise 5.8

1. Find the balance factor of each node of the following binary search trees and state whether it is an AVL tree or not.

(a)

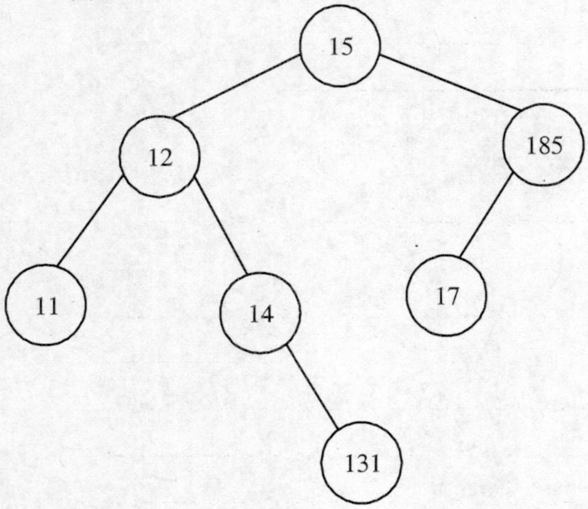

(b)

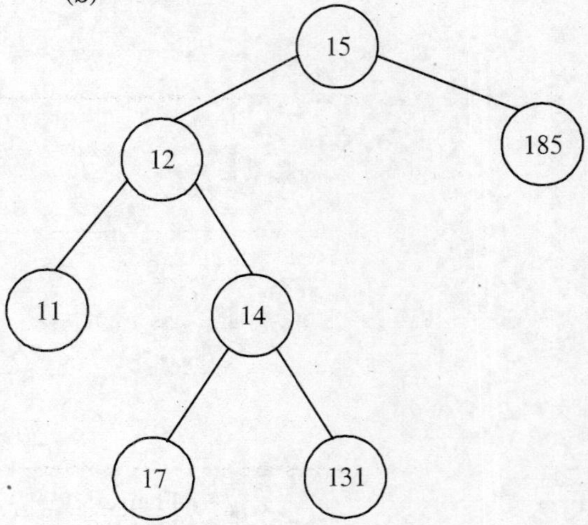

(c)

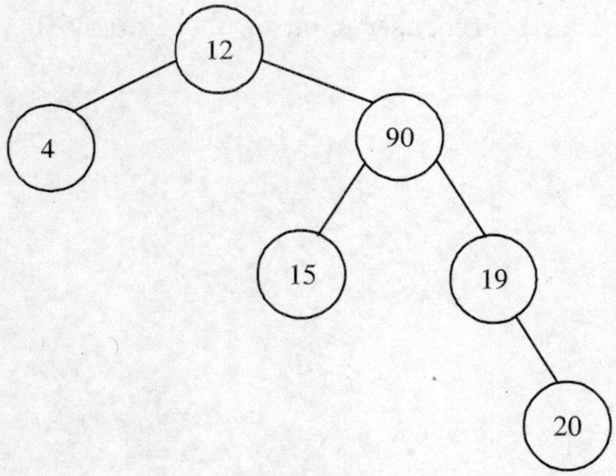

(d)

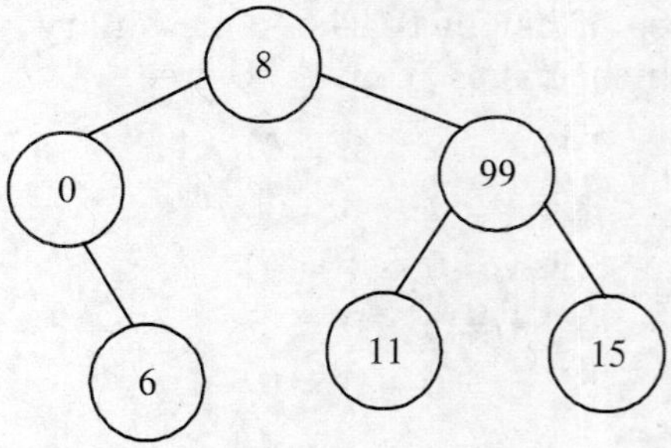

Chapter 6

Graphs

6.1 INTRODUCTION

In Chapter 5, we discussed the hierarchical data structure, trees. In this chapter, we look into a non-hierarchical data structure known as *graph*. The term 'graph' is a very familiar one, even from our school days, and is usually associated with a drawing showing the relation between two variable quantities. For example, between average temperature and months of the year in your town; pass percentage of a particular exam obtained in different colleges conducting the same course, etc. Generally, a graph is a pictorial representation of a relation of data.

Let us look at another situation, say, an airlines system. Consider the flight details between the cities — Thiruvanathapuram (TVM), Cochin (COC), Madras (MDS), Bombay (BOM), Delhi (DEL) and Bangalore (BAN). Assume that there are flights from TVM and COC to MDS and BAN. Also assume that there is a flight from BAN and MDS to COC and TVM. One of the ways in which this situation can be graphically represented is as follows (Figure 6.1):

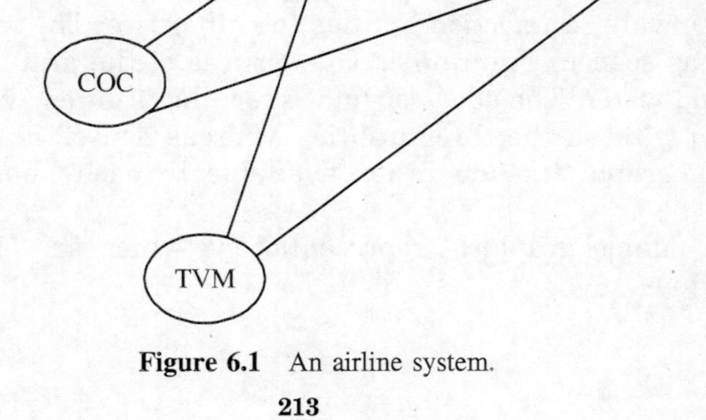

Figure 6.1 An airline system.

In the above figure, the cities are represented as circles. A line joining two cities indicates the existence of a flight between them. There is a line joining COC and BAN because there are flights between these two cities. If there is a flight connecting BAN, to BOM and DEL, then the route map will be as shown in Figure 6.2.

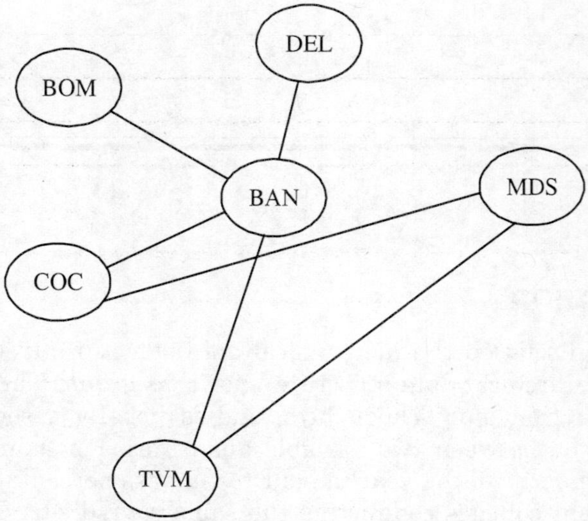

Figure 6.2 An airline system.

It is evident from Figures 6.1 and 6.2 that these graphic representations are made up of two sets — one is the set of circles and the other is the set of lines. Circles represent the elements on which the relation is defined. Lines represent the relation itself between the elements. The elements are usually known as *vertices*, *nodes,* or *points*, which can be represented as rectangles or circles. Lines representing the relation are known as *edges* or *links*, which can be represented as lines or curves. The relation can be bi-directional or single-directional. In the airlines system, the relation is bi-directional since we have assumed that if there is a flight from TVM to BAN, then there is one from BAN to TVM. From the graphic representation, it is very easy to conclude that to go to DEL from TVM, one has to go to BAN because there is only flight from BAN to DEL.

Let us look at another example which depicts the relation between utilities available in two houses. One of them has electricity, gas and water connection. The second one has no water connection but has the other two. The relation is given in the form of a graph as seen in Figure 6.3. The vertices of the graph are house1, house2, electricity, gas and water. The edges or lines show the utilities available in each house. House1 is related with all the three utilities whereas house2 is related only to two of them. From this graph, the amenities available in each house can be made out effortlessly.

Graphs are simple graphical representations which are expected to make the obscure very obvious.

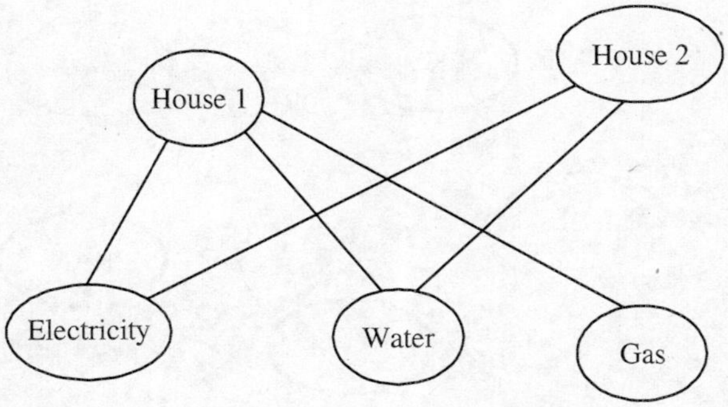

Figure 6.3 A Utility graph.

Exercise 6.1

1. For the information given in each step, complete the corresponding graphical representation for a courier company having its branches in five cities — TVM, KOL, EKM, KAN and PAL.

(a) Between TVM and KOL, there is a direct transport service.

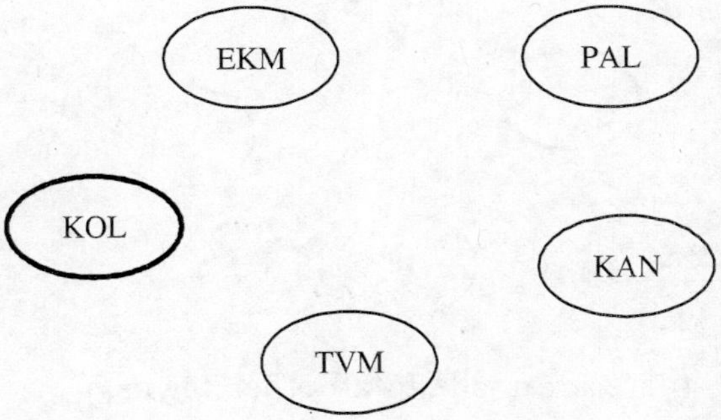

(b) From PAL, there is a direct transport service to all other cities.

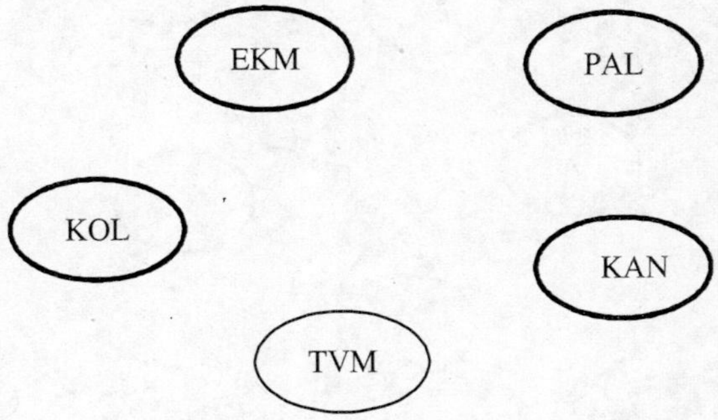

(c) From KAN, there is a direct transport service to EKM and TVM.

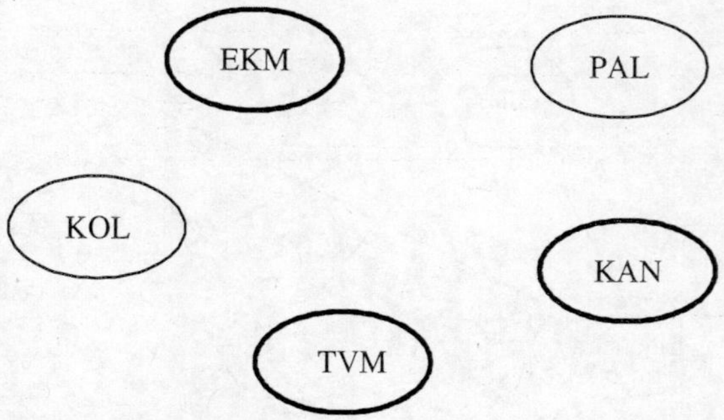

2. In the following problem, at each step a relation between the roads connecting towns A, B, C, D and E is given. Find the graphical representation of the situation as given in each step.

(a) There is a road between towns A and B.

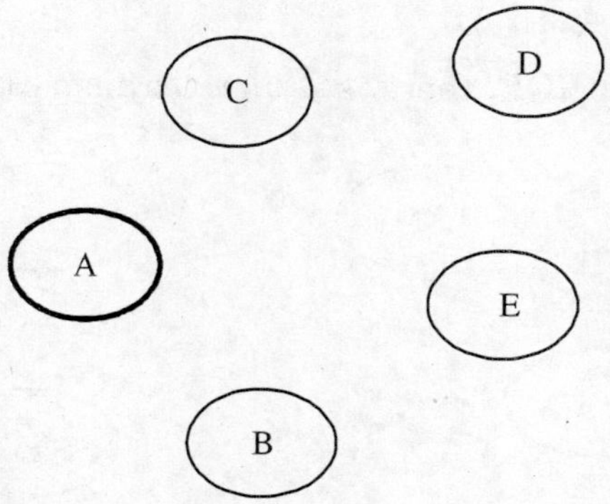

(b) From town D, there are roads to all other towns.

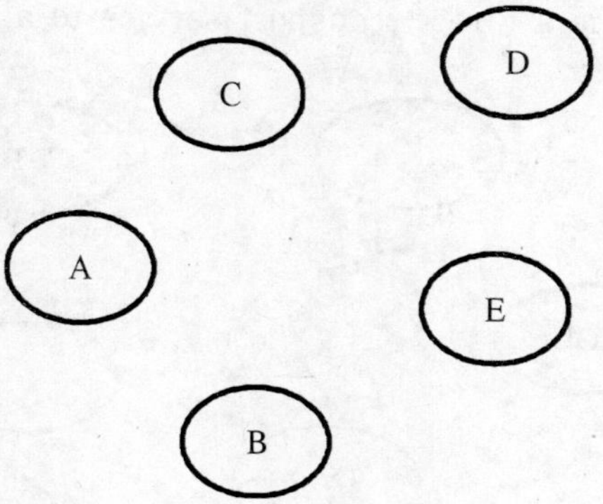

(c) From C, there are roads to A, B and E.

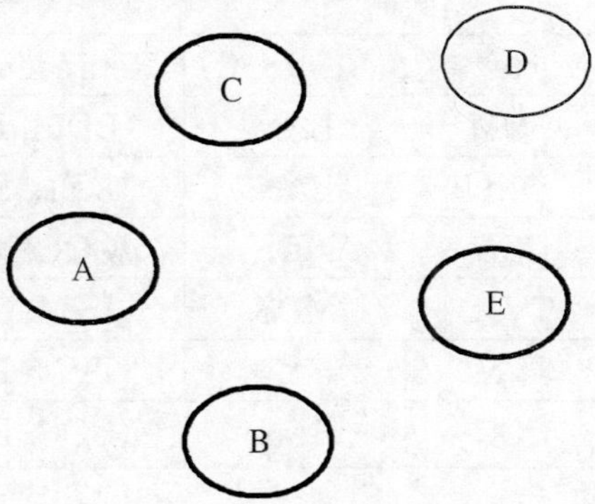

6.2 DEFINITION

A graph can be formally defined as consisting of two sets — set of vertices and set of edges. Each edge has at its end points two vertices from the set of vertices. An edge shows a relation between the vertices. Let us consider the airlines system example once more. The nodes have names as is evident from Figure 6.4. A graph is said to be a labelled graph if the edges are also named. The edges are usually named as E_1, E_2, etc.

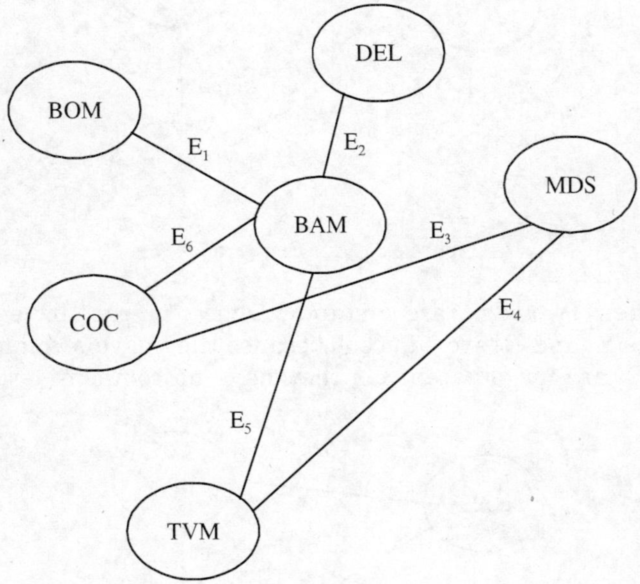

Figure 6.4 A graph.

The edge E_1 connects the nodes BOM and BAN. It can be written as E_1 = (BOM, BAN). In the same manner the remaining edges can be written as given in Table 6.1.

Table 6.1 Edge representation in a graph

Edge	Vertex 1	Vertex 2	Represented as
E_1	BOM	BAN	(BOM, BAN)
E_2	DEL	BAN	(DEL, BAN)
E_3	COC	MDS	(COC, MDS)
E_4	TVM	MDS	(TVM, MDS)
E_5	TVM	BAN	(TVM, BAN)
E_6	COC	BAN	(COC, BAN)

The following are the important terminologies associated with graphs.

Adjacent vertices: Two vertices are said to be adjacent if they have an edge between them. In Figure 6.5, vertices A and B are adjacent since there is an edge between them, whereas vertices C and D are not adjacent, for there is no edge between them.

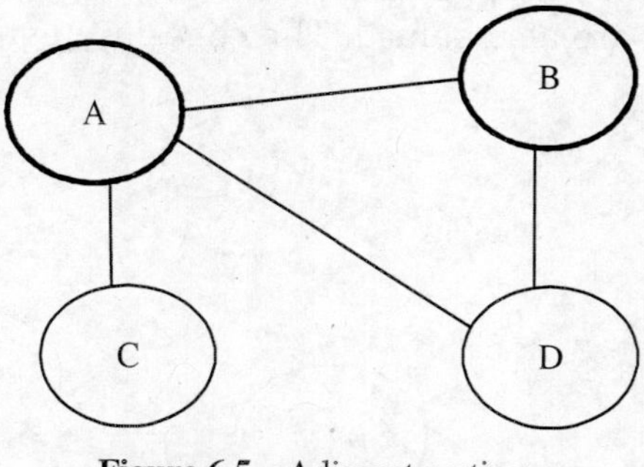

Figure 6.5 Adjacent vertices.

Adjacent edges: Two edges are said to be adjacent if they have a common vertex. In Figure 6.6, edges E_1 and E_2 are adjacent because they have a common vertex B. But the edges E_2 and E_4 are not adjacent, as they have no common vertex.

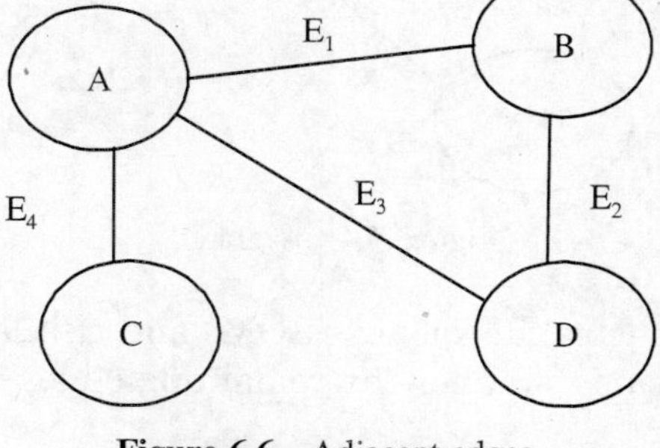

Figure 6.6 Adjacent edges.

Degree of a vertex: It is the number of vertices adjacent to the vertex. That is, it is the number of edges incident on a vertex. For example, in Figure 6.7, the degree of vertex B is 2 since there are two edges incident on B — one joining B to A and another joining B to D. The degree of the remaining vertices is shown in Figure 6.7.

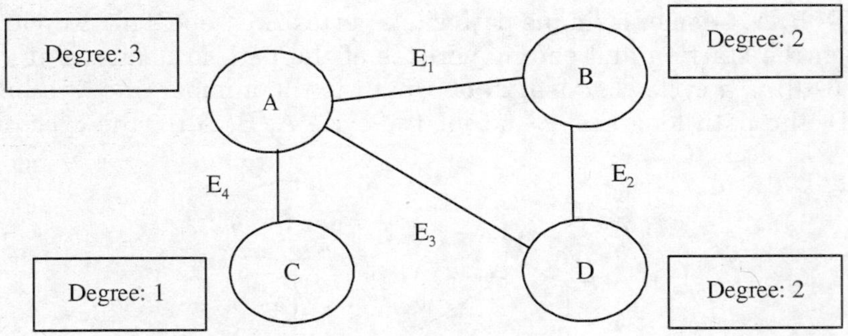

Figure 6.7 Degree of a vertex.

Pendant vertex: A vertex of degree one is called a pendant vertex. For such a vertex, there will only be one edge incident on it. In Figure 6.8, C is a pendent vertex since there is only one edge incident on it.

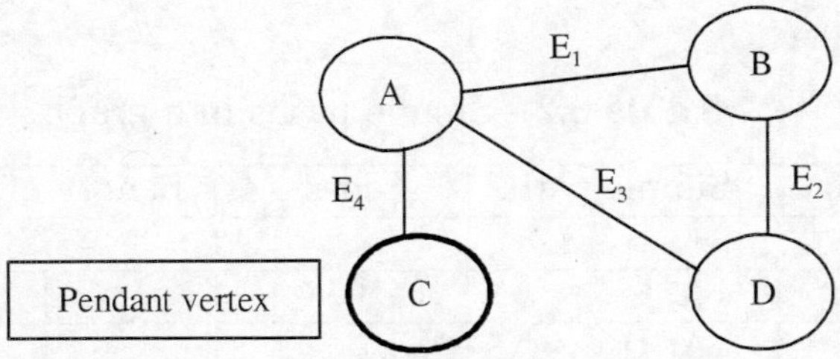

Figure 6.8 Pendant vertex.

Isolated vertex: A vertex of degree zero is said to be an isolated vertex. For such a vertex, there will be no edge incident on it. Consider the graph given in Figure 6.9. In this graph, vertex C is the isolated vertex since it has no edges incident on it.

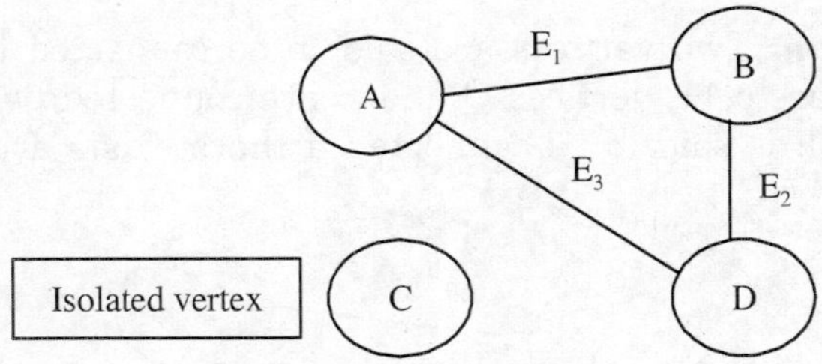

Figure 6.9 Isolated vertex.

Path of a graph: It is the sequence of vertices that are adjacent to each other. In other words, given two vertices, it is possible to start from one vertex, traverse through edges passing through other vertices till the second vertex is reached. In Figure 6.10, A, B, D is a path whereas A, C, D is not a path. A path is said to be a simple path if all the vertices in the path are distinct. Path A, B, D (see Figure 6.10) is a simple path whereas A, D, B, A, C is not a simple path since vertex A is repeated. A cycle is a simple path in which the starting and ending vertices of the path are same. Path A, B, D, A (see Figure 6.10) is a cycle. The length of a path is the number of edges in it. For the path A, B, D, the path length is 2 and for the cycle A, B, D, A, the cycle length is 3.

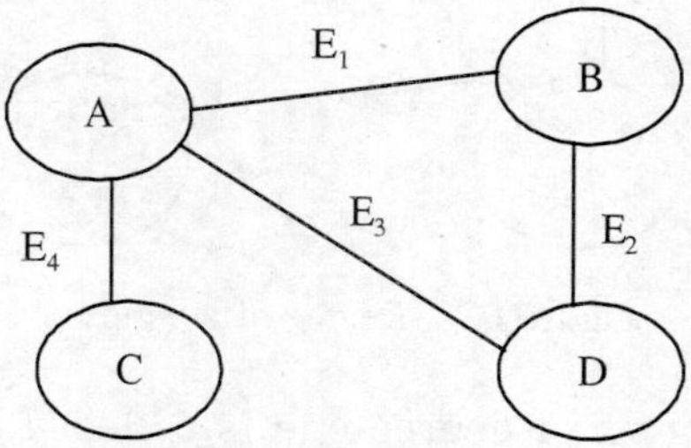

Figure 6.10 Path in a graph.

The following table (Table 6.2) lists some more simple paths of Figure 6.10 along with their path lengths.

Table 6.2 Simple paths in a graph

Sl. No	Simple path	Edges	Length of path
1	A, B	E_1	1
2	A, C	E_4	1
3	A, D	E_3	1
4	B, D	E_2	1
5	A, B, D	E_1, E_2	2
6	C, A, D	E_4, E_3	2
7	C, A, B	E_4, E_1	2
8	C, A, B, D	E_4, E_1, E_2	3

Connected graph: Two vertices are said to be connected if there exists a path between them. In Figure 6.11, vertices C and B are connected because there is a path between them. A graph is said to be connected if there exists a path for every pair of vertices.

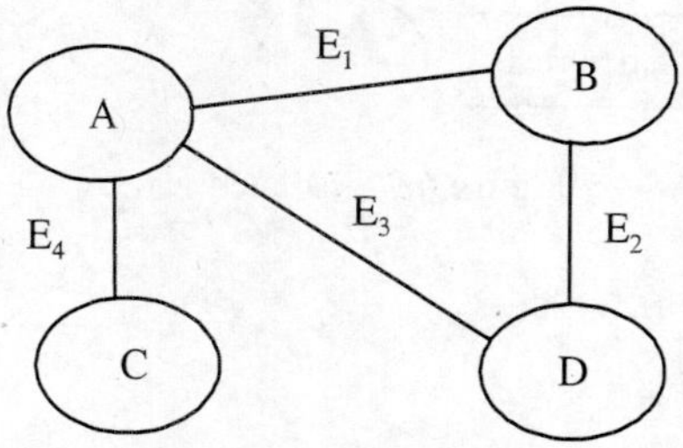

Figure 6.11 A simple connected graph.

The graph of Figure 6.11 is connected since there exists at least one path connecting any two vertices. In the following table (Table 6.3), all pairs of vertices are listed along with the paths joining them.

Table 6.3 All pairs of vertices in a graph

Pairs of vertices	Path joining the vertices	Length of the path
A, B	E_1	1
A, C	E_4	1
A, D	E_3	1
B, C	E_2	1
B, D	E_1, E_4 OR E_2, E_3, E_4	2 OR 3
C, D	E_4, E_3 OR E_4, E_1, E_2	2 OR 3

Loop: An edge is called a loop if both its end points are the same. Two edges are said to be parallel if their end points are the same. In Figure 6.12, vertex B has an edge, E_5, incident on itself. Hence, that edge is a loop. Between vertices B and D, there are two edges, E_2 and E_3. These two edges have the same end points and hence they are parallel edges. For our example, it means that there are two roads joining the towns B and D.

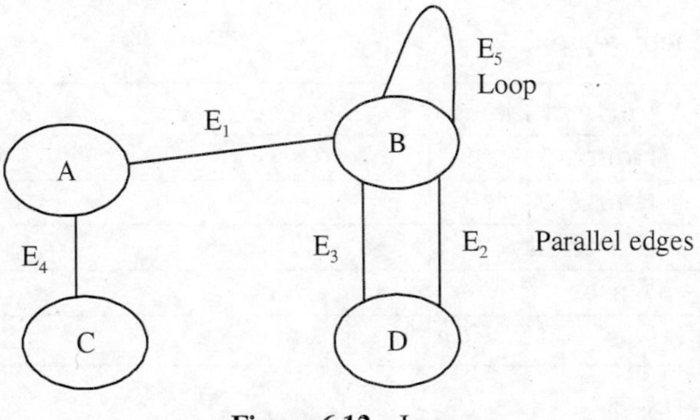

Figure 6.12 Loop.

Exercise 6.2

1. Consider the example of houses and utilities discussed previously (see Figure 6.3). Answer the following questions:

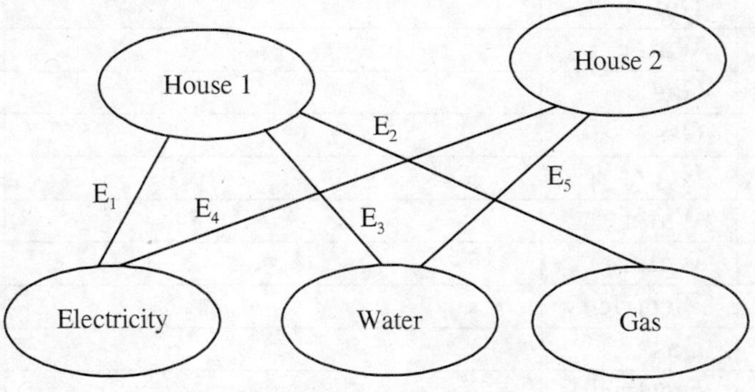

Figure 6.13 A graph.

(a) Set of vertices:
(b) Set of edges:
(c) Adjacent vertices:

Vertex (V)	Adjacent vertices of V
House 1	
House 2	
Electricity	
Water	
Gas	

(d) Adjacent edges:

Edges (E)	Adjacent edges of E
E_1	
E_2	
E_3	
E_4	
E_5	

(e) Degree of each vertex:

Vertex (V)	Degree of V
House 1	
House 2	
Electricity	
Water	
Gas	

(f) Pendant vertex:
(g) Isolated vertex:
(h) Path of the graph:

Vertex 1	Vertex 2	Path between vertex 1 and vertex 2	Edges sequence
House 1	House 2		
House 2	Water		
Electricity	Gas		
Water	Gas		
Gas	House 2		
Electricity	Water		
House1	Water		
House1	Electricity		
House1	Gas		
House2	Electricity		

(i) List a cycle in the graph:
(j) Is the graph connected?

2. Consider the railway line graph which connects 8 cities as given below:

Railway line R_1 connects Trivandrum (TVM) to Kayamkulam (KYM). To reach Ernakulam (EKM) from KYM, there are two railway lines, R_2 and R_3. There is a railway line R_4 which starts at EKM and stops at the same station. R_5 goes from EKM to Palaghat (PGT). To reach Chennai (MDS) from PGT, R_6 is used. R_7 is between MDS and Madurai (MDU). In MDU, there is a metre gauge R_8 to Rameswaram (RWM). R_9 is from MDU to TVM. Draw the graph for this situation. Also, answer the following questions based on the graph obtained.

Step 1: R_1 connects Trivandrum (TVM) and Kayamkulam (KYM).

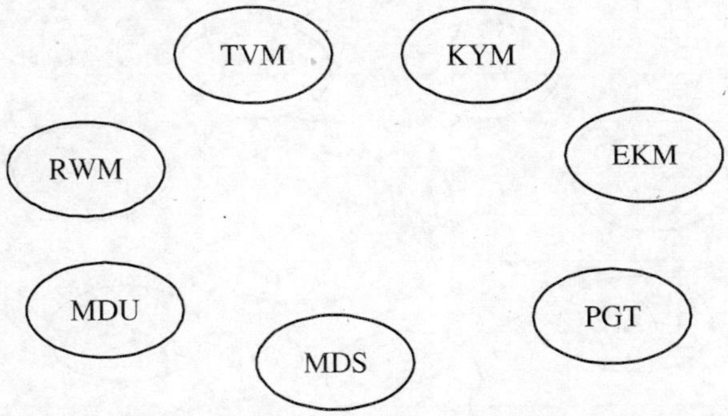

Step 2: There are two railway lines from Ernakulam (EKM) to Kayamkulam (KYM).

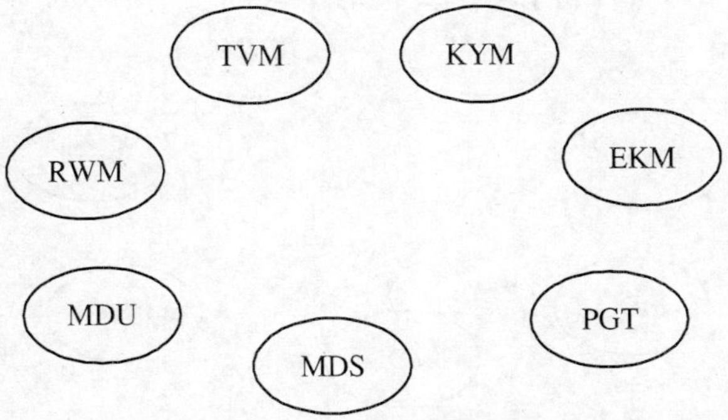

Step 3: R_4 which starts at Ernakulam (EKM) and stops at the same station.

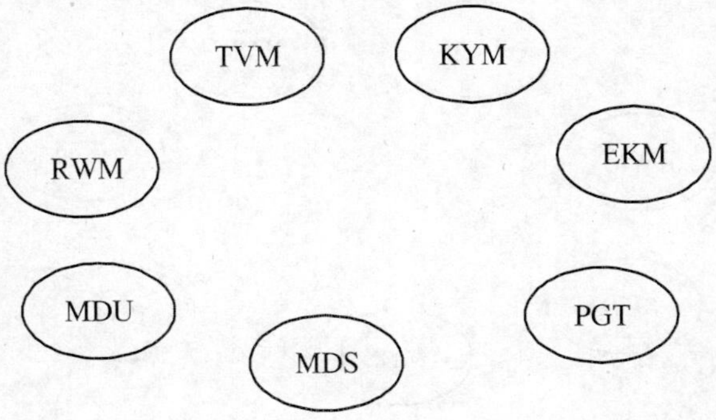

Step 4: R_5 goes from Ernakulam (EKM) to Palaghat (PGT).

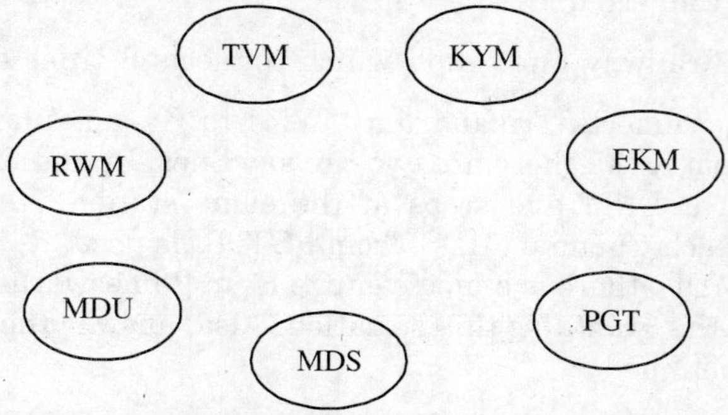

Step 5: To reach Chennai (MDS) from Palaghat (PGT), R_6 is used.

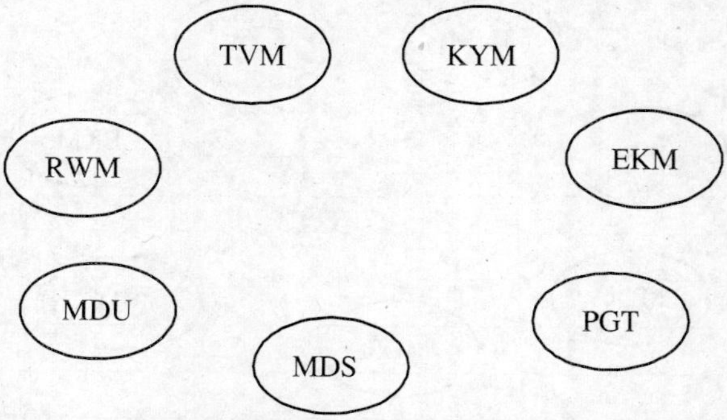

Step 6: R_7 is between Chennai (MDS) and Madurai (MDU).

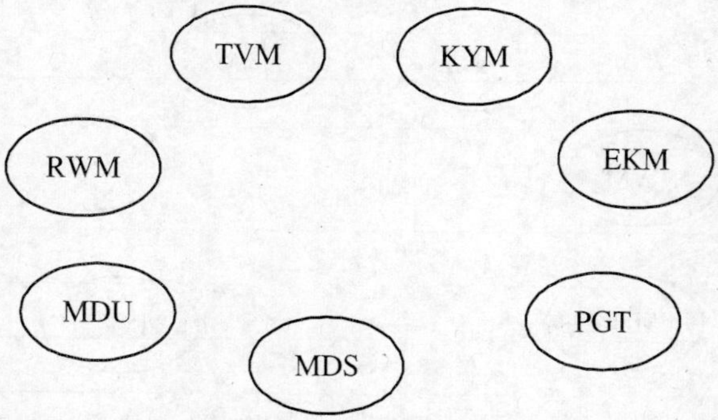

Step 7: From Madurai (MDU), there is a metre gauge R_8 to Rameswaram (RWM).

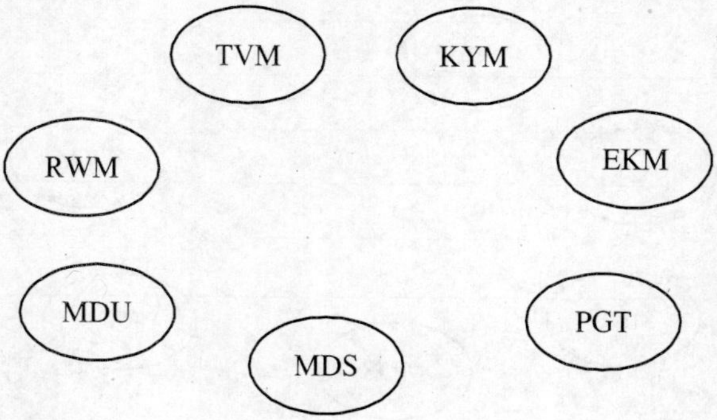

Step 8: R_9 is from Madurai (MDU) to Trivandrum (TVM).

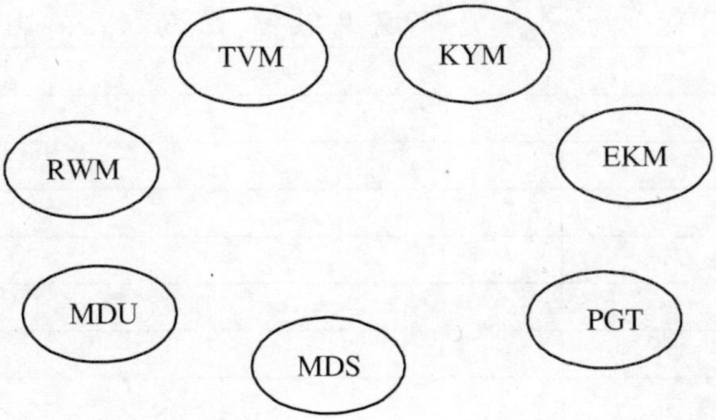

(a) Set of vertices:
(b) Set of edges:
(c) Adjacent vertices:

Vertex (V)	Adjacent vertices of V

(d) Adjacent edges:

Edges (E)	Adjacent edges of E
R_1	
R_2	
R_3	
R_4	
R_5	
R_6	
R_7	
R_8	
R_9	

(e) Degree of each vertex:

Vertex (V)	Degree of V

(f) Pendant vertex:
(g) Isolated vertex:
(h) Path of the graph:

Vertex 1	Vertex 2	Path between vertex 1 and vertex 2	Edges sequence
TVM	MDS		
KYM	MDU		
EKM	PGT		
KYM	RWM		
MDS	EKM		
TVM	RWM		

(i) Find any 4 cycles:
1.
2.
3.
4.

(j) Is the graph connected?

6.3 DIGRAPH

In our discussion so far, we assumed that the graph possesses a bi-directional relationship between the vertices. That is, if vertex A is related to B, then vertex B is related to A. As in the example of airlines system, if there is a flight from BOM to DEL, then we assumed the availability of flight from DEL to BOM. There can be relations which are unidirectional too. Such graphs are represented by edges with arrow to indicate the direction. A graph with directed edges is known as **directed graphs** or **digraph**.

Consider the road map given in Figure 6.14. From a point A, it is possible to go to point B. Suppose that it is not possible to go from point B to point A. The arrowhead in the edge indicates this information. That is, it is possible to traverse through the edge where the arrowhead is pointing to, and not in the other opposite direction. Some of the terminologies associated with a digraph are as follows.

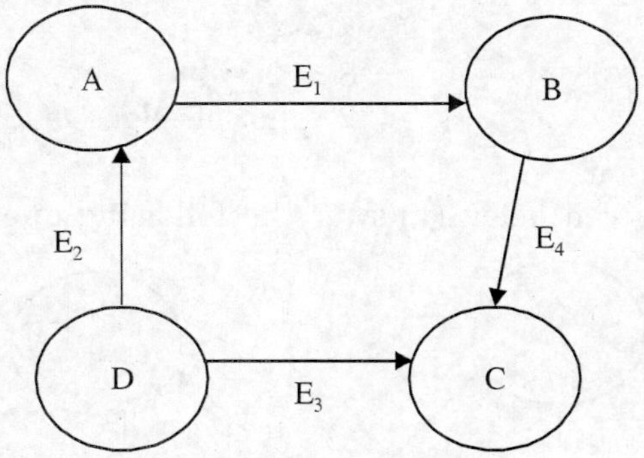

Figure 6.14 A diagraph.

Tail and head: In a diagraph, the arrow (in an edge) pointed towards the vertex is known as head and the other end vertex of the edge is known as tail. In Figure 6.14, B is the head and A is the tail of the edge E_1. The head and tail of all the edges in Figure 6.14 are given in Table 6.4.

Table 6.4 Head and tail of each edge of a graph

Edge	Head	Tail
E_1	B	A
E_2	A	D
E_3	C	D
E_4	C	B

Adjacent vertices: A is adjacent to B if there is an edge from A to B with A as the tail and B as the head. In Figure 6.14, A is adjacent to B but not vice versa.

Indegree and outdegree of a vertex: The indegree of a vertex is the number of edges incident on it. The outdegree of the vertex is the number of edges that start from the vertex. In Figure 6.14, the indegree of A is one and so is the outdegree. For vertex C, the outdegree is zero and the indegree is 2. The indegree and the outdegree of each vertex in Figure 6.14 are given in Table 6.5.

Table 6.5 Degree of a node-in a diagraph

Vertex (V)	Adjacent vertices of V	Indegree of V	Outdegree of V
A	B	1	1
B	C	1	1
C	–	2	0
D	A, C	0	2

Note: The sum of the degree of all vertices of a graph = 2 * no. of edges of the graph.

For a diagraph, the degree of a vertex is the sum of its indegree and outdegree. For the graph in Figure 6.14,

Sum of the degree of all vertices = (Indegree + Outdegree) of all vertices
= 4 + 4
= 8 = 2 * 4
= 2 * no. of edges of the graph.

Exercise 6.3

1. For the graph given below, answer the following questions.

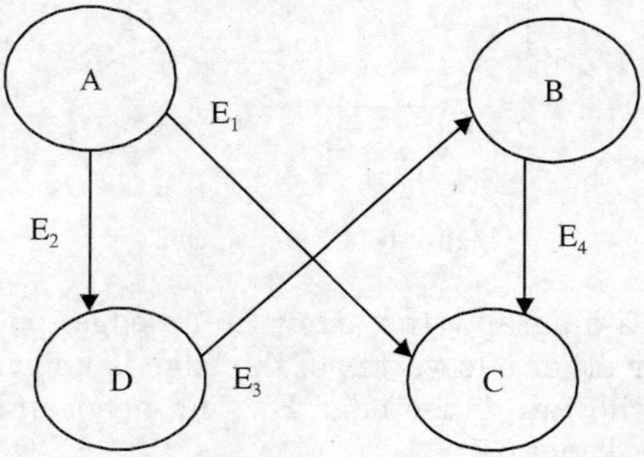

(a) Head and tail of each edge.

Edge	Head	Tail
E_1	C	A
E_2		
E_3		
E_4		

(b) Indegree and outdegree of each vertex.

Vertex	Indegree	Outdegree
A	0	2
B		
C		
D		

(c) Vertices adjacent to each vertex.

Vertex	Adjacent vertices	Edge
A		
B		
C		
D		

(d) Edges adjacent to each edge.

Edge	Adjacent edges	Vertices
E_1		
E_2		
E_3		
E_4		

(e) Path between vertices.

Vertex 1	Vertex 2	Path	Edge sequence
A	B		
B	C		
C	D		
D	A		
B	A		
B	D		
A	C		
D	C		
C	B		

(f) Find any cycle, if possible:
(g) Is the graph connected?

2. For the following graph, answer the following.

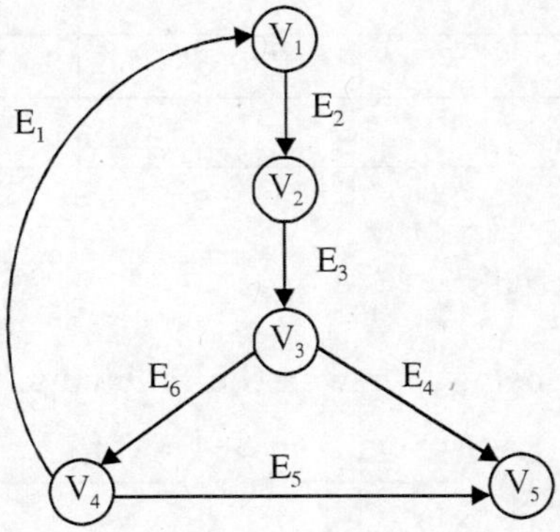

(a) Edges adjacent to each edge and head and tail of each edge.

Edge	Adjacent edges	Head	Tail
E_1			
E_2			
E_3			
E_4			
E_5			
E_6			

(b) Vertices adjacent to each vertex and indegree and outdegree of each vertex.

Vertex	Adjacent vertices	Indegree	Outdegree
V_1			
V_2			
V_3			
V_4			
V_5			

(c) Path between vertices.

Vertex 1	Vertex 2	Path from vertex 1 to vertex 2	Path from vertex 2 to vertex 1
V_1	V_5		
V_2	V_4		
V_3	V_5		
V_4	V_1		
V_5	V_2		

(d) Find cycle, if any:
(e) Is the graph connected?

3. For the graph given below, answer the following.

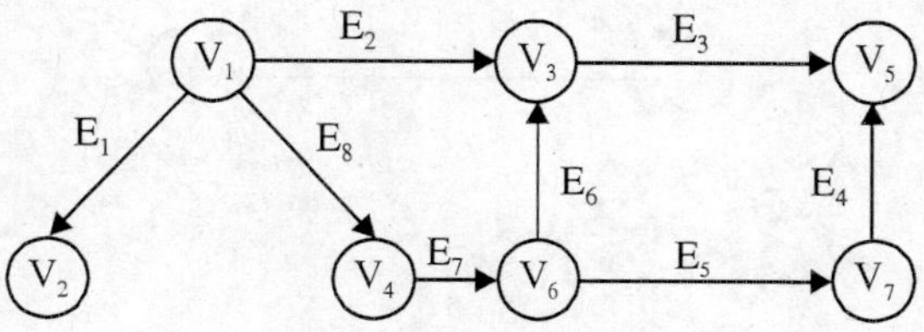

(a) Edges adjacent to each edge and head and tail of each edge.

Edge	Adjacent edges	Head	Tail
E_1			
E_2			
E_3			
E_4			
E_5			
E_6			
E_7			
E_8			

(b) Vertices adjacent to each vertex and indegree and outdegree of each vertex.

Vertex	Adjacent vertices	Indegree	Outdegree
V_1			
V_2			
V_3			
V_4			
V_5			
V_6			
V_7			

(c) Path between vertices.

Vertex 1	Vertex 2	Path from vertex 1 to vertex 2	Path from vertex 2 to vertex 1
V_1	V_6		
V_2	V_7		
V_3	V_5		
V_5	V_1		
V_6	V_2		

(d) Find cycle, if any:
(e) Is the graph connected?

3. Consider the food chain process — grass, rabbit, snake, and eagle. This can be pictorially represented as a graph as given below. This shows the relationship of eating habits of some animals.

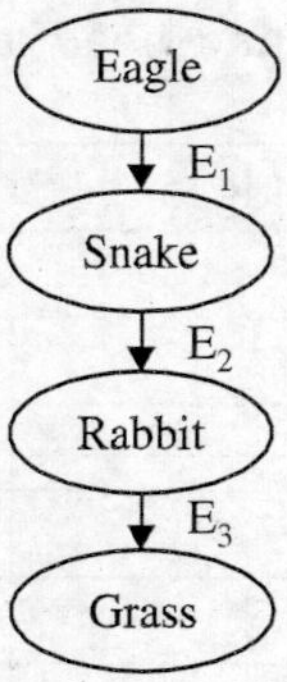

Answer the following questions:

(a) Adjacent vertices and degree of each vertex.

Vertex	Adjacent vertices	Indegree	Outdegree
Eagle			
Snake			
Rabbit			
Grass			

(b) Adjacent edges.

Edge	Adjacent edges	Head	Tail
E_1			
E_2			
E_3			

(c) Path of the graph.

Vertex 1	Vertex 2	Path from vertex 1 to vertex 2	Path from vertex 2 to vertex 1
Eagle	Grass		
Snake	Rabbit		
Rabbit	Eagle		
Grass	Snake		

(d) Is the graph connected?

6.4 GRAPH REPRESENTATION

For storing a graph in the memory of a computer, it is usually represented in one of the following two ways:

- Adjacency matrix
- Adjacency list

The adjacency matrix can be considered a sequential representation of a graph, and the adjacency list can be considered a linked representation of the graph.

6.4.1 Adjacency Matrix

Consider the graph given in Figure 6.15. It contains four vertices and four edges. The adjacency matrix of a graph is a square matrix with rows and columns equal to the number of vertices. Each row and column is represented by each vertex. The elements of the vertices are either 0 or 1, depending upon the existence of an edge between the vertex in the row and the vertex in the column. For the graph of Figure 6.15, the adjacency matrix is given by an 4×4 matrix (see Table 6.6) with rows and columns as Suma, Ann, Mini and Jane. The row and the column names are same as those of the vertex name. The element at position [Suma, Suma] of the matrix is 0 because there is no edge between them, whereas the element at position [Ann, Mini] is one since there is an edge. In this manner, the remaining elements can be obtained.

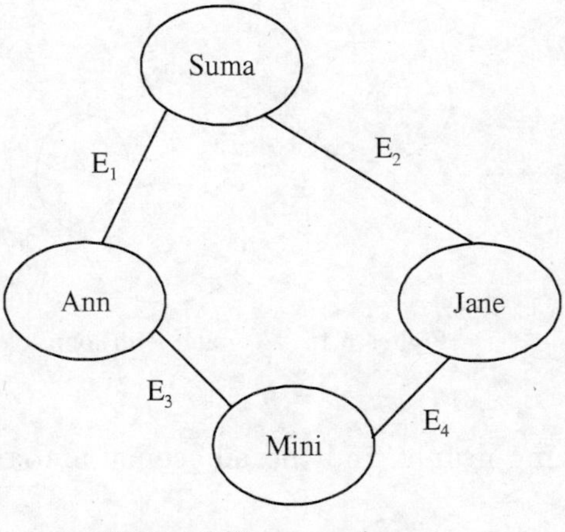

Figure 6.15 A graph.

Table 6.6 Adjacency matrix

	Suma	Ann	Mini	Jane
Suma	0	1	0	1
Ann	1	0	1	0
Mini	0	1	0	1
Jane	1	0	1	0

The properties of the adjacency matrix are as follows:

- For an undirected graph the adjacency matrix will be symmetrical since the relation is bi-directional. The row total or column total gives the degree of each vertex. The matrix in Table 6.6 is a symmetric matrix.
- If any diagonal element is one, it indicates the existence of a loop. Consider the graph given in Figure 6.16. Its adjacency matrix is given in Table 6.7. The diagonal element (C, C) is 1, indicating the existence of an edge from C to itself. This is true because of the edge E_4 in Figure 6.16.

Table 6.7 Adjacency matrix of a graph with loop

Row \ Column	A	B	C
A	0	1	0
B	1	0	1
C	0	1	1

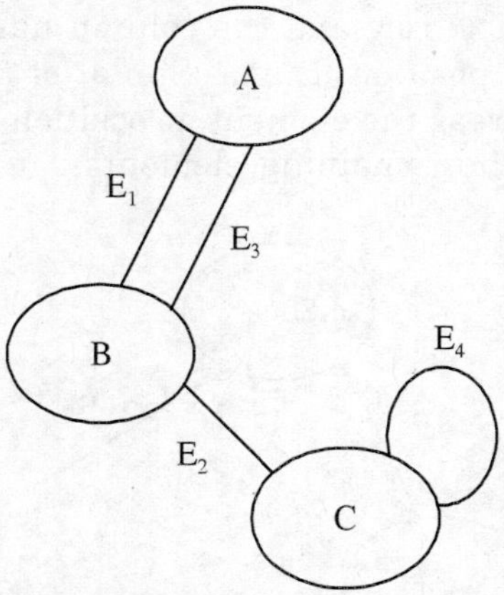

Figure 6.16 A graph with loop.

Exercise 6.4

1. For the following graph, find the adjacency matrix.

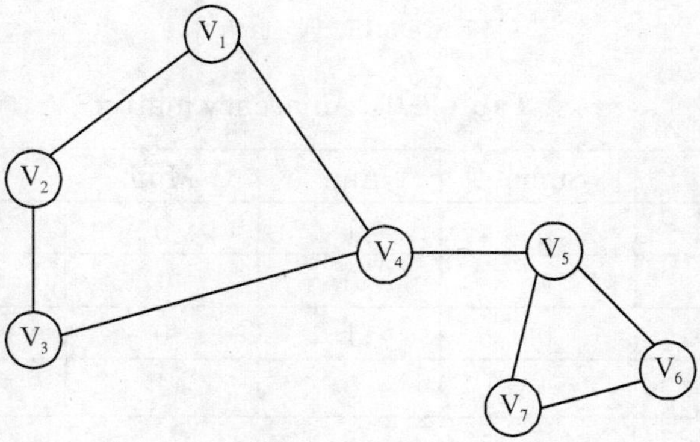

Row \ Column	V_1	V_2	V_3	V_4	V_5	V_6	V_7	Total	Degree of vertex
V_1	0	1	0	1	0	0	0	2	2
V_2									
V_3									
V_4									
V_5									
V_6									
V_7									
Total									
Degree of vertex									

2. For the diagraph given below, find the adjacency matrix.

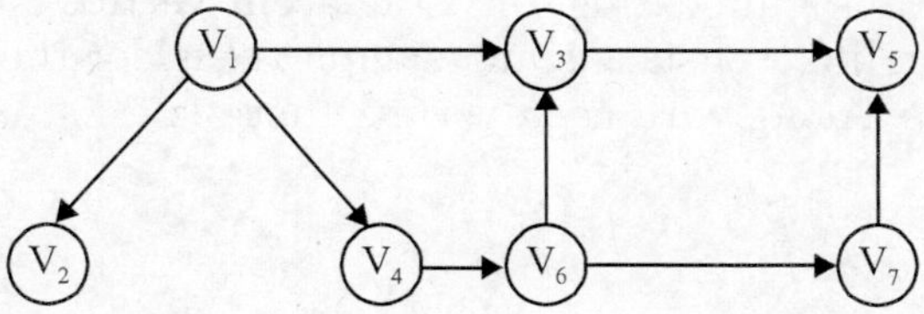

Row \ Column	V_1	V_2	V_3	V_4	V_5	V_6	V_7	Total	Outdegree of vertex
V_1	0	1	1	1	0	0	0	3	3
V_2									
V_3									
V_4									
V_5									
V_6									
V_7									
Total									
Indegree of vertex									

3. Draw a graph corresponding to the following adjacent matrix.

Row \ Column	A	B	C	D
A	0	1	1	1
B	1	1	0	1
C	1	0	1	0
D	1	1	0	0

4. Draw a digraph corresponding to the following adjacency matrix.

Row \ Column	A	B	C	D	E	F
A	0	1	1	1	0	1
B	1	0	0	1	1	1
C	1	0	0	0	0	1
D	1	0	1	0	1	1
E	0	1	1	0	1	0
F	1	0	0	1	0	1

6.4.2 Adjacency List

In the adjacency list, the graph is stored as a linked list. Corresponding to each vertex of a graph, there is a linked list of its adjacent vertices. So, for a graph with n vertices, there will be n linked lists. As an example, consider the graph in Figure 6.17. There are four vertices. Along with each vertex, there is a list containing the vertices adjacent to it.

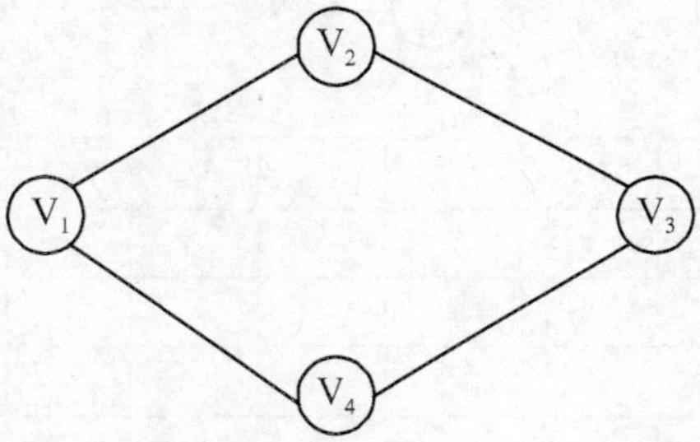

Figure 6.17 A graph.

Consider the vertex V_1. Its adjacent vertices are V_2 and V_4. So, there will be a list containing two nodes with values V_2 and V_4. In the same manner, for each of the other vertices, there will be a list. Table 6.8 gives all the lists associated with each vertex of the graph given in Figure 6.17.

Table 6.8 Ajacency list

Vertex (V)	Linked list containing vertices adjacent to V
V_1	V_2, V_4
V_2	V_1, V_3
V_3	V_2, V_4
V_4	V_1, V_3

The adjacency list structure for the graph of Figure 6.17 can be pictorially represented as given in Figure 6.18. The first position contains the vertex V_1. The second position gives the location of the adjacency vertices of V_1. The third position contains the vertex V_2. The next position gives the location of the adjacency vertices of V_2. In this manner, the remaining positions are obtained.

1	2	3	4	5	6	7	8	9	10	11	12	13	14	15	16	17	18	19	20	21	22	23	24
V_1	9	V_2	13	V_3	17	V_4	21	V_2	11	V_4	NULL	V_1	15	V_3	NULL	V_2	18	V_4	NULL	V1	23	V3	NULL

Figure 6.18 Graphical representation of an adjacency list.

Exercise 6.5

1. For the following graph, find the adjacency list and adjacency matrix representation.

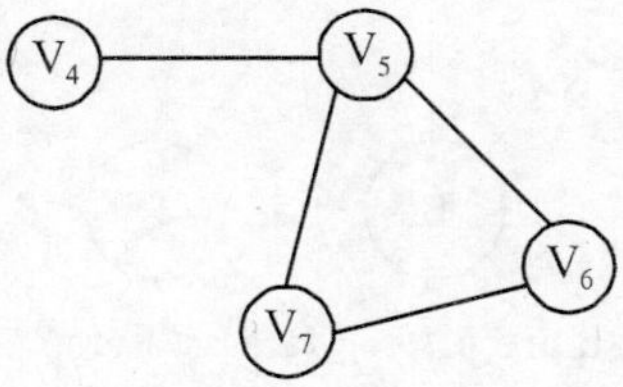

1	2	3	4	5	6	7	8	9	10	11	12	13	14	15	16	17	18	19	20	21	22	23	24
V_1																							

Row \ Column	V_4	V_5	V_6	V_7
V_4				
V_5				
V_6				
V_7				

2. For the graph given below, find the adjacency list and adjacency matrix representation by labelling the edges suitably.

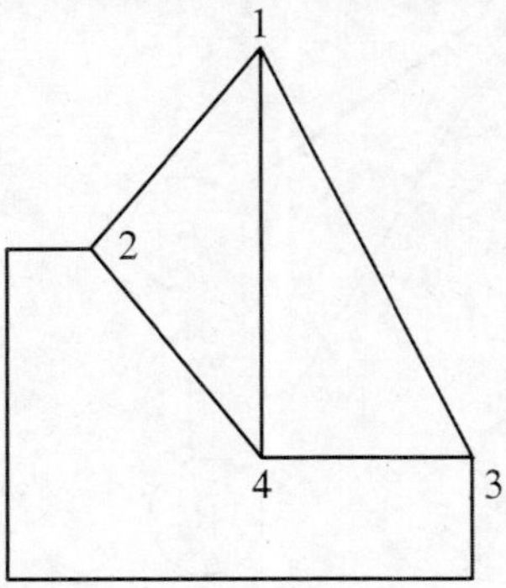

6.5 GRAPH TRAVERSAL

Traversal means the act of traversing, or moving or passing along or through. The term 'graph traversal' means to visit all the vertices of the graph. It is a technique for processing the vertices of a graph in a systematic order. Since there are many paths leading from one vertex to another, the toughest part about traversing a graph is to make sure that you do not process (visit) some vertices twice. Using graph traversal, we can find the shortest route that visits all the vertices.

Suppose that a maze is represented in the form of a graph as given in Figure 6.19.

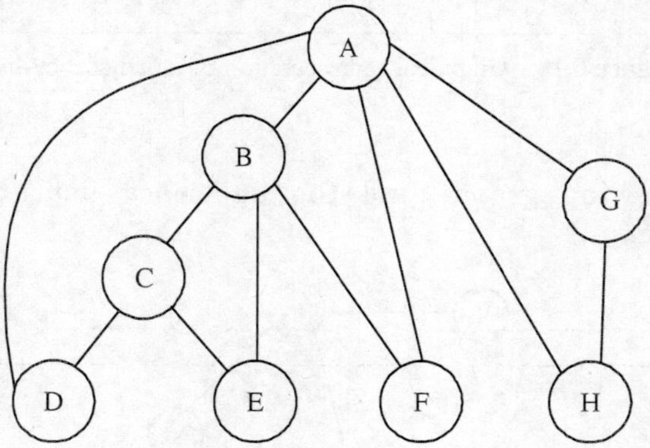

Figure 6.19 Maze as a graph.

Each vertex in the maze contains precious stones denoted by A, B, ..., H. It is required to collect all these stones by visiting the vertices. This process can be carried out in a systematic manner in one of the following two ways:

1. Depth First Search (DFS)
2. Breadth First Search (BFS)

6.5.1 Depth First Search (DFS)

The DFS technique is explained by means of an example and is illustrated in Figures 6.20 through 6.26.

Step1: Suppose you start from vertex A. Then you can visit any of the vertices adjacent to A, and in this case the adjacent vertices are B, D, F, G and H. Suppose that B is selected. At this point, it should be remembered that there are other unvisited vertices that are adjacent to A.

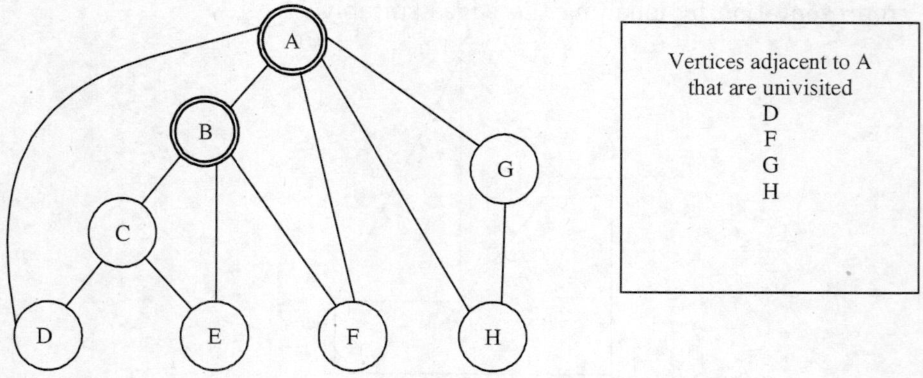

Figure 6.20 DFS—Step 1.

Step 2: From B, it is possible to go to A, C, E or F. Among these, A is not a suitable choice since the stone from A has been collected. Among the other choices, suppose C is selected.

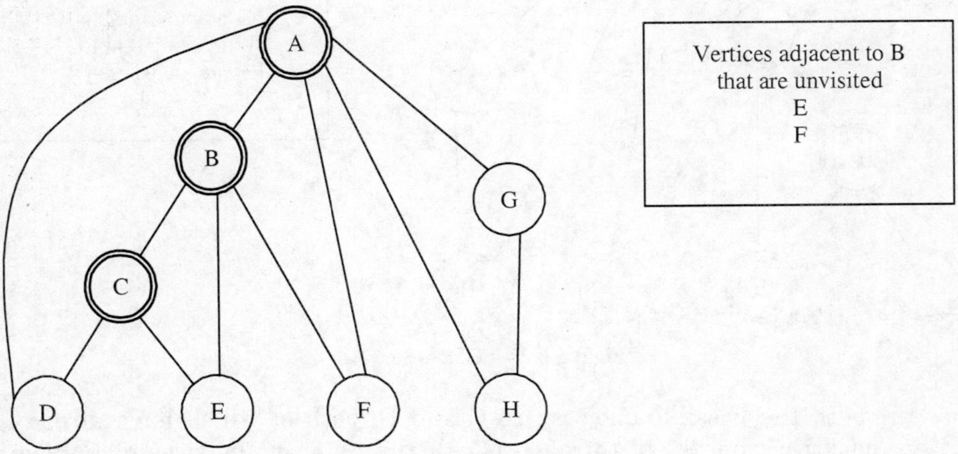

Figure 6.21 DFS—Step 2.

Step 3: From C, it is possible to go to B, D or E, and D is selected. It is to be remembered that E is an unvisited vertex from C.

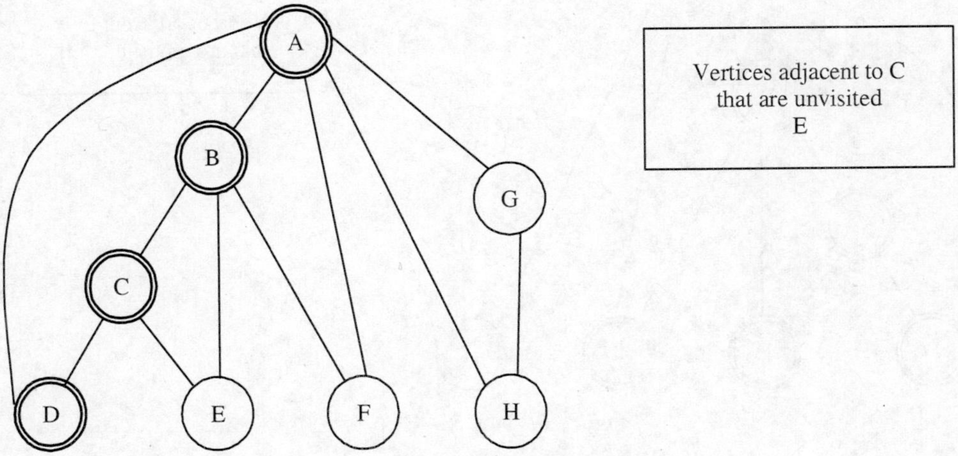

Figure 6.22 DFS—Step 3.

Step 4: From D, it is possible to go to either C or A only, both of which have been visited, that is, the stones have been collected from them. Now you are in a dilemma of what to do. There is no way you can move forward as in the previous step. But we know there are other unvisited vertices in the previous steps. So, you decide to go back one step (backtracking). We are in now D, which was reached from C. So, go back to C and find other unvisited vertices. We see from step 3 that E is our only choice. So, E is selected.

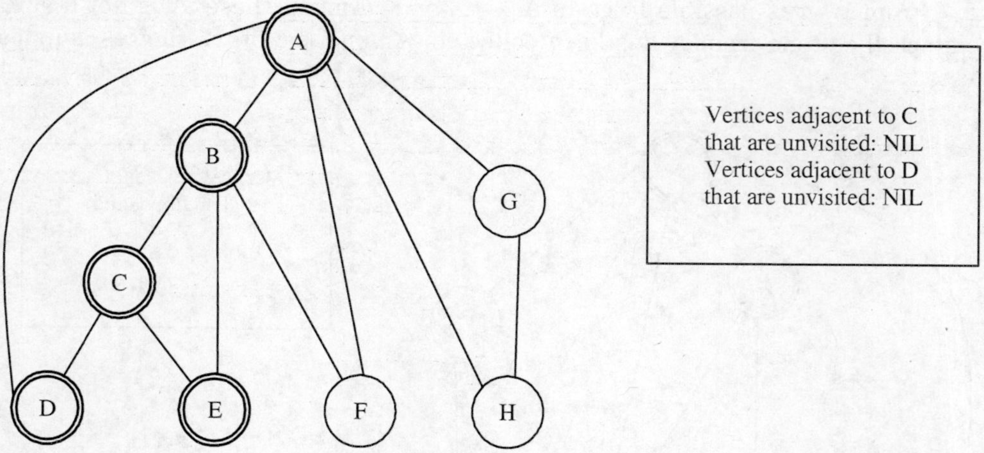

Figure 6.23 DFS—Step 4.

Step 5: From E, the possible choices are C and B, both of which have already been visited. So, backtrack one step, to reach C. All the adjacent vertices of C have been visited. So, once more backtrack and B is reached. From B, among the adjacent vertices only F is unvisited. So, select F.

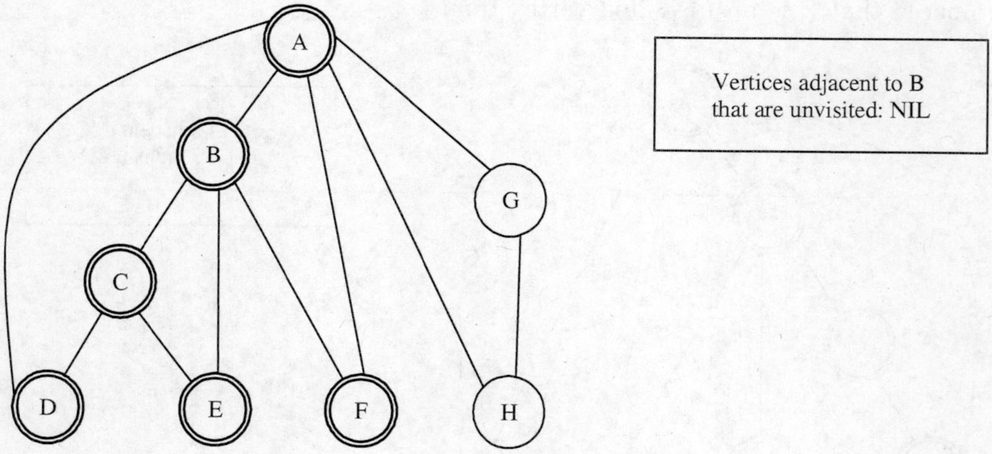

Figure 6.24 DFS—Step 5.

Step 6: From F, the possible choices are A and B, both of which have been visited. So, backtracking takes you to B. There are no vertices adjacent to B that have been unvisited. So, backtracking once again you reach A. Among the adjacent vertices of A, it is found that G and H are unvisited. So, select one of them, say, G.

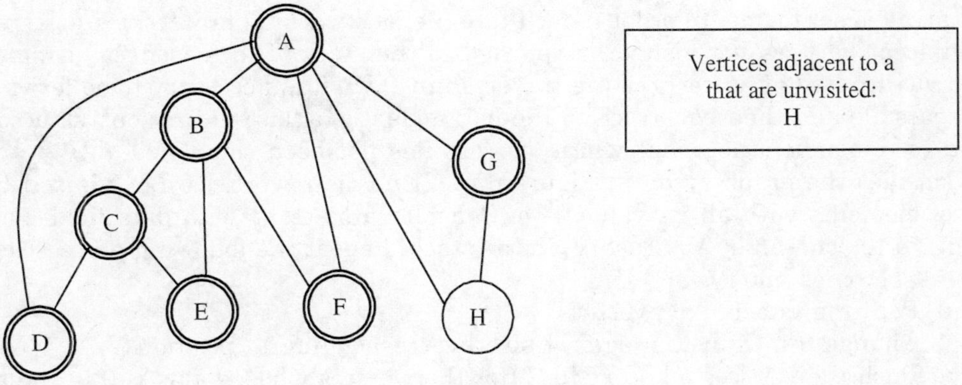

Figure 6.25 DFS—Step 6.

Step 7: The adjacent unvisited vertex of G is H. Hence, G is selected next.

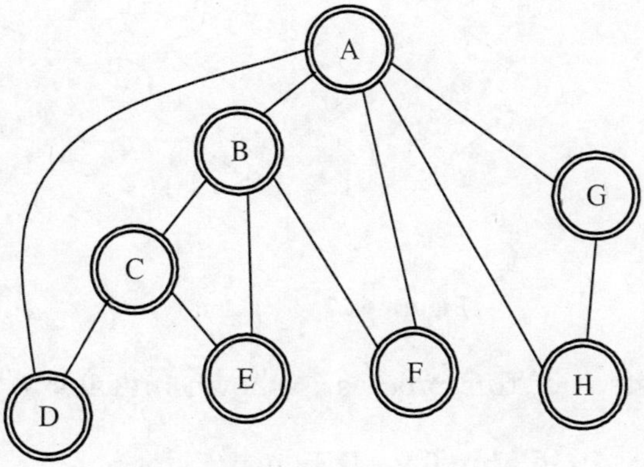

Figure 6.26 DFS—Step 7.

Step 8: From H, it is found that all the adjacent vertices of H have been visited. Now all the vertices of the maze have been visited and precious stones have been collected, and that is the end of this method.

The order in which the vertices were visited is as follows:

A B C D E F G H

The systematic approach that is followed in DFS is to move forward using unvisited adjacent vertices until no further forward movement is possible. At this stage, backtrack to the previous vertex and the process is repeated once again. This technique of graph traversal is known as *depth first search* (DFS).

6.5.2 Implementation of Depth First Search (DFS)

In order to keep track of the information about whether a vertex has been visited or not, an array is used. This array has the size equal to that of the number of vertices, and initially its value is zero. Each time the vertex is visited, the corresponding element in the array is set to one. In order to facilitate the backtracking process, a stack is used. The adjacent vertices not visited are pushed to the stack. The reason for using stack data structure is that as vertices are traversed in DFS, it is necessary to go forward as far as possible and then backtrack to the last node. So, a 'last in first out' structure is needed to remember the nodes whose process has not been completed.

Consider the graph given in Figure 6.27. It has four vertices. Let **visited** be an array of elements with all its value zero. Consider a stack s1 with data field. Let the starting vertex chosen be V_1. Push V_1 to the stack. Repeat the following processes until the stack becomes empty:

(a) Pop from stack, say, vertex V.
(b) Change 0 to 1 in the array **visited** corresponding to position V.
(c) Push the vertices adjacent to V (for the vertices whose value is 0 in the array **visited**).

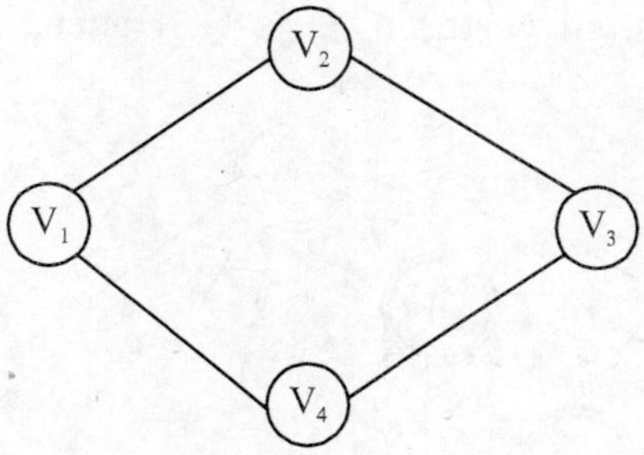

Figure 6.27 A graph.

The sequence of steps of this process is shown in Table 6.9.

Table 6.9 DFS using stack

Sl. No	data[0]	data[1]	data[2]	data[3]	top	Remarks	Visited
1					–1	Empty	0, 0, 0, 0
2	V_1				0	Push(& s1, V_1)	0, 0, 0, 0
3					–1	Pop(& s1, 0)	1, 0, 0, 0
4	V_2				0	Push(& s1, V_2)	1, 0, 0, 0
5	V_2	V_4			1	Push(&s1, V_4)	1, 0, 0, 0
6	V_2				0	Pop(&s1, 1)	1, 0, 0, 1
7	V_2	V_3			1	Push(&s1, V_3)	1, 0, 0, 1
8	V_2				0	Pop(&s1, 1)	1, 0, 1, 1
9	V_2	V_2			1	Push(&s1, V_2)	1, 0, 1, 1
10	V_2				0	Pop(&s1, 1)	1, 1, 1, 1
11					–1	Pop(&s1, 0)	

Steps 1 and 2 in Table 6.9 do initialization of the process for DFS. In step 3, vertex v_1 is popped and **visited**[1] = 1. Adjacent vertices of V_1, which are V_2 and V_4, are pushed into the stack in steps 4 and 5. In the next step, V_4 is popped and **visited**[4] = 1. In step 7, adjacent vertex V_3 of V_4 is pushed to the stack. Another adjacent vertex of V_4, V_1, is not pushed to stack since **visited**[1] = 1. In step 8, V_3 is popped and the above process is repeated until the stack becomes empty.

Exercise 6.6

1. Apply DFS for the following graph.

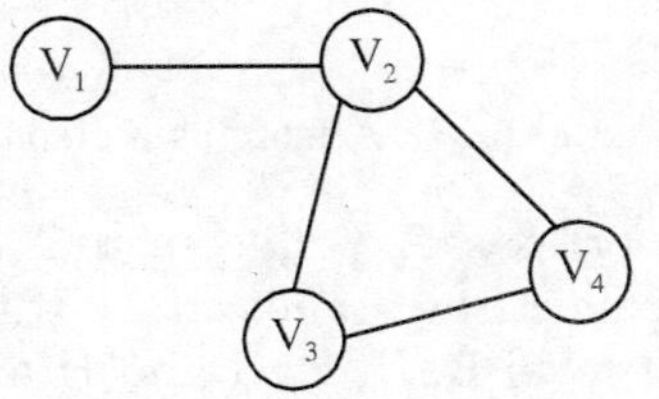

data[0]	data[1]	data[2]	data[3]	**top**	**Remarks**	**Visited**
				–1	Empty	0, 0, 0, 0
V_1				0	Push(& s1, V_1)	0, 0, 0, 0

6.5.3 Breadth First Search (BFS)

Consider the maze figure discussed in Section 6.5.1, which has precious stones in its vertices. Let us look into another method of traversing this graph to collect the stones and is illustrated in Figures 6.28, 6.29 and 6.30.

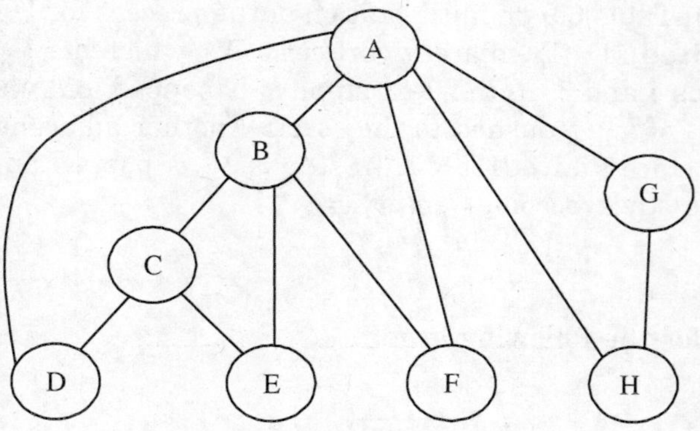

Figure 6.28 A maze as a graph.

Step 1: Suppose the starting vertex is A. Adjacent to A are the vertices B, D, F, G and H. Visit all these vertices and collect the stones. If we think A as in level 1, then at this step all the vertices in the next level B, D, F, G and H are visited. Among the vertices, choose any one, to go for the next level, say, B is selected. It is necessary to remember the remaining vertices since their process is not yet completed.

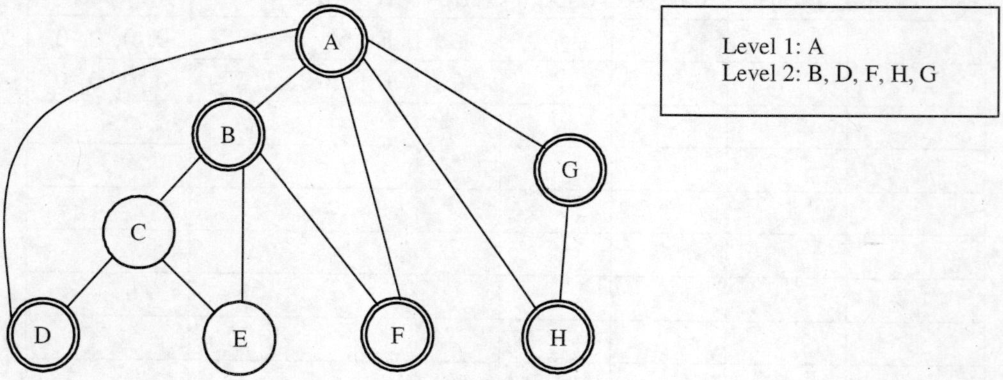

Figure 6.29 BFS—Step 1.

Step 2: The vertices adjacent to B are A, C, E and F. Among these, unvisited vertices are C and E. So, these are to be visited at this step to collect the stones. Now all the vertices have been visited and the process terminates.

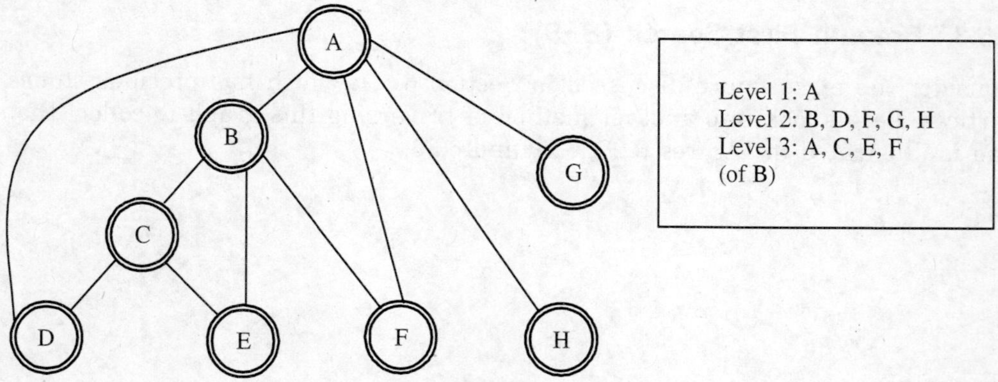

Figure 6.30 BFS—Step 2.

If there are any more unvisited vertices, then select vertex from level 2 and visit all its adjacent vertices. Only when all the vertices of level 2 have been considered, adjacent vertices of the vertex from the next level are to be considered for the process.

6.5.4 Implementation of Breadth First Search (BFS)

In breadth first search from the starting vertex, all its adjacent vertices are visited first before going to the next level. So, in this traversal data structure, the queue is used instead of the stack (as in DFS). In other words, it is necessary to remember the vertices as 'first in first out' because the nodes are processed levelwise (breadthwise or spread out) unlike DFS, where it is done depthwise.

Consider the graph given in Figure 6.31. It has four vertices. Let **visited** be an array of elements with all its value zero. Consider a queue q_1 with data field. Let the starting vertex chosen be V_1. Insert V_1 to the queue. Repeat the following processes until the queue becomes empty:

- Delete from the queue, say, vertex V.
- Change 0 to 1 in the array **visited** corresponding to position V.
- Insert the vertices adjacent to V (for the vertices whose value is 0 in the array **visited**).

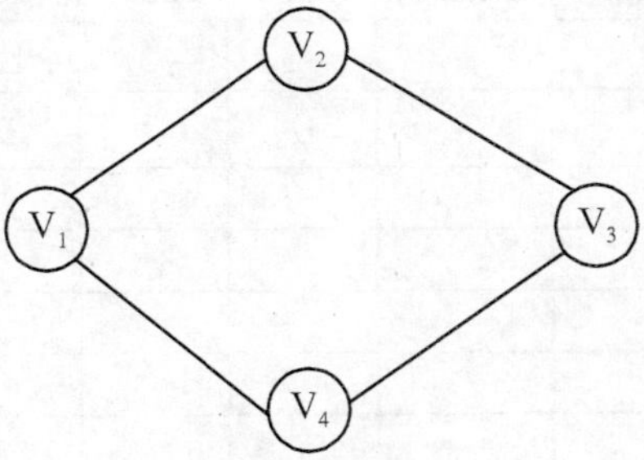

Figure 6.31 A graph.

The sequence of steps of this process is shown in Table 6.10.

Table 6.10 BFS using queue

Sl.No	data[0]	data[1]	data[2]	data[3]	front	rear	Remarks	Visited
1					–1	–1	Empty	0, 0, 0, 0
2	V_1				0	–1	Add(&q1, V_1)	0, 0, 0, 0
3					0	0	Delete(&q1)	1, 0, 0, 0
4		V_2			1	0	Add(&q1, V_2)	1, 0, 0, 0
5		V_2	V_4		2	0	Add(&q1, V_4)	1, 0, 0, 0
6			V_4		2	1	Delete(&q1)	1, 1, 0, 0
7			V_4	V_3	3	1	Add(&q1, V_3)	1, 1, 0, 0
8				V_3	3	2	Delete(&q1)	1, 1, 0, 1
9					3	3	Delete(&q1	1, 1, 1, 1

In steps 1 and 2, initialization process for BFS is done. In step 3, the element from the front of the queue, V_1, is deleted and **visited**[1] = 1. Adjacent vertices of V_1, V_2 and V_4 are inserted into the queue in steps 4 and 5. In step 6, the element from the front of queue, V_2 , is deleted and **visited**[2] = 1. Adjacent vertex of V_2 , whose value in visited is zero, is added to the queue in step 7. These steps are repeated until the queue becomes empty.

Exercise 6.7

Apply BFS for the following graph.

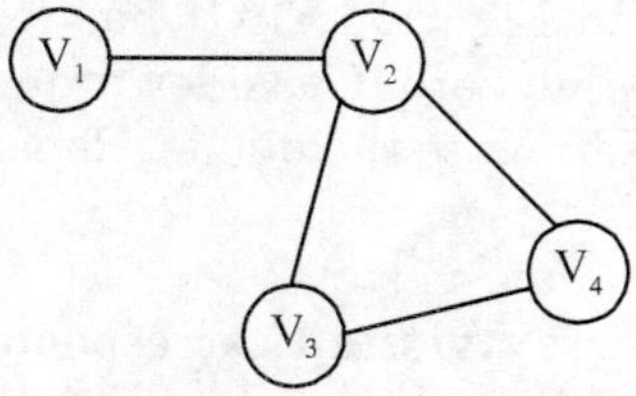

data[0]	data[1]	data[2]	data[3]	front	rear	Remarks	Visited
				–1	–1	Empty	0, 0, 0, 0
V_1				0	–1	Add(&q_1, V_1)	0, 0, 0, 0

6.5.5 Difference between DFS and BFS

1. Depth first search selects any one of the adjacent vertices as the start vertex. Then any one of its adjacent vertices is visited. When no further movement is possible, backtracking takes place to visit the unvisited adjacent vertices. In breadth first search, we first visit all the adjacent vertices of the start vertex and then visit all the unvisited vertices adjacent to these, and so on.
2. Depth first search wends its way through the graph, storing on the stack the points where other paths branch off. Breadth first search 'sweeps through' the graph, using a queue to remember the frontier of the visited places.
3. Depth first search 'explores' the graph by looking for a new vertex far away from the start point, taking closer vertices only when dead ends are encountered. Breadth first search completely covers the area close to the starting point, moving further away only when everything close has been looked at.

Chapter 7

Searching, Sorting and Files

7.1 INTRODUCTION

Searching and sorting are two topics that are discussed along with data structures. Both of them are interrelated and also related to data structures. When you have a collection of data and you want to know if a particular data is present in the collection, we need **searching**. When a collection of data is required to be ordered according to some criteria, we do **sorting**. Searching is easier if data is sorted. The ease of searching and sorting of data depends on the data structure used to store the data. We discuss a few methods for each in this chapter. After that, files are discussed.

7.2 SEARCHING

We have already indicated that the searching method will depend on (a) whether the data is kept sorted and (b) which structure is used to store data. We consider the array data structure under both sorted and unsorted conditions.

7.2.1 Linear Search

Consider an array with unsorted data. The following program (Program 7.1) reads the value of k (**key value**) and search for the key in the array.

Program 7.1

```
#include<stdio.h>
void main( )
{
    int k, i, result=0;
    int data[8]={23, 45, 67, 3, 56, 44, 94, 12}; //Unsorted
    printf("Type the value you would like to search\n");
    scanf("%d", &k);
    for(i=0; i<8; i++)
    {
        if(data[i]==k) {result=1; break;}
    }
    if(result==1) {printf("Search Successful");}
    else          {printf("Search Not Successful");}
}
```

The above search is known as a **linear search**. If we are lucky, in one comparison we can find the key (if it is the first element in the array). If the key is not in the array, the search result will be known only after eight comparisons are done. So, on an average, we need about four comparisons (1 + 8/2). If there is more data, the average number of comparison goes up proportionately. This kind of analysis about an algorithm is known as the analysis of **algorithm complexity**. We can make the following statements about the linear search algorithm (having 8 elements):

- The best case comparison is 1.
- The worst case comparison is 8.
- The average number of comparison is 4.
- The complexity is **O(n)** — this means, as the number of data increases, the number of comparison increases proportionately (Figure 7.1).

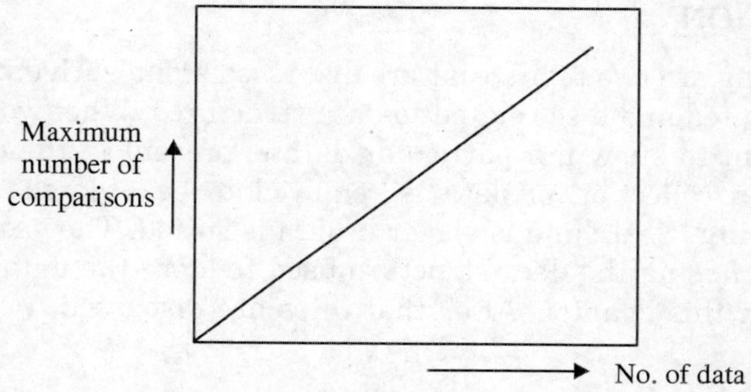

Figure 7.1 Time complexity graph.

Exercise 7.1

1. Write a program to declare and initialize an array of characters, then read the key value (character) and then search for the key and print out the result.
2. Write a program to declare and initialize an array of struct student{int id; int mark; char grade;}; and then read a key student id and search for the corresponding data and print out the result.

7.2.2 Binary Search

Suppose there is a set of sorted data and a key. It is required to search the key in the given sorted list. One way to do this is as follows:

Compare key with the value of the middle element of the list. Then there can arise one of the following three situations. In each case what action is to be taken is given as well.

- If key== middle value, Success, Stop
- If key <middle value, search Left half of data
- If key >middle value, search Right half of data

The above steps can be applied repeatedly to search very effectively. This is illustrated in Figures 7.2(a)–(c) for an int array {10, 24, 32, 46, 47, 67, 76, 79}; and key = 10.

KEY = 47

0	1	2	3	4	5	6	7	Left	Right	Mid	Remarks
10	24	32	**46**	47	67	76	79	0	7	3	data[mid]=46, not 47, look right
10	24	32	46	47	**67**	76	79	4	7	5	data[mid]=67, not 47, look left
10	24	32	46	**47**	67	76	79	4	4	4	data[mid]=47, equal to 47 ☺

Figure 7.2(a) Binary search – An example with key value 47.

KEY = 10

0	1	2	3	4	5	6	7	Left	Right	Mid	Remarks
10	24	32	**46**	47	67	76	79	0	7	3	data[mid]=46, not 10, look left
10	**24**	32	46	47	67	76	79	0	2	1	data[mid]=24, not 10, look left
10	24	32	46	47	67	76	79	0	0	0	data[mid]=10, equal to10 ☺

Figure 7.2(b) Binary search – An example with key value 10.

KEY = 48

0	1	2	3	4	5	6	7	Left	Right	Mid	Remarks
10	24	32	**46**	47	67	76	79	0	7	3	data[mid]=46, not 47, look right
10	24	32	46	47	**67**	76	79	4	7	5	data[mid]=67, not 47, look left
10	24	32	46	**47**	67	76	79	4	4	4	data[mid]=47, not 47 ☹

Figure 7.2(c) Binary search – An example with key value 48.

Notes: 1. You need maximum of three searches only whatever be the value of the key. When left==right, the search is over.

Exercise 7.2

1. Fill up the following table using the Binary Search method, for key values specified:

(a) KEY = 77

0	1	2	3	4	5	6	7	Left	Right	Mid	Remarks
10	24	32	46	47	67	76	79	0	7	3	
10	24	32	46	47	67	76	79				
10	24	32	46	47	67	76	79				

(b) KEY = 33

0	1	2	3	4	5	6	7	Left	Right	Mid	Remarks
10	24	32	46	47	67	76	79	0	7	3	
10	24	32	46	47	67	76	79				
10	24	32	46	47	67	76	79				

(c) KEY = 77

0	1	2	3	4	5	6	7	Left	Right	Mid	Remarks
10	24	32	46	47	67	76	79	0	7	3	
10	24	32	46	47	67	76	79				
10	24	32	46	47	67	76	79				

(d) KEY = 95

0	1	2	3	4	5	6	7	8	9	10	11	12	13	14	15	Left	Right	Mid	Remarks
11	34	36	40	49	53	58	71	72	73	80	85	91	96	97	99				

(e) KEY = 58

0	1	2	3	4	5	6	7	8	9	10	11	12	13	14	15	Left	Right	Mid	Remarks
11	34	36	40	49	53	58	71	72	73	80	85	91	96	97	99				

(f) KEY = 40

0	1	2	3	4	5	6	7	8	9	10	11	12	13	14	15	Left	Right	Mid	Remarks
11	34	36	40	49	53	58	71	72	73	80	85	91	96	97	99				

7.2.3 Implementation of Binary Search

Here is a program which implements the Binary Search method described in Section 7.2.2. Please note that this will work only if we start with the data whose total number is a power of two (like 1, 2, 4,8, 16, 32, 64, 128, 256, etc.) If the number of data is not a power of two, we need to add some dummy values to make it so. See the following example: (Program 7.2).

Program 7.2

```
#include <stdio.h>
void main( )
{
    int left, right, mid, k, i, result=0;
    int data[8]={10, 24, 32, 46, 47, 67, 76, 79};
```

```
    printf("Type the value you would like to search\n");
    scanf("%d", &k);
    left=0;  right=7;
    while(left<=right)
    {
        mid=(left+right)/2;
        if(k==data[mid]) {result=1;  break;}
        if(k>data[mid])  {left=mid+1;}  else  {right=mid-1;}
    }
    if(result==1) {printf("Search Successful");}
    else          {printf("Search Not Successful");}
}
```

(i) Data: {2, 3, 4, 34, 45, 78, 90, **<u>90</u>**} 8 data, with 1 dummy OR
(ii) Data: {**<u>0</u>,** 2, 3, 4, 34, 45, 78, 90} 8 data, with 1 dummy

This search technique is known as a **binary search**. If we are lucky, in one comparison we can find the key (if it is the middle element in the array). If the key is not in the array, the search result will be known only after four comparisons are done. So, on an average, we need about two comparisons (1 + 4/2). If there are more data, the average number of comparison goes up only as **$\log_2(n)$**. We can make the following statements about the linear search algorithm (having 8 elements):

- The best case comparison is 1.
- The worst case comparison is 4.
- The average number of comparison is 2.
- The complexity is **$O(\log_2(n))$** — this means, as the number of data increases, the number of comparison increases only **$\log_2(n)$** times. If n=8, comparisons=3, if n=16, comparisons=4, if n=32, comparison=5, and so on. So, we see that **if the data doubles, only one extra comparison is required** (Figure 7.3).

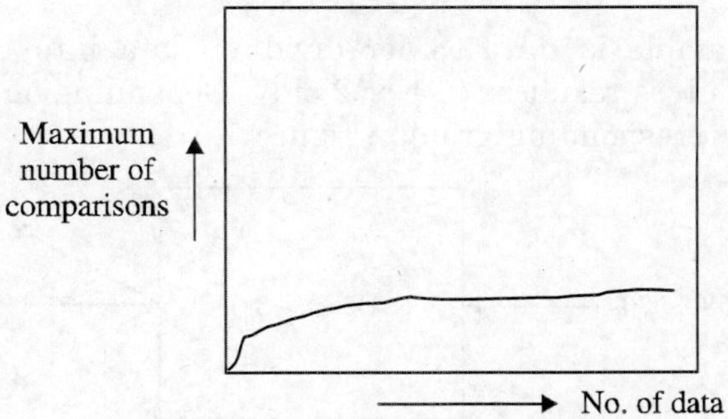

Figure 7.3 Time complexity Graph.

You may note that had the data been entered into a **binary search tree,** we could use the recursive search procedure described in Section 5.4 to search for the data.

Exercise 7.3

1. Write a program to declare an array of characters and initialize it with sorted characters. Then read a key value (character) and search for the key and print out the result.
2. Write a program to declare and initialize an array of struct student {int id; int mark; char grade;}; with sorted student data (based on id). Then read a key student id and search for the corresponding data and print out the result.
3. Rewrite the binary search program using recursion.

7.3 HASHING FOR IMPROVING SEARCH

Even when the data to be searched is unsorted, it can be organized in a better way to reduce the search time. In a college, if the result slip of every student is kept sorted, the search can be very efficient. However, even if sorting is not used, we can still improve the situation. If the result slip of each class (intake) is kept separately as a group, then we need to search only within those groups. If a set of data is divided into **n** groups, the search time would come down to **1/n**. In computer terminology, each such group is known as a **bucket**. Dividing a set of data into different groups (buckets) is known as **hashing**. Whereas result slips, etc. can be easily grouped, raw data need some procedure for grouping. We use hashing functions for this (Figure 7.4).

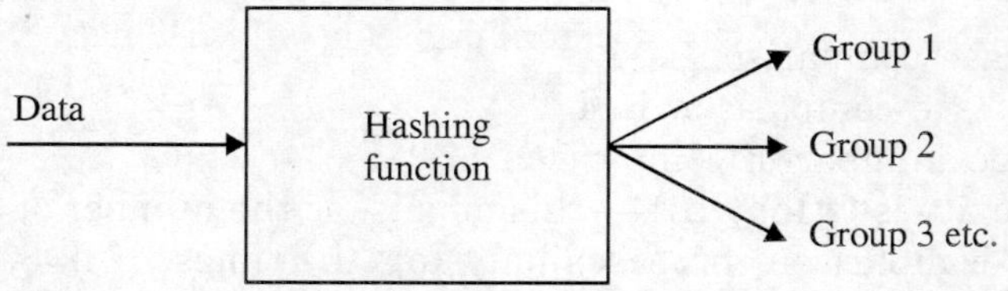

Figure 7.4 Hashing function.

Different hashing functions can be used for grouping.

1. A simple example is **data%3** for dividing data into three groups. Modulo division by 3 gives result as 0, 1 or 2 only. Depending on this value, we assign data to the corresponding group, (Figure 7.5).

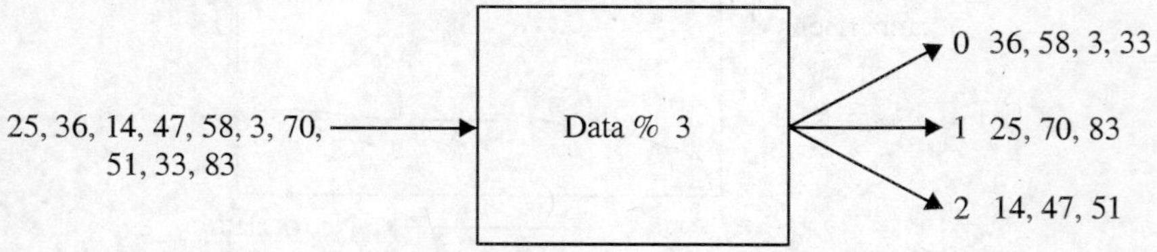

Figure 7.5 Illustration of hashing function.

When you need to search, we apply the same hashing function on the key and search only one group. For example, in the above case, if we need to search for the key 59, we search only bucket 1 (since 59%3=1). Only three comparisons are required, as opposed to maximum of ten if we had not used hashing. Here are some other hash functions that can be used.

2. **Selecting digits:** Depending on the first digit of the data, it can be assigned to a bucket. 0–9 buckets if each digit is used for each bucket. We can also modify this for, say, two buckets. If the first digit is 0–4, we can assign bucket 0, else bucket 1
3. **Folding digits:** Digits of the data can be added together to decide the bucket. For data 347, we calculate 3+4+7=14 ->1+4=5, indicating bucket 5 for the data. We can further apply modulo division to modify the hashing function.

Exercise 7.4

1. For each of the following hash functions and data sets, specify: (i) the number of buckets and (ii) the data in each bucket:
   (a) Hashing function= Data%4, Data = 34, 54, 12, 78, 90, 125, 46, 79, 678, 32, 77, 67, 89, 4, 44.
   (b) Hashing function= Data%2, Data = 34, 54, 12, 78, 90, 125, 46, 79, 678, 32, 77, 67, 89, 4, 44.
   (c) Hashing function= (Sum of digits of data) %3, Data = 34, 54, 12, 78, 90, 125, 46, 79, 678, 32, 77, 67, 89, 4, 44.
   (d) Hashing function= (First digit + Last digit of data) %4, Data = 34, 54, 12, 78, 90, 125, 46, 79, 678, 32, 77, 67, 89, 4, 44.
2. With the linear search for the data used in question 1 above, a maximum of fifteen comparisons are required since there are fifteen data. For each hashing function, find the number of comparisons required for searching the following keys: (a) 44, (b) 678, and (c) 125.

7.3.1 Implementation of Hashing Functions

Here is a program which uses the hashing function **data%3** to group data into three buckets and then reads a key and searches for it. For the sake of clarity, the efficiency of the program has been ignored. Also, it is easier to use an array of pointers than a two-dimensional array.

Program 7.3

```
#include<stdio.h>
void main( )
{   int data[15]={24, 110, 27, 60, 46, 47, 17, 16, 79, 54, 11, 44,
    55, 1, 7};
    int bucket[3][15];
    int i,k, pos0=0, pos1=0, pos2=0, result, group;
    for(i=0;i<15;i++)
    {   group=data[i]%3;
        switch(group)
        {   case 0: bucket[group][pos0++]=data[i]; break;
            case 1: bucket[group][pos1++]=data[i]; break;
            case 2: bucket[group][pos2++]=data[i]; break;
        }
    }
```

```
    printf("Enter value to search\n");
    scanf("%d", &k);
    group=k%3;
    result=0;
    switch(group)
    {   case 0:  for(i=0;i<pos0;i++)
            {   if  (bucket[group][i]==k)
                {   result=1; break;
                }
            }
            break;
        case 1:  for(i=0;i<pos1;i++)
                {   if  (bucket[group][i]==k)
                    {   result=1; break;
                    }
                }
            break;
        case 2:  for(i=0;i<pos2;i++)
                    {   if  (bucket[group][i]==k)
                        { result=1; break;
                        }
                    }
                break;
            }
        if  (result==0)
                printf("Search Not Successful");
        else
                printf("Search Successful");
    }
```

7.4 SORTING

We have already seen why we need to sort data. Searching can be efficiently done only if sorted data is available. For sorting again, data structure is crucial. We have seen that a binary search tree can contain data which, when traversed **in-order**, will be in sorted order. Let us now assume that unsorted data is already available in an array and that we want to sort it. Let us further assume that we want to do the sorting without using another temporary array. This is called **in-place sorting**.

We discuss some sort methods in the following section. Sorting can be in ascending or descending order. We consider only sorting in descending order here. It is a trivial effort to modify the program for descending order.

7.4.1 Selection Sort (Insertion Sort)

Selection sort works by first finding the biggest element in the array and then placing it in the first position. What is already in the first position will be moved to the position of the biggest. This is, then, repeated for the array starting from 2nd position, 3rd position, etc. Let us try to understand the sorting method step by step.

Finding biggest element of the array: Look at the following program (Program 7.4). It declares an array data[10] and finds out the biggest element.

Program 7.4

```
#include<stdio.h>
main( )
{
    int a[10]= {34, 56, 26, 11, 89, 32, 55, 90, 11, 88};
    int i, big;
    for (i=0; i<10; i++)
            {
                if(data[i] >big)
                {
                    big=data[i];
                }
            }
    printf("Biggest Element=%d\n", big);
}
The output of the above program will be Biggest Element=90
```

Exercise 7.5

1. Write a program to declare an array of characters and initialize it with characters of the word "Monica Levinsky" and print out the biggest character (sorry for the pun!). Please recall that characters are small integers (their ASCII codes) and can be compared just like integers.
2. Write a program to declare and initialize an array of struct student{int id; int mark; char grade;}; and then print out the id, mark and grade of the student with maximum marks.

7.4.1.1 Finding position of biggest element of the array

Look at the following program (Program 7.5). It declares an array data[10] and finds out the position of the biggest element.

Program 7.5

```
# include <stdio.h>
main( )
{
int a[10]= {34, 56, 26, 11, 89, 32, 55, 90, 11, 88};
int i, big, bigposition;
big=0;
for (i=0; i<10; i++)
        {
            if(data[i] >big) {big=data[i]; bigposition=i;}
        }
printf("Biggest Element is in position=%d\n", bigposition);
}
The output of the above program will be Biggest Element
is in position=7
```

Exercise 7.6

1. Write a program to declare an array of characters and initialize it with characters of the word "Green Earth" and print out the position(index) of the biggest character. Please recall that characters are small integers (their ASCII codes) and can be compared just like integers.
2. Write a program to declare and initialize an array of struct student{int id; int mark; char grade;}; and then print out the index of the student with maximum marks.

7.4.1.2 Exchanging biggest element with first element

Look at the following program (Program 7.6). It declares an array data[10] and finds out the position of the biggest element and exchanges it with the first element.

Program 7.6

```
#include<stdio.h>
main( )
{   int  a[10]= {34,  56,  26,  11,  89,  32,  55,  90,  11,  88};
    int  i,  big,  bigposition;
    big=0;
    for  (i=0;  i<10;  i++)
    {    if(data[i]  >big)
         {    big=data[i];  bigposition=i;
         }
    }
    data[bigposition]=data[0];
    data[0]=big;
}
```

Exercise 7.7

1. Write a program to declare an array of characters and initialize it with characters of the word "Green Earth" and exchange the biggest character with the first character. Please recall that characters are small integers (their ASCII codes) and can be compared just like integers.
2. Write a program to declare and initialize an array of struct student{int id; int mark; char grade;}; and then exchange the data of the student with maximum marks with that of the first data.

7.4.1.3 Combining Program 7.4, 7.5, 7.6 program

We will now put together the knowledge of the Programs 7.4, 7.5, 7.6 to implement selection sort. Program 7.7 is the complete program. The program's working is explained in Table 7.1.

Table 7.1 Illustration of selection sort

Find biggest in positions 0 – 9	Exchange biggest with position 0
Find biggest in positions 1 – 9	Exchange biggest with position 1
Find biggest in positions 2 – 9	Exchange biggest with position 2
Find biggest in positions 3 – 9	Exchange biggest with position 3
Find biggest in positions 4 – 9	Exchange biggest with position 4
Find biggest in positions 5 – 9	Exchange biggest with position 5
Find biggest in positions 6 – 9	Exchange biggest with position 6
Find biggest in positions 7 – 9	Exchange biggest with position 7
Find biggest in positions 8 – 9	Exchange biggest with position 8
By now, the last data will be in the correct position	

Program 7.7

```
#include<stdio.h>
main( )
{   int data[10]= {34, 56, 26, 11, 89, 32, 55, 90, 13, 88};
    int i, j, big, bigposition;
    for(i=0; i<=8; i++)
    {       big=0;
            for(j=i; j<=9; j++)
        {       if(data[j] >big)
            {       big=data[j]; bigposition=j;
            }
        }
        data[bigposition]=data[i];
        data[i]=big;
    }
    printf("Array in sorted order is:\n");
    for(i=0; i<10; i++)
        printf("%d ", data[i]);
}
```

The result of the program will be: Array in sorted order is: 90 89 88 56 55 34 32 26 13 11

The different steps of the program are related in Table 7.2

Table 7.2 Illustration of selection sort program

a[0]	a[1]	a[2]	a[3]	a[4]	a[5]	a[6]	a[7]	a[8]	a[9]	Remarks
34	56	26	11	89	32	55	90	13	88	Exchange 0 and 7
90	56	26	11	89	32	55	34	13	88	Exchange 1 and 4
90	89	26	11	56	32	55	34	13	88	Exchange 2 and 9
90	89	88	11	56	32	55	34	13	26	Exchange 3 and 4
90	89	88	56	11	32	55	34	13	26	Exchange 4 and 6
90	89	88	56	55	32	11	34	13	26	Exchange 4 and 6
90	89	88	56	55	34	11	32	13	26	Exchange 5 and 7
90	89	88	56	55	34	32	11	13	26	Exchange 6 and 7
90	89	88	56	55	34	32	26	13	11	Exchange 7 and 9

Exercise 7.8

1. Write a program to declare an array of characters and initialize it with characters of the word "Green Earth" and then sort it using selection sort. Please recall that characters are small integers (their ASCII codes) and can be compared just like integers.
2. Write a program to declare and initialize an array of struct student{int id, int mark, char grade}; and then sort it using selection sort.
3. Rewrite the selection sort for integers to sort in ascending order.

7.4.2 Bubble Sort (Exchange Sort)

Bubble sort works by comparing two adjacent elements at a time, and exchanging them if necessary. In each iteration, the biggest value will have *bubbled up* to the end of the array. Table 7.3 shows one iteration of the algorithm:

Table 7.3 One iteration of bubble sort algorithm

21	21									21
34	34	16								16
16		34	25							25
25			34	11						11
11				34	34					34
89					89	35				35
35						89	78			78
78							89	12		12
12								89	9	9
9									89	**89**

Unlike in selection sort, where we need to complete the process even if the array is sorted in one or two iterations, in bubble sort it is easy to detect an early completion of sorting. We use a variable **ready** to check this. If the value of **ready** is 1 in any iteration, this is taken as an indication that the array has been sorted. You may study this program 7.8 by printing out **i** inside the loop and changing the data to nearly sorted values. Then you can see the advantage of bubble sort.

Program 7.8

```
# include<stdio.h>
main( )
{
    int data[10]= {34, 56, 26, 11, 89, 32, 55, 90, 13, 88};
    int i, j, temp, ready;
    for (i=0; i<=8; i++)
    {
        ready=1;
        for (j=0; j<=8-i; j++)
        {
            if( data[j]> data[j+1])
            {
                temp= data[j];
                data[j]=data[j+1];
                data[j+1]=temp;
                ready=0;
            }
        }
        if(ready==1)
            break;
}
printf("The array elements after sorting:");
for (i=0;i<10;i++
         printf("%d\n ",a[i]);
}
```

Exercise 7.9

1. Write a program to declare an array of characters and initialize it with characters of the word "Green Earth" and then sort it using bubble sort. Please recall that characters are small integers (their ASCII codes) and can be compared just like integers.
2. Write a program to declare and initialize an array of struct student{int id, int mark, char grade}; and then sort it using Bubble sort.
3. Rewrite the bubble sort program for integers to sort in ascending order.
4. Complete the remaining tables similar to Table 7.3 for the same data.

7.4.3 Shuttle Sort

Consider an array A with n elements. The shuttle sort method requires n-1 passes. In the first pass, the first & zeroth elements are compared. If the elements are not in order (ascending or descending as required) then an exchange will take place. In the second pass starting from the second element, the comparison is done backwards till the zeroth element is reached. That is, the comparison is between the second and the first and between the first and zeroth element. So by the time *i*th pass reached, the elements from zero to i-1 are sorted. The process is repeated till the end of the array is reached. Table 7.4 shows the implementation of the method on a set of elements.

Table 7.4 Illustration of bubble sort program

a[0]	a[1]	a[2]	a[3]	a[4]	a[5]	Comparison		Remarks
						From	To	Initial array
15	8	17	12	38	19	1	0	Compare 1, 0
8	15	17	12	38	19	2	0	Compare 2, 1 and 1, 0
8	15	17	12	38	19	3	0	Compare 3, 2
8	15	12	17	38	19			Compare 2, 1
8	12	15	17	38	19			Compare 1, 0
8	12	15	17	38	19	4	0	Compare 4, 3 & 3, 2, 2, 1 & 1, 0
8	12	15	17	19	38	5	0	Compare 5, 4 & 4, 3 & 3, 2 & 2, 1 & 1, 0

Exercise 7.10

1. Write a program for the shuttle sort method.
2. For the following given set of elements, create tables similar to Table 7.4 using the shuttle sort method.
   (a) 7, 95, 36, 40, 17, 25
   (b) 29, 25, 38, 7, 45, 16, 28
   (c) 67, 18, 9, 17, 99

7.4.4 Shell Sort

In shell sort, the whole list of elements are divided into sub list. In each sub list shuttle sort is applied. The division of the list into sub list is done by means of a number called increment. This process of partitioning is repeated for lesser values of increment. The following program (Program 7.9) gives implementation of the shell sort method.

Program 7.9

```
# include<stdio.h>
void shellsort(int[]);
void main()
{
```

```
    int arr[10]= {34, 56, 26, 11, 89, 32, 55, 90, 13, 88};
    int i;
    shellsort(arr);
    printf("\nAfter sorting ");
    for(i=0;i<10;i++)
        printf("\n%d",arr[i]);
}
/*   DEFINITION OF SHELLSORT FUNCTION*/
void shellsort(int arr[])
{
    int i,j,k,l;
    int temp;
        for(l=10/2;l>0;l/=2)
    {   for(j=l;j<10;j++)
        {   for(i=j-l;i>=0;i-=l)
            {   if(arr[i+l]>=arr[i])
                            break;
        else
        {
            temp=arr[i];
            arr[i]=arr[i+l];
            arr[i+l]=temp;

                }
            }
        }
    }
}
```

Shell sort is efficient when compared with insertion sort. Figure 7.6(a) – 7.6(e) gives an example of the implementation of the shell sort method. In this example, at the first step, increment is taken as 5, in the second step, the increment is taken as 3, and in the third step the increment is taken as 1.

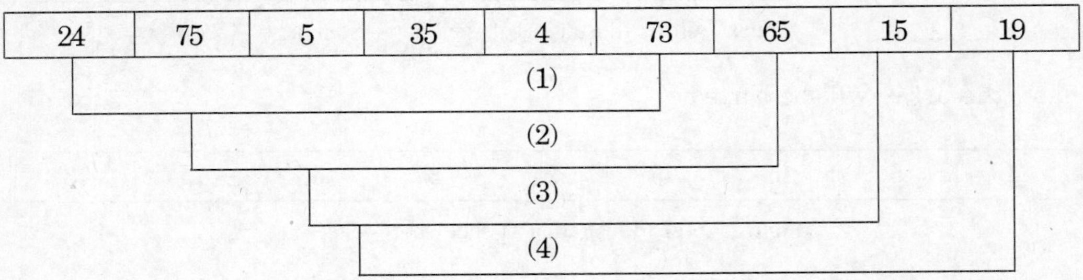

Figure 7.6(a) Illustration of shell sort—Step 1.

(1) 1st sub list is 24, 73. On applying shuttle sort the sorted elements are 24, 73.
(2) 2nd sub list is 75, 65. On applying shuttle sort the sorted elements are 65, 75.
(3) 3rd sub list is 5, 15. On applying shuttle sort the sorted elements are 5, 15.
(4) 4th sub list is 35, 19. On applying shuttle sort the sorted elements are 19, 35.

After comparing, the array will be changed to as follows.

24	65	5	19	4	73	75	15	35

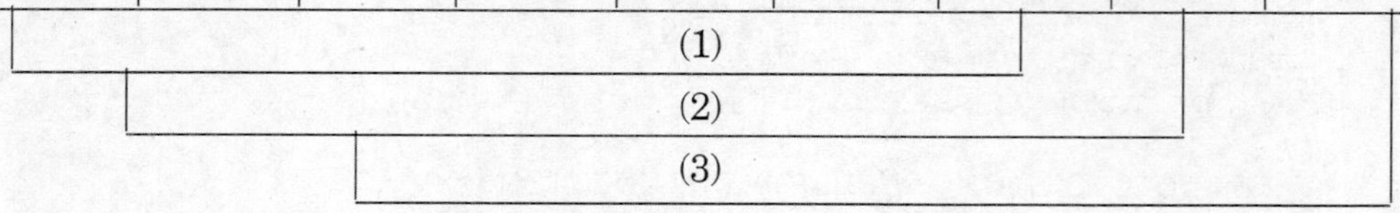

Figure 7.6(b) Illustration of shell sort—Step 2.

(1) 1st sub list is 24, 19, 75. On applying shuttle sort the sorted elements are 19, 24, 75.
(2) 2nd sub list is 65, 4, 15. On applying shuttle sort the sorted elements are 4, 15, 65.
(3) 3rd sub list is 5, 73, 35. On applying shuttle sort the sorted elements are 5, 35, 73.

After comparing, the array will be changed to as follows.

19	4	5	24	15	35	75	65	73

Figure 7.6(c) Illustration of shell sort—Step 3.

Applying shuttle sort, the array becomes as follows.

19	4	5	24	15	35	75	65	73

4	19	5	24	15	35	75	65	73

4	5	19	24	15	35	75	65	73

4	5	15	19	24	35	75	65	73

4	5	15	19	24	35	65	75	73

Figure 7.6(d) Illustration of shell sort—Step 4.

At last, the array will be sorted.

4	5	15	19	24	35	65	75	73

Figure 7.6(e) Illustration of shell short—Step 5.

7.4.5 Quick Sort

Quick sort is also known as **partition exchange sort**. Consider an array A with n elements is to be sorted. In quick sort method, a control element is needed which plays an important role in this sorting method. Any element of the array can be considered the control element. Let us suppose that the control element cl=A[1]. The array A will be split in such a way that A[1:r-1] will contain all elements smaller than cl and A[r+1:n] will contain all elements greater than cl. After this splitting process the control element cl will be placed at its proper position with respect to the entire array. The next step is to sort the two sub arrays. The above mentioned procedure is to be repeated for the two sub arrays. Program 7.10 gives the implementation of the quick method. In the next sub section, an example is given which illustrates the working of the quick sort method.

Program 7.10

```
#include "stdio.h"
#include "conio.h"
void qsort(int [],int,int);
int partition (int[],int,int);
void main()
{
    int arr[10]= {34, 56, 26, 11, 89, 32, 55, 90, 13, 88};
    int n,i,upper=9;
    clrscr();
    qsort(arr,0,upper);
    for(i=0;i<10;i++)
        printf("\n%d",arr[i]);
}
void qsort(int arr[],int lower,int upper) /* Definition Of Qsort */
{
    int i;
    if(upper>lower)
    {
        i=partition(arr,lower,upper);
        qsort(arr,lower,i-1);
        qsort(arr,i+1,upper);
    }
}
int partition(int arr[],int lower,int upper) /* Definition Of
Partition Function*/
{
    int piv,l,u,t;
    l=lower;
    u=upper+1;
    piv=arr[lower];
    while(u>=l)
    {
        while(arr[++l]<piv);
        while(arr[—u]>piv);
        if(u>l)
        { t=arr[l];
          arr[l]=arr[u];
          arr[u]=t;
```

```
        }
    }
    t=arr[lower];
    arr[lower]=arr[u];
    arr[u]=t;
    return u;
}
```

7.4.5.1 Analysis of quick sort

Let **A** be an array of five elements, which is to be sorted. Select an element from the array as control element(piv). Let **piv=A[1]**.

25	**46**	**80**	**9**	**48**

Figure 7.7(a) Illustration of quick sort—Step 1.

It is required to partition this array by placing the control element at the proper position. Consider two indices **up** and **down** where up indicates A[1] and **down** indicates A[n] initially. The **up** index moves forward till it finds an element larger than the control element. The **down** index moves downward till it finds an element smaller than the control element. When such elements are found, an exchange takes place. This step terminates when **down** crosses **up** or vice versa.

Piv=A[down] thus **piv = 25**

There are two pointers **up** and **down**. **Up** will be incremented only if the element of the array **<=piv**, **down** gets incremented only if the element of array is **>piv.**

Piv, down ⇓				up ⇓
25	46	80	9	48

Figure 7.7(b) Illustration of quick sort—Step 2.

Here **piv** is equal to **A[down]**, so down moves forward and **piv** is **> A[down]**. Since A[up]=48, up will move backward.

Piv ⇓	down ⇓		up ⇓	
25	46	80	9	48

Figure 7.7(c) Illustration of quick sort—Step 3.

Here **piv is not < A[down]** and **piv is not >=A[up]**, so no further movement takes place. Thus, it exchanges the value of **up** and **down**.

Piv ⇓	down ⇓		up ⇓	
25	9	80	46	48

Figure 7.7(d) Illustration of quick sort—Step 4.

Again, **down** will move forward and **up** will move backward.

Piv ⇓	up ⇓	down ⇓		
25	9	80	46	48

Figure 7.7(e) Illustration of quick sort—Step 5.

Now **up** crosses **down** and so an exchange of the values of piv and A[up] takes place.

Piv ⇓	up ⇓	down ⇓		
9	25	80	46	48

Figure 7.7(f) Illustration of quick sort—Step 6.

Now the array is split into two parts logically. Again the above process is applied with the **upper bound** and **lower bound** of these two logical parts till **down>up**.

In this case, the first sub array is A[1:1] and the second sub array is A[3:5]. When the above method is applied to A[1:1], it is a sorted array since there is only one element. Now consider the sub array A[3:5]. Let the control element **Piv=A[3]=80**. The following figures show the movement of **up** and **down** indices.

		Piv, down ⇓		up ⇓
9	25	80	46	48

Figure 7.7(g) Illustration of quick sort—Step 7.

		Piv ⇓		down, up ⇓
9	25	80	46	48

Figure 7.7(h) Illustration of quick sort—Step 8.

		Piv ⇓		down, up ⇓
9	25	48	46	80

Figure 7.7(i) Illustration of quick sort—Step 9.

Now the control element 80 has been fixed. There is only one sub array since the control element just fixed occupies the last position. The new sub array is A[3:4]. The control element **Piv** is 48. The following figure shows the sequence of steps that takes place next.

		Piv, down ⇓	up ⇓	
9	25	48	46	80

Figure 7.7(j) Illustration of quick sort—Step 10.

In this case, we interchange the values of **piv and up**.

		Piv, up ⇓	down ⇓	
9	25	48	46	80

Figure 7.7(k) Illustration of quick sort—Step 11.

Thus, the array is sorted.

9	25	46	48	80

Figure 7.7(l) Illustration of quick sort—Step 12.

Exercise 7.11

1. Apply the quick sort process to the following set of elements:

   (a) 25, 7, 95, 4, 1
   (b) 13, 12, 19, 18, 17, 16
   (c) 1, 2, 3, 4, 5, 6

In each case, do the problem using at least two different control elements.

7.4.6 Merge Sort

Consider a shop with four branches. Each branch sends to the head office a sorted list in descending order of the sales of items each month. At the main office, these four sorted lists have to be combined to get the exact picture. The operation of combining two or more sorted lists into a single sorted lists is known as *merge sort*.

The steps required for the merge sorting method are as follows:

1. An array (not sorted) is the input of the problem.
2. The array is broken into two at the middle.
3. Using recursive operation, each part of the array is sorted. The breaking process continues until a single element is reached. Single element is a sorted one.
4. Once the initial broken arrays are sorted, they are combined.
   Program 7.11 gives the implementation of the above algorithm. It is a recursive procedure.

Program 7.11

```
# include<stdio.h>
# include<conio.h>
void main()
{ int a[8]= {26, 30, 17, 15, 20, 36, 21, 8};
  int i;
  clrscr();
  mer(a, 0, 7);
  for(i=0;i<8;i++)
      printf("\n%d",a[i]);
}
mer(int a[ ], int l, int h)
{
  int mid;
  mid=(l+h)/2;
  if (l<h)
  {
      mer(a, l, mid);
      mer(a, mid+1, h);
      merge(l, mid, h, a);
  }
  return;
}
merge(int l, int m, int h, int s[])
{
  int a, b, c, d, f[20];
  a=l;
  b=l;
  c=m+1;
  while(a<=m && c<=h)
  {
  if(s[a]<=s[c])
      f[b++]=s[a++];
  else
      f[b++]=s[c++];
  }
/*if (a<m)*/
  for(d=c;d<=h;d++)
      f[b++]=s[d];
/*else*/
  for(d=a;d<=m;d++)
      f[b++]=s[d];
  for(a=I;a<=h;a++)
      s[a]=f[a];
}
```

Let us consider an example, to see how the program works (Table 7.5).

Table 7.5 Illustration of merge sort program

a[0]	a[1]	a[2]	a[3]	a[4]	a[5]	a[6]	a[7]	Action
26	30	17	15	20	36	21	8	Initial array
26	30	17	15	20	36	21	8	Split after 4th element
26	30	17	15	20	36	21	8	Split after 2nd element
26	30	17	15	20	36	21	8	Split after 1st element
26	30	17	15	20	36	21	8	Merge 1st and 2nd elements
26	30	17	15	20	36	21	8	Split after 3rd element
26	30	15	17	20	36	21	8	Merge 3rd and 4th elements
15	17	26	30	20	36	21	8	Merge first four elements
15	17	26	30	20	36	21	8	Split after 6th element
15	17	26	30	20	36	21	8	Split after 5th element
15	17	26	30	20	36	21	8	Merge 5th and 6th elements
15	17	26	30	20	36	21	8	Split after 7th element
15	17	26	30	20	36	8	21	Merge 7th and 8th elements
15	17	26	30	8	20	21	36	Merge last four elements
8	15	17	20	21	26	30	36	Merge the two halves

Exercise 7.12

1. Implement the Program 7.11 without using the recursive method.
2. For the following set of data find out how the program works.
   (a) 30, 28, 65, 71, 26
   (b) 29, 90, 25, 80
   (c) 10, 25, 28, 46, 55, 5, 2

7.5 FILES

Data stored in the disks (or other secondary storage such as CDs, VCDs, and Tape, etc. under unique names are called **files**. There are many types of files. Simplest of them, **text files** is already familiar to you (through C Primer). These are files which can be opened and read with plain editors such as Notepad. There is another class of files, known as **binary files**, which are very powerful. We quickly revise text files before discussing binary files.

7.6 PROCESSING TEXT FILES

Every file has an associated **file pointer**. The file pointers are declared and associated with disk filenames as shown below:

```
FILE *fp;
fp=fopen("address.txt", "r");
```

FILE *fp is a declaration of file pointer named fp in this example. FILE is a data type created specially for handling files. **fopen**("address.txt", "r") opens the file in the disk with the name "address.txt" for reading, indicated by "r". For writing, we use "w", and for both operations we use "rw". The function returns a file pointer which is stored in **fp**. We must have a file pointer declaration and **fopen** statement for each file used in a program.

7.6.1 fscanf Function

We are familiar with **scanf** statement for reading from the keyboard. We have a similar statement for reading from files. It requests the file pointer to be included as an argument, as in the example below (x is a char variable):

fscanf(fp, "%c", &x);

This statement is to read the value of x from the file (indicated by the file pointer fp), using %c format (since we are considering only text files now, only %c format is applicable). Since we may usually have many characters inside files, we need to read repeatedly. For this, we need the help of another function — **feof( )**. **feof (fp)** will return 1 (true) or 0(false), depending on whether the end of the file referred to by file pointer **fp** has been reached. Now that we know how to use **fscanf** and **feof** functions, we proceed to write a program (Program 7.12) that reads the contents of the file "address.txt" and displays it on the screen.

Program 7.12

```
# include<stdio.h>
main ( )
{
    FILE *fp;
    char x;
    fp= fopen("address.txt", "r");
    do
{
        fscanf(fp, "%c", &x);
        printf("%c", x);
}while (feof(fp)==F);
}
```

When this program is run, it will display the contents of the "address.txt" file on the screen. Now you have a way to read files without the help of editors like Notepad! You may give the name of any file of your choice and rerun the program.

We can make small modifications to the body of the **while** loop to achieve many different things. Consider the following program (Program 7.13), which shows the count of the characters in the file after displaying it.

Program 7.13

```
# include<stdio.h>
main ( )
{
    FILE *fp;
    char x;
    int count;
    fp= fopen("address.txt", "r");
    count=0;
    do
    {
        fscanf(fp, "%c", &x);
        printf("%c", x);
        count++;
    }while (feof(fp)==F);
}
    printf("\n Your file had %d characters in it\n", count);
```

The following program displays the file, but all in capital letters:

```
# include<stdio.h>
main ( )
{
    FILE *fp;
    char x;
    fp= fopen("address.txt", "r");
    do
    {
        fscanf(fp, "%c", &x);
        if ((x >= 'a') && (x<= 'z'))
            printf("%c", x-32);
        else
            printf("%c", x);
    }while (feof(fp)==F);
}
```

Note: Recall the ASCII codes of capital letters are different from the small letters by 32. Refer to the Appendix for ASCII table.

Exercise 7.13

1. Write a program to open and read a file named "letter.txt" and display it on the screen.
2. Write a program to open and read a file named "letter.txt" and display the count of characters in it on the screen.
3. Write a program to open and read a file named "letter.txt" and display the count of alphabets in it on the screen.
4. Write a program to open and read a file named "letter.txt" and display the count of upper alphabets in it on the screen.

5. Write a program to open and read a file named "letter.txt" and display the count of the character 'e' in the file. [It may be of interest to note that a British novelist once wrote a novel running into a few hundred pages without even once using 'e', which usually happens to be one of the most frequently used characters.]
6. Write a program to open and read a file named "letter.txt" and display the count of vowels in it on the screen.
7. Write a program to open and read a file named "letter.txt" and convert all upper case characters to lower case characters and display it on the screen.
8. Write a program to open and read a file named "letter.txt" and convert all lower case characters to upper case characters and vice versa, then display it on the screen.
9. Write a program to open and read a file named "letter.txt" and print out all alphabet characters without changes, but printing a '.' in place of non-alphabet characters. For example, the word "Room # 25A" will be shown as "Room....A".
10. Write a program to open and read a file named "letter.txt" and print it out in a coded way such that a is replaced by b, b is replaced by c, and so on. For example: 'Malaysia' will be printed as 'Nbmbztjb'.

7.6.2 fprintf Function

Similar to **fscanf**, we have **fprintf** function to write into a file. We can write a char variable x into a file referred to by the file pointer fp as:

fprintf (fp, "%c", x);

We can use this function along with **fscanf** to copy from one file to another. This is shown in the following program (Program 7.14).

Program 7.14

```
# include<stdio.h>
main ( )
{
    FILE *fp1, *fp2;
    char x;
    fp1 = fopen("letter.old", "r");
    fp2 = fopen("letter.new", "w");
    do
    {
        fscanf(fp1, "%c", &x);
        fprintf(fp2, "%c", x);
    }while (feof(fp1)==0);
}
```

Exercise 7.14

1. Write a program to read the characters from the file "in.dat" and copy into a file "out.dat".

2. Write a program to read the characters from the file "in.dat" and copy only the alphabet characters into the file "out.dat".
3. Write a program to read the characters from the file "in.dat" and copy only the alphabet characters into file "out1.dat"and non-alphabet characters into "out2.dat".
4. Write a program to read characters from a file "note.txt" and convert all lower case alphabets into upper case characters and write it to the file "capitalnotes.txt".

7.6.3 fclose Function

All files which are opened must be closed. In our previous programs, we did not do this since it is not mandatory. We can close a file with the following statement:

fclose(*file pointer*)

You may from now on use this in all file-related programs. It becomes mandatory to use this when you want to re-open a file as in the following example. Program 7.15 reads and displays a file "in.dat" which is simultaneously copied into "out.dat" after converting all alphabet characters into upper case. Read the "out.dat" after converting all alphabet characters into upper case. Then out.dat file is printed out.

Program 7.15

```
# include<stdio.h>
main ( )
{
    FILE *f1, *f2;
    char x;
    f1 = fopen("in.dat", "r");
    f2 = fopen("out.dat", "w");
    do
    {
        fscanf(f1, "%c", &x);
        if (( x > 'a') && (x <= 'z'))
            fprintf(f2, " %c ", x-32);
        else
            fprintf (f2, " %c ", x;
    } while (feof(f1) ==0);
    fclose(f1);
    fclose(f2);
    f2= fopen("out.dat", "r");
    do
    {
        fscanf(f2, " %c ", &x);
        printf(" %c ", x);
    }while (feof(f2)==0);
}
```

7.7 BINARY FILES

Whereas text files are processed as a character stream, binary files can read and write any data type. Since they can also read or write structures, it becomes the most flexible kind of file handling. (In text files, you can **fprintf** using %d or %f, but they cannot be read back in the same format.) Binary files have two powerful file handling functions —**fwrite** and **fread**.

7.7.1 Declaring File Pointers

The file pointers are declared and associated with disk filenames in the same way as text files. However, read/write mode has the character **b** also added as shown below:

```
FILE *fp;
fp=fopen("student.dat", "rb");
```

fopen("student.dat", "rb") opens the file in the disk with the name "address.txt" for reading in the binary mode, indicated by "rb". For writing, we use "wb", and for both operations we use "rwb". For appending during writing, we can use "wb+". The function returns a file pointer, which is stored in **fp**. We must have a file pointer declaration and **fopen** statement for each file used in a program.

7.7.2 fwrite and fread

The **fread** and **fwrite** are general file read/write functions and can handle any data type or a structure. This means that they can read/write a huge chunk of data in one operation. The syntax of **fread** and **fwrite** is:

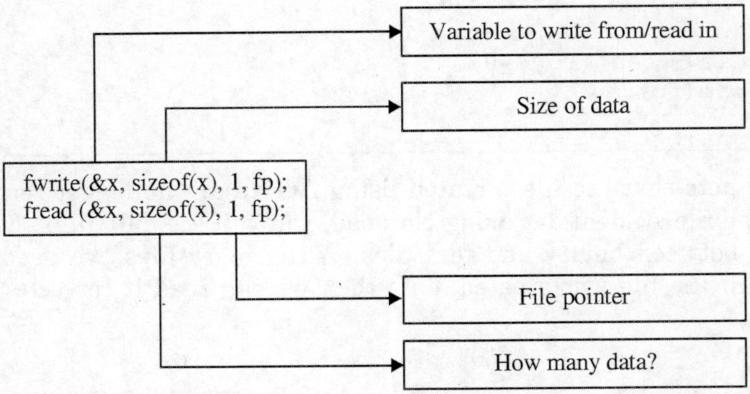

Figure 7.8 Syntax of fread and fwrite.

Here are two example programs. The first one (Program 7.16) creates a file student.dat, consisting of student id of students in a college. The second one reads and displays it (Program 7.17).

1. Accept data and write into the binary file.

Program 7.16

```
# include<stdio.h>
main ( )
{
    FILE *fp;
    int x;
    fp= fopen("student.dat", "wb");
    do
    {
        printf("Enter Student id (0 to stop)\n");
        scanf("%d", &x);
        fwrite(&x, sizeof(int), 1, fp);
    }while (x!=0);
    fclose(fp);
}
```

2. Read data from the binary file and display.

Program 7.17

```
# include<stdio.h>
main ( )
{
    FILE *fp;
    int x;
        fp= fopen("student.dat", "rb");
    do
    {
        fread(&x, sizeof(x), 1, fp);
        printf("%d\n", x);
    }while (feof(fp)==0);
    fclose(fp);
}
```

You may note that the files created using **fwrite** are no longer readable as text. Try opening the file student.dat using Notepad, you will see only junk. That is exactly the difference between binary and text files. With binary files, we need to know the format in which the file was created, only then we can read it correctly using **fread**.

Exercise 7.15

1. Write a program to create a binary character file "in.dat" and copy into a file "out.dat". Can the file in.dat be read using notepad? Why?
2. Write a program to read the student id and marks from the keyboard (until id is 0) and write them to the binary file "student.dat". (*Hint*: Use two **fwrite** commands.)

7.7.3 Reading and Writing Structures from Files

The **fread** and **fwrite** can easily handle structures. See the following program (Program 7.18) where the student data (id, age, marks and grade) are read until student id is entered as 0 and each record is written into a file "student.dat". Finally, the records are all printed out from the file.

Program 7.18

```
#include<stdio.h>
void main( )
{   FILE *fp;
    struct stud
    {   int id;
        int age;
        float mark;
        char grade;
    }; struct stud s1;
    fp=fopen("student.dat", "wb");
    do
    { //Read from Keyboard, Write to file
          printf("Enter student data: \n");
          scanf("%d%d%f %c", &s1.id, &s1.age, &s1.mark, &s1.grade);
          fwrite(&s1, sizeof(s1), 1, fp);
    }while(s1.id!=0);
    fclose(fp);

    fp=fopen("student.dat", "rb");
    printf("Here is student data from file: \n");
    while(!feof(fp))
    {   //Read from file, display on Screen
           fread(&s1, sizeof(s1), 1, fp);
           printf("Id=%d\tAge=%d\tMark=%f\tGrade=%c\n",
           s1.id, s1.age, s1.mark, s1.grade);
    };
    fclose(fp);
}
```

Exercise 7.16

1. Modify programs for creating linked lists and trees of struct student data such that the data is read from files rather than keyboard.
2. Modify programs for stack and queues such that when the user quits, the stack/queue is saved in a file and the user is given an option to load the stack/queue from the file.

Appendix

ASCII (American Standard Code for Information) Table

Char: Character
Dec : Decimal
Hex: Hexadecimal

Char	Dec	Hex
NUL	0	0
SOH	1	1
STX	2	2
ETX	3	3
EOT	4	4
ENQ	5	5
ACK	6	6
BEL	7	7
BS	8	8
HT	9	9
LF	10	a
VT	11	b
FF	12	c
CR	13	d
SO	14	e
SI	15	f
DLE	16	10
DC1	17	11
DC2	18	12
DC3	19	13
DC4	20	14
NAK	21	15
SYN	22	16
ETB	23	17
CAN	24	17
EM	25	19
SUB	26	1a
ESC	27	1b
FS	28	1c
GS	29	1d
RS	30	1e
US	31	1f

Char	Dec	Hex
SP	32	20
!	33	21
“	34	22
#	35	23
$	36	24
%	37	25
&	38	26
‘	39	27
(	40	28
)	41	29
*	42	2a
+	43	2b
,	44	2c
-	45	2d
.	46	2e
/	47	2f
0	48	30
1	49	31
2	50	32
3	51	33
4	52	34
5	53	35
6	54	36
7	55	37
8	56	38
9	57	39
:	58	3a
;	59	3b
<	60	3c
=	61	3d
>	62	3e
?	63	3f

Char	Dec	Hex
@	64	40
A	65	41
B	66	42
C	67	43
D	68	44
E	69	45
F	70	46
G	71	47
H	72	48
I	73	49
J	74	4a
K	75	4b
L	76	4c
M	77	4d
N	78	4e
O	79	4f
P	80	50
Q	81	51
R	82	52
S	83	53
T	84	54
U	85	55
V	86	56
W	87	57
X	88	58
Y	89	59
Z	90	5a
[	91	5b
\	92	5c
]	93	5d
^	94	5e
_	95	5f

Char	Dec	Hex
‘	96	60
a	97	61
b	98	62
c	99	63
d	100	64
e	101	65
f	102	66
g	103	67
h	104	68
i	105	69
j	106	6a
k	107	6b
l	108	6c
m	109	6d
n	110	6e
o	111	6f
p	112	70
q	113	71
r	114	72
s	115	73
t	116	74
u	117	75
v	118	76
w	119	77
x	120	78
y	121	79
z	122	7a
{	123	7b
|	124	7c
}	125	7d
~	126	7e
DEL	127	7f

Index